W9-AOQ-809

Collins
Gage
Canadian
School
Thesaurus

 Collins

 THOMSON ™

NELSON

Australia   Canada   Mexico   Singapore   Spain   United Kingdom   United States

THOMSON
NELSON™

School distribution by Nelson, **a division of Thomson Canada Limited**
1120 Birchmount Road, Toronto, Ontario, M1K 5G4
www.nelson.com

Trade distribution by
HarperCollins Canada
2 Bloor Street East,
Toronto, ON M4W 1A8
www.collinsdictionaries.ca

Nelson, a division of Thomson Canada Limited, is licensed to use the Collins trademark by HarperCollins Publishers Limited.

Collins is one of the world's leading reference publishers. **The Collins Word Web** contains 125 million words of Canadian English and grows at over 1.5 million words per month.

Gage represents a 40-year tradition of Canadian dictionary making. Today, Gage is the reference division of **Thomson Nelson**, Canada's foremost educational publisher.

Library and Archives Canada Cataloguing in Publication

Collins Gage Canadian School Thesaurus
ISBN-13: 978-0-17-635474-9
ISBN-10: 0-17-635474-3

1. English language—Synonyms and antonyms—Juvenile literature

PE1591. G33 1997 j423.1
C97-930981-6

Reviewers
Gloria Gustafson
Coquitlam School District 43

Irene Heffel
Edmonton Public Schools

Brenda Newcombe
Annapolis Valley Regional School Board

Annemarie Petrasek
Huron Perth Catholic District School Board

Tara Rajaram-Donaldson
Toronto District School Board

Susan Sienema
Winnipeg School Division

Editorial and Production

Associate VP, Publishing and Customer Solutions
Bev Buxton

General Manager, Literacy and Reference
Kevin Martindale

Director of Publishing, Literacy and Reference
Joe Banel

Publisher, Supplementary Literacy and Reference
David Friend

Executive Managing Editor, Development
Darleen Rotozinski

Senior Program Manager, Supplementary Literacy and Reference
Ann Downar

Project Editor
Lisa Peterson

Contributing Editor
Sandra Manley

Executive Director, Content and Media Production
Renate McCloy

Director, Content and Media Production
Lisa Dimson

Senior Content Production Manager
Sujata Singh

Production Coordinator
Susan Ure

Creative Director
Ken Phipps

Cover Design
Jan John Rivera
Glenn Toddun

Page Design
Peter Papayanakis

Compositor
Zenaida Diores

Printer
Transcontinental Printing

CONTENTS

Look for REPLACE AN OVERUSED WORD on these pages

	Page		Page
bad	22	**little**	126
better/best	25	**look**	128
big	26	**mark**	131
break	31	**move**	139
call	34	**new**	142
close	39	**nice**	143
cry	52	**old**	147
cut	50	**right**	178
eat	67	**say**	182–183
end	70	**short**	188
fat	78	**small**	192
good	92	**strong**	201
great	94	**thin**	210
happy	98	**very**	227
high	101	**walk**	231–232
hit	102	**wide**	237
laugh	122		

WHAT IS A THESAURUS?

What is a thesaurus? It looks a bit like a dictionary. In a dictionary, you look up a word to find its *meaning*. In a thesaurus, you look up a word to find its *synonyms*—words that have a similar meaning.

sounds like
thih-SAW-russ

WHY SHOULD I USE A THESAURUS?

Why should I use a thesaurus? It can help you find a more interesting word to replace a word that you think is boring. For example, instead of the verb ***cry***, you could use the verb ***bawl***:

My little brother started to cry.
*My little brother started to **bawl**.*

It can also help you find a substitute for a word that you have used too often. For example, there are lots of words you could use instead of the word ***said***:

One person in the class said that the school shouldn't sell pop. Another person said we should have a choice of pop or milk. I said the school could sell fruit juice instead of pop, and someone said that fruit juice doesn't go with pizza.

*One person in the class said that the school shouldn't sell pop. Another person **replied** that we should have a choice of pop or milk. I **pointed out** that the school could sell fruit juice instead of pop, and someone **retorted** that fruit juice doesn't go with pizza.*

HOW WILL THIS THESAURUS HELP ME?

How will this thesaurus help me? This thesaurus will let you:

- find the word that expresses **exactly what you want to say**
- choose **alternatives to words that you use too often**
- build up your vocabulary so that you have **lots of words to choose from** when you write

WHAT IS SPECIAL ABOUT THIS THESAURUS?

What is special about this thesaurus? The *Collins Gage School Thesaurus* gives you **the words that you need most often** in your schoolwork and in your personal writing.

Each entry word is followed by a **sentence that uses that word**. Then, coloured in blue, you get a list of the most useful synonyms for that word.

In addition to the synonyms, many entries also give the best **antonym** for the entry word. (An antonym is a word that is opposite in meaning.)

HOW TO USE THIS THESAURUS

Each entry follows the same format, so you can easily locate the information you need. Also, every synonym can be easily interchanged with the entry word in the sample sentence. Here is the entry for **perfect**:

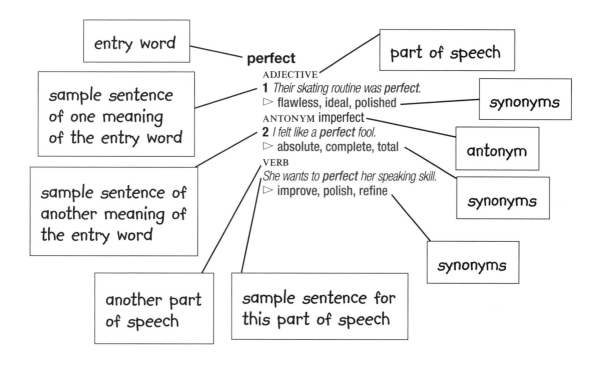

FEATURE BOXES

There are two types of feature box in this thesaurus. Each one will help you with some of the more difficult aspects of the English language.

Make It More Formal

When you are **talking**, you are using **informal** language most of the time. When you are **writing**, you are usually using more **formal** language.

Some informal expressions mean something special, that you wouldn't be able to figure out from the individual words. For example, when you say that yesterday's homework was *a piece of cake*, you are not really talking about cake. If you wanted to write that, it would be better to describe the homework as *a very easy task*.

> **MAKE IT MORE FORMAL**
>
> **a piece of cake** a very easy task
> **a piece of my mind** a scolding
> **a piece of work** a difficult person to deal with
> **go to pieces** break down
> **piece together** assemble
> **speak your piece** express your opinion

Replace an Overused Word

Some words are used so often, that they have lost all their effectiveness. For example: *good, bad, big, happy, nice*. You can improve your writing by choosing a more precise word to replace an overused word.

Here's part of the box for the adjective **good**. You can find a list of all the **REPLACE AN OVERUSED WORD** boxes on page 3.

> **REPLACE AN OVERUSED WORD: GOOD**
>
> Like the word **bad**, the word **good** is used in so many ways to describe so many things that it has lost a great deal of its strength. Try using one of these adjectives instead.
>
> - **good quality**
>   The food in Montréal was **excellent**.
>   Our team played a **first-class** game.
>   This is a **great** story, full of interesting people.
>   All the actors in the school play were **superb**.
>
> - **a good experience**
>   We spent an **agreeable** afternoon sightseeing.
>   My friend and I had a **delightful** time at the party.
>
>   My uncle is a **skilled** carpenter.
>   She was introduced as one of Canada's most **talented** writers.
>
> - **good behaviour**
>   I like dogs that are **obedient**.
>   During a fire drill, **orderly** behaviour is most important.
>   Please be **polite** at all times.
>   The child was **well-behaved** throughout the

ACTIVITY 1: VIVID VERBS

The following activity will help you find more vivid verbs.

One synonym for **say** is **murmur**, which tells you that the speaker's voice is quite **soft** and **calm**.

1. On a piece of paper, sketch (or trace) a pair of thermometers for the following synonyms for **say**:

   ### announce, babble, gasp, groan, retort

2. Now, look up the REPLACE AN OVERUSED WORD box for **move**. Choose any three synonyms for the verb **move**, and sketch (or trace) pairs of thermometers that show how a person moves. Use *slow-fast* on one thermometer, and *smooth-jerky* on the other. Compare your results with a classmate.

ACTIVITY 2: MORE VIVID VERBS

You can put more meaning into your writing by using a vivid verb instead of a basic verb. For example, instead of writing:

> *Max **laughed** when I told him the story.*

you might want to show the way in which Max laughed:

> *Max **chuckled** when I told him the story.*

1. Use your thesaurus to help you find a more vivid replacement for the bold word in each sentence. Rewrite the sentence in your notebook, using the synonym that you chose.

   > *It's not polite to **laugh** when someone makes a mistake.*

   > *If they **call** your name, you have made it to the next round of the competition.*

   > *My mom is planning to **walk** through Highlands National Park.*

   > *He **moved** out of the way when he saw the car coming.*

   > *She **hit** the ball with the bat and **ran** to first base.*

2. Now, choose **one** of the verbs from the sentences above and list three synonyms for that verb. Write a short paragraph using all three synonyms.

ACTIVITY 3: SPECIFIC NOUNS

Sometimes when you don't know or can't remember the exact name for something, you can find it in a thesaurus.

1. For the following objects, use your thesaurus to find a noun that is more specific:

   boat, hate, lake, mark, picture, pain

2. Write a short paragraph that uses some of the synonyms above.

ACTIVITY 4: ADJECTIVES — SIZE, APPEARANCE

We use adjectives to describe what we see. We might say, for example, that the Arctic is a **gigantic**, **frozen** desert. Words like **gigantic** and **frozen** are adjectives that describe **size** and **appearance**.

Each word inside the triangles below has three synonyms around it.

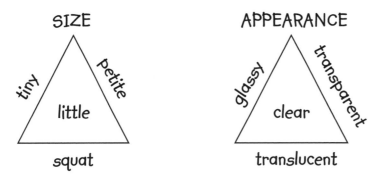

You can choose adjectives from around any triangle and write an interesting sentence:

*The **tiny, translucent** earrings glinted in the candlelight.*

1. On a piece of paper, sketch (or trace) triangles for the following adjectives:

   wide, old

   short, orange

   For each adjective, find three synonyms and write them around the sides of its triangle.

2. Sometimes we're not content to describe things the way they actually are. We want to exaggerate the way they look to make a point, or to be humorous. For example:

   *This food isn't just **bad**, it's **inedible**!*

   Write some sentences that exaggerate, using words from the triangles above. Be creative and have fun!

ACTIVITY 5: ADJECTIVES — SMELL, TASTE, SOUND, FEEL

In addition to describing what we **see**, adjectives also tell us how things **smell**, **taste**, **sound**, and **feel**.

Here are some word webs that show how something smells, tastes, sounds, or feels.

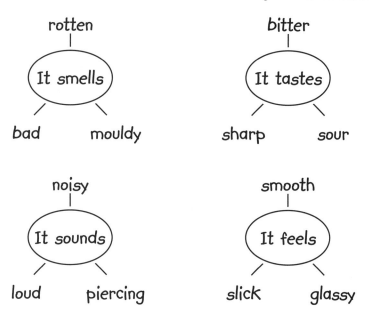

Now, find an adjective to describe how the following objects might smell, or taste, or sound, or feel. Write the whole phrase in your notebook.

1. a __ desk   (feel)

2. a __ flower (smell)

3. a __ cat   (feel)

4. a __ crowd (sound)

5. a __ drink   (taste)

6. a __ song   (sound)

7. a __ meal   (smell)

8. a __ candy (taste)

A thesaurus can help you find the opposite of a word. For example, an antonym for **greedy** is **unselfish**:

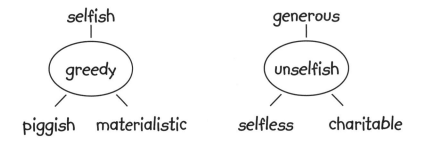

greedy
ADJECTIVE
A person can be greedy in many ways.
▷ materialistic, piggish, selfish
ANTONYM unselfish

The following word webs show the word **greedy** and the antonym **unselfish**. Around these are three synonyms for **greedy**, and three synonyms for **unselfish**.

selfish
|
(greedy)
/ \
piggish   materialistic

generous
|
(unselfish)
/ \
selfless   charitable

In your notebook, sketch (or trace) the word webs below, and complete by finding an antonym and as many synonyms as you can for each set.

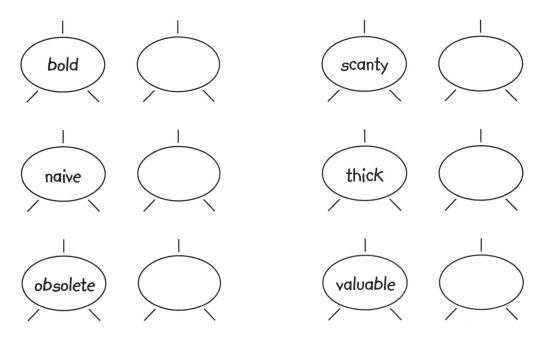

A a

abandon
VERB
*It was wrong to **abandon** the cat by the side of the road.*
▷ desert, leave, leave behind

abate
VERB
*The high winds did not **abate** for three days.*
▷ decrease, diminish, lessen, subside

abbreviate
VERB
*Try to **abbreviate** that long paragraph.*
▷ cut, reduce, shorten

abdicate
VERB
*Please don't **abdicate** as president of the club.*
▷ quit, resign, retire

ability
NOUN
*You have the **ability** to do this project.*
▷ capability, competence, expertise, skill, talent
ANTONYM inability

able
ADJECTIVE
*He is a very **able** photographer.*
▷ accomplished, capable, competent, expert, skilled, talented
ANTONYM incompetent

abnormal
ADJECTIVE
*Snowstorms in May are **abnormal** in southern Canada.*
▷ odd, strange, uncommon, unusual
ANTONYM normal

abolish
VERB
*The new government will **abolish** the unfair law.*
▷ cancel, eliminate
ANTONYM restore

about
PREPOSITION
*My mom spoke to the class **about** her job.*
▷ concerning, regarding, relating to
ADVERB
*Moose Jaw is **about** 230 kilometres from Saskatoon.*
▷ almost, approximately, around, nearly, roughly
ANTONYM exactly

above
PREPOSITION
1 *The wind took the kite **above** the trees.*
▷ beyond, over
ANTONYM below

2 *The school raised more than $500 **above** its goal for the Fall Fair.*
▷ beyond, exceeding, over

abrupt
ADJECTIVE
1 *He had an **abrupt** change of mind and decided not to go to the party.*
▷ sudden, unexpected
2 *I was hurt by her **abrupt** reply.*
▷ curt, short, terse
ANTONYM polite

absent
ADJECTIVE
*I said you had been **absent** that day.*
▷ away, elsewhere, missing
ANTONYM present

absent-minded
ADJECTIVE
*The **absent-minded** man got off the bus at the wrong stop.*
▷ distracted, forgetful

absolute
ADJECTIVE
*Her whole story was an **absolute** lie.*
▷ complete, downright, pure, sheer, total

absorb
VERB
*Skin can **absorb** Vitamin D from sunlight.*
▷ soak up, take in
ANTONYM emit

absorbed
ADJECTIVE
*I was **absorbed** in the story and forgot the time.*
▷ fascinated, involved
ANTONYM uninterested

abstain from
VERB
*It is wise to **abstain from** smoking.*
▷ avoid, give up, refrain from, refuse
ANTONYM indulge in

absurd
ADJECTIVE
*He wore an **absurd** hat that made us laugh.*
▷ foolish, ludicrous, nonsensical, ridiculous, silly

abundant
ADJECTIVE
*The Prairie Provinces produce an **abundant** supply of wheat.*
▷ ample, copious, plentiful, rich
ANTONYM scarce

A

abuse
NOUN
1 *The abuse that the dog suffered was terrible.*
▷ harm, hurt, ill-treatment
2 *I refuse to listen to abuse.*
▷ curses, derision, insults
VERB
If you abuse the referee, you will be thrown out of the game.
▷ curse, insult

accent
NOUN
1 *Put the accent on the first syllable of the word.*
▷ emphasis, stress
2 *We thought her accent was charming.*
▷ drawl, pronunciation, twang

accept
VERB
1 *We will not accept the change in plans.*
▷ agree to, approve, concur with, consent to
ANTONYM refuse
2 *I accept that I may have been wrong.*
▷ acknowledge, admit, believe
ANTONYM reject

accident
NOUN
The accident was caused by a careless person.
▷ calamity, disaster, misfortune, mishap

accommodation
NOUN
In big cities, accommodation is expensive.
▷ housing, lodgings, quarters

accomplice
NOUN
She was my accomplice in planning the surprise party.
▷ ally, helper, partner

accomplish
VERB
How did they accomplish so much in such a short time?
▷ achieve, complete, finish

accord
NOUN
We were in complete accord regarding the changes in the club rules.
▷ agreement, harmony

account
NOUN
Her account of the accident is true.
▷ report, statement, story, tale

accumulate
VERB
I don't have room to accumulate more books.
▷ collect, gather, hoard, store

accurate
ADJECTIVE
Is that clock accurate?
▷ correct, exact, precise, true
ANTONYM inaccurate

accuse
VERB
Do not accuse him unless you can prove that he is guilty.
▷ blame, censure, charge, denounce

achieve
VERB
Did you achieve your goal?
▷ accomplish, complete, fulfill

achievement
NOUN
Being made team captain is quite an achievement.
▷ accomplishment, deed, exploit, feat

acknowledge
VERB
I acknowledge that you are a better skier.
▷ accept, admit, recognize

acquaintance
NOUN
He is not a close friend, just an acquaintance.
▷ associate, contact, friend

acquire
VERB
I would like to acquire a new cellphone.
▷ obtain, purchase

acquit
VERB
The judge will acquit her due to lack of evidence.
▷ clear, discharge, excuse, free
ANTONYM convict

act
VERB
1 *Employees should act honestly.*
▷ behave, function, operate, perform, work
2 *It was fun to act in the school musical.*
▷ perform, play
NOUN
Your kind act was much appreciated.
▷ action, deed, feat

MAKE IT MORE FORMAL

act against counteract
act out act
act up be troublesome
clean up your act improve your behaviour
get into the act get involved
get your act together get organized

action
NOUN
*Your quick **action** helped us win the game.*
▷ activity, deed, move, reaction

active
ADJECTIVE
1 *My hamster is extremely **active**.*
▷ energetic, lively, vigorous
2 *She is an **active** girl, and belongs to six clubs.*
▷ busy, enthusiastic, involved

activity
NOUN
1 *You can see lots of **activity** in a kindergarten class.*
▷ action, bustle, energy, liveliness
2 *One **activity** that I like is collecting hockey cards.*
▷ hobby, interest, pastime, pursuit

actual
ADJECTIVE
*Is that an **actual** rock from the moon?*
▷ authentic, genuine, real, true
ANTONYM fake

acute
ADJECTIVE
1 *There is an **acute** water shortage in our area.*
▷ critical, extreme, grave, intense, serious, severe, urgent
2 *His **acute** mind sensed something was wrong.*
▷ alert, astute, bright, keen, perceptive, quick, sharp, shrewd

adapt
VERB
*Scientists are testing ways to **adapt** cars to run on a renewable fuel.*
▷ adjust, alter, convert, modify

adaptable
ADJECTIVE
*Our plan is **adaptable** enough for us to make changes.*
▷ adjustable, flexible

add
VERB
1 *Add a conclusion to your report.*
▷ attach, include
2 *Add our expenses and divide by three.*
▷ combine, total
ANTONYM subtract

MAKE IT MORE FORMAL
add to supplement
add up make sense

address
NOUN
*The **address** given by the prime minister was televised.*
▷ lecture, speech, talk

adept
ADJECTIVE
*She is quite **adept** in the kitchen.*
▷ capable, expert, handy, skilful

adequate
ADJECTIVE
*Do you have **adequate** clothing for this cold weather?*
▷ acceptable, enough, satisfactory, sufficient
ANTONYM inadequate

adjacent
ADJECTIVE
*The field **adjacent** to our school is for sale.*
▷ beside, bordering, touching

adjust
VERB
*I would like to **adjust** what I wrote yesterday.*
▷ amend, change, revise

administer
VERB
1 *They must **administer** the office according to company rules.*
▷ command, control, direct, govern, manage, run, supervise
2 *Will she **administer** the punishment fairly?*
▷ apply, conduct, impose, perform

admirable
ADJECTIVE
*It is **admirable** to help others in need.*
▷ commendable, excellent, praiseworthy

admiration
NOUN
*We showed our **admiration** by cheering.*
▷ appreciation, approval, esteem, regard, respect

admire
VERB
*I **admire** people who refuse to gossip.*
▷ appreciate, esteem, praise, respect, value
ANTONYM despise

admit
VERB
1 *She did **admit** that she broke the window.*
▷ acknowledge, confess
ANTONYM deny
2 *The craft teacher may **admit** me if the class is not full.*
▷ accept, allow
ANTONYM exclude

adore
VERB
*I **adore** the lead guitar player.*
▷ admire, idolize, love
ANTONYM despise

adorn
VERB
*We plan to **adorn** the cake with flowers.*
▷ decorate, garnish

adrift
ADJECTIVE
*The damaged boat was **adrift** in the ocean.*
▷ astray, loose, lost

adult
NOUN
*At what age does a person become an **adult**?*
▷ grown-up, man, woman
ANTONYM child
ADJECTIVE
*The youngsters acted in an **adult** manner.*
▷ grown-up, mature
ANTONYM immature

advance
VERB
*The knights decided to **advance** as far as the castle gate.*
▷ press on, proceed, progress
NOUN
*Insulin was a great **advance** in the control of diabetes.*
▷ development, gain, progress

advantage
NOUN
*Our team has the **advantage** because we have better players.*
▷ benefit, edge, superiority, upper hand
ANTONYM disadvantage

adventure
NOUN
*Our canoe trip down the Saint John River in New Brunswick was an exciting **adventure**.*
▷ experience, exploit, undertaking, venture

adversary
NOUN
*Who is my first **adversary** in the wrestling competition?*
▷ competitor, enemy, foe, opponent, rival
ANTONYM ally

advice
NOUN
*Your **advice** is very helpful.*
▷ guidance, help, opinion, suggestion

advise
VERB
1 *I **advise** that you leave early or you will miss the last bus.*
▷ caution, counsel, recommend, suggest, urge
2 *Please **advise** me when you are ready to leave.*
▷ inform, notify

affect
VERB
*Global warming will **affect** the whole world.*
▷ alter, change, influence

affection
NOUN
*We all have great **affection** for the new baby.*
▷ attachment, fondness, liking, love, warmth
ANTONYM dislike

affectionate
ADJECTIVE
*The **affectionate** aunt hugged everyone.*
▷ caring, fond, loving, tender, warm
ANTONYM cold

affliction
NOUN
*That **affliction** is called depression.*
▷ disorder, illness, sickness, trouble

afraid
ADJECTIVE
*I'm not **afraid** of the dark.*
▷ alarmed, apprehensive, fearful, frightened, nervous, scared, terrified

again
ADVERB
*I had to do the test **again**.*
▷ afresh, anew, once more

against
PREPOSITION
1 *She is **against** eating cooked food.*
▷ averse to, hostile to, opposed to
2 *Protect yourself **against** the cold by wearing a warm jacket.*
▷ in anticipation of, in expectation of, in preparation for

aggravate
VERB
1 *She will only **aggravate** her foot injury if she keeps running.*
▷ exaggerate, increase, intensify, worsen
ANTONYM lessen
2 *Please do not **aggravate** your older sister.*
▷ annoy, exasperate, provoke
ANTONYM soothe

aggressive
ADJECTIVE
*The **aggressive** bullies were taken to the principal's office.*
▷ hostile, quarrelsome, offensive, pushy
ANTONYM peaceful

A

agile
ADJECTIVE
The agile man hopped easily over the fence.
▷ active, lithe, nimble, sprightly, supple
ANTONYM clumsy

agitate
VERB
1 *The hockey players agreed to agitate for better contracts.*
▷ campaign, demonstrate, protest, push
2 *Please do not agitate yourself about being late.*
▷ bother, disturb, excite, fluster, trouble, upset, worry

agony
NOUN
My agony ended when I heard she was not hurt in the accident.
▷ anguish, distress, suffering, torment, woe

agree
VERB
1 *Does everyone agree?*
▷ assent, concur
ANTONYM disagree
2 *My results agree with yours.*
▷ accord, conform, correspond, match
ANTONYM differ

agreeable
ADJECTIVE
When I was nine, I discovered that reading is a very agreeable pastime.
▷ enjoyable, lovely, pleasant, pleasurable
ANTONYM disagreeable

agreement
NOUN
They had an agreement to share the cost of the trip.
▷ arrangement, contract, pact

aid
VERB
Regular exercise will aid us in staying healthy.
▷ assist, help, support
NOUN
Thank you for giving me aid when I needed it.
▷ assistance, help, relief, support

aim
VERB
I aim to improve my score every time I play this game.
▷ aspire, attempt, intend, mean, plan, propose, strive
NOUN
Our aim is to reach Winnipeg by July 10.
▷ ambition, goal, intention, object, objective, plan, purpose, target

aisle
NOUN
Do not block the aisle with your backpacks.
▷ corridor, passageway, path

alarm
NOUN
1 *I felt alarm when she was late getting home.*
▷ anxiety, apprehension, fright, nervousness, panic
ANTONYM calm
2 *When the alarm sounds, leave the building by the nearest exit.*
▷ alert, warning
VERB
Do not alarm my parents, because my ankle is only sprained, not broken.
▷ frighten, panic, scare, startle, unnerve
ANTONYM calm

alert
ADJECTIVE
The alert salesperson caught the shoplifter.
▷ attentive, observant, vigilant, wary, watchful
ANTONYM unaware
VERB
Please call Mom and alert her that we are bringing some friends home with us.
▷ inform, notify, signal, warn

alien
ADJECTIVE
My baby sister refuses to eat food that is alien to her.
▷ strange, unfamiliar

alike
ADJECTIVE
The two friends are alike in many ways.
▷ identical, like, matching, similar
ANTONYM different

alive
ADJECTIVE
1 *My turtle was still alive after five years.*
▷ breathing, living
ANTONYM dead
2 *Music always makes me feel alive.*
▷ active, alert, animated, energetic, lively, vivacious
ANTONYM dull

all (the)
ADJECTIVE
Did you eat all the pizza?
▷ (the) complete, (the) entire, (the) total, (the) whole

MAKE IT MORE FORMAL
all but almost
go all out use all your resources

A

allow
VERB
1 *If you will **allow** us to have a party, we promise to clean up.*
▷ authorize, permit
ANTONYM forbid
2 ***Allow** two tickets per student.*
▷ allocate, allot, assign, grant

all right
ADJECTIVE
*My report was **all right**, but my presentation was bad.*
▷ acceptable, adequate, average, fair, satisfactory

ally
NOUN
*She is my **ally** in all my activities.*
▷ accomplice, colleague, supporter
ANTONYM enemy

almost
ADVERB
*He has **almost** enough money to take the train to Halifax.*
▷ about, approximately, around, barely, nearly, practically, roughly

alone
ADJECTIVE
*One tree stood **alone** at the top of the hill.*
▷ isolated, lone, separate, solitary

aloud
ADVERB
*We gave our opinion **aloud** so all could hear.*
▷ audibly, out loud

also
ADVERB
*She offered to babysit the other child **also**.*
▷ as well, into the bargain, too

alter
VERB
*I want to **alter** the ending of the story.*
▷ change, convert, modify, transform, vary
ANTONYM preserve

always
ADVERB
*Do you **always** eat the same food for breakfast?*
▷ continually, eternally, forever, invariably, perpetually

amass
VERB
*The pioneers had to **amass** a lot of food for the winter.*
▷ accumulate, collect, gather, stockpile

amaze
VERB
*You **amaze** me with your knowledge of Canadian history.*
▷ astonish, astound, stagger, stun, surprise

ambition
NOUN
*Her **ambition** is to be a police officer.*
▷ aim, dream, goal, hope

amend
VERB
*Please **amend** that confusing sentence.*
▷ correct, improve, remedy, revise

amiable
ADJECTIVE
*He is an **amiable** person and we all like him.*
▷ agreeable, friendly, kindly, pleasant
ANTONYM unfriendly

among
PREPOSITION
*There were a few weeds **among** the flowers.*
▷ amid, amidst, in the middle of, in the thick of, surrounded by

amount
NOUN
*What **amount** of sugar do we need to make twelve muffins?*
▷ quantity, sum, total, volume

ample
ADJECTIVE
*We have **ample** space to plant vegetables.*
▷ abundant, enough, generous, plentiful, substantial, sufficient
ANTONYM insufficient

amuse
VERB
*My uncle likes to **amuse** us with magic tricks.*
▷ delight, entertain, please
ANTONYM bore

ancestor
NOUN
*I have an **ancestor** who came to Canada before 1900.*
▷ forebear, predecessor
ANTONYM offspring

ancient
ADJECTIVE
*We saw several **ancient** maps at the museum.*
▷ aged, antique, old-fashioned
ANTONYM modern

anger
NOUN
*Try to control your **anger** and stay calm.*
▷ fury, outrage, rage, wrath
VERB
*Do not **anger** me by telling lies.*
▷ annoy, enrage, infuriate, outrage
ANTONYM calm

angry

ADJECTIVE

The angry child kicked at his broken toy.

▷ cross, enraged, furious, infuriated, resentful

anguish

NOUN

When her cat died, she was filled with anguish.

▷ agony, distress, suffering, torment, woe

animal noises

NOUN

See picture at bottom of page.

announce

VERB

I'm ready to announce the winner of the contest.

▷ declare, proclaim, reveal, tell

announcement

NOUN

We heard the announcement on the radio.

▷ bulletin, declaration, report, statement

annoy

VERB

Do not annoy your brother while he is studying.

▷ bother, disturb, irritate, pester, tease, vex

answer

VERB

I refuse to answer that question.

▷ reply to, respond to

ANTONYM ask

NOUN

Please give me your answer now.

▷ reply, response

ANTONYM question

MAKE IT MORE FORMAL

answer back reply disrespectfully

answer for accept the consequences of

anticipate

VERB

The media tried to anticipate what the prime minister would say.

▷ foresee, predict, prepare for

anxious

ADJECTIVE

The anxious mother took her child to the hospital.

▷ apprehensive, bothered, concerned, fearful, nervous, troubled, uneasy, worried

ANTONYM confident

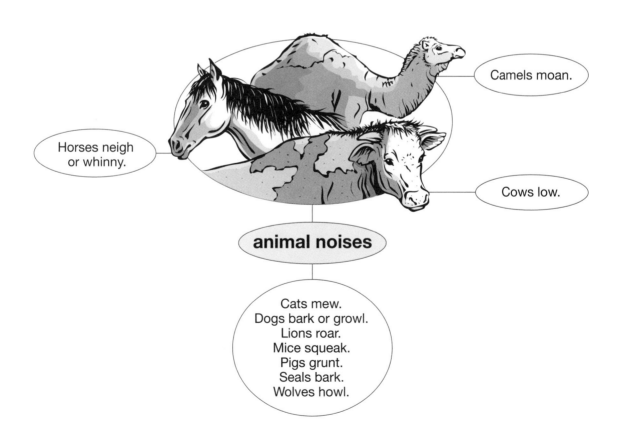

Camels moan.

Horses neigh or whinny.

Cows low.

animal noises

Cats mew.
Dogs bark or growl.
Lions roar.
Mice squeak.
Pigs grunt.
Seals bark.
Wolves howl.

apologize
VERB
*You should **apologize** for your rudeness!*
▷ ask forgiveness, beg someone's pardon, express regret

apparent
ADJECTIVE
*It is **apparent** that you do not like peas.*
▷ clear, conspicuous, evident, obvious, plain

appeal
NOUN
*We presented an **appeal** to save the trees.*
▷ petition, plea, request

appeal to
VERB
1 *My brother does not often **appeal to** me for help with his homework.*
▷ beg, implore, plead with, urge
2 *This jacket in another colour would **appeal to** me more.*
▷ attract, fascinate, interest, please

appear
VERB
*A clown will **appear** out of a big box.*
▷ arrive, emerge, surface
ANTONYM disappear

appearance
NOUN
***Appearance** is important to him.*
▷ bearing, image, look, looks

appetite
NOUN
*I have an **appetite** for strawberries today.*
▷ craving, desire, hunger, longing

applaud
VERB
*We **applaud** your efforts to improve your math skills.*
▷ approve, encourage, praise

apply
VERB
*Will you **apply** your artistic skill to decorate his birthday cake?*
▷ employ, use, utilize

appointment
NOUN
1 *The reporter has an **appointment** with the lacrosse coach.*
▷ interview, meeting, rendezvous
2 *The **appointment** of student council members took place yesterday.*
▷ election, naming, nomination, selection
3 *He received an **appointment** to work in Europe.*
▷ assignment, job, place, position, post

appreciate
VERB
1 *They **appreciate** what their parents did for them.*
▷ admire, prize, respect, treasure, value
ANTONYM scorn
2 *Do you **appreciate** the value of this laptop?*
▷ realize, recognize, understand

appropriate
ADJECTIVE
*Be sure to use **appropriate** tools for the job.*
▷ apt, correct, fitting, proper, suitable
ANTONYM inappropriate

approval
NOUN
1 *I have my parents' **approval** to go to hockey camp.*
▷ agreement, authorization, endorsement
2 *We do not always need **approval** from others.*
▷ admiration, esteem, favour, praise, respect
ANTONYM disapproval

approve
VERB
1 *I strongly **approve** your decision.*
▷ admire, favour, praise, respect
ANTONYM disapprove
2 *The teacher has to **approve** the trip.*
▷ authorize, endorse, permit
ANTONYM veto

approximate
ADJECTIVE
*I can give you an **approximate** total.*
▷ estimated, rough
ANTONYM exact

ardent
ADJECTIVE
*Teenagers are **ardent** fans of the singer.*
▷ avid, devoted, enthusiastic, fervent, intense, keen, passionate

arduous
ADJECTIVE
*The climb up the hill was **arduous**.*
▷ difficult, hard, laborious, strenuous, tough

area
NOUN
1 *I like living in this **area**.*
▷ district, locality, neighbourhood, region, zone
2 *The total **area** of Vancouver's Stanley Park is huge.*
▷ expanse, extent, range, size

argue
VERB
*Do not **argue** about whose turn it is.*
▷ bicker, disagree, discuss, fight, quarrel, squabble, wrangle

argument
NOUN
*The neighbours got into an **argument** over the loud music.*
▷ clash, dispute, feud, fight, row, squabble

arid
ADJECTIVE
*The land is **arid** from lack of rain.*
▷ barren, dry, parched, sterile

arise
VERB
*No arguments will **arise** if we explain our decision.*
▷ begin, occur, start

army
NOUN
*He has joined the Canadian **army**.*
▷ armed forces, soldiers, troops

arouse
VERB
*The speaker tried to **arouse** the crowd.*
▷ excite, provoke

arrange
VERB
*We could **arrange** the class library by subject.*
▷ classify, order, organize, sort

arrangement
NOUN
*Readers liked the **arrangement** of topics in the newsletter.*
▷ layout, sequence, structure

arrest
VERB
*The police were able to **arrest** the thieves.*
▷ apprehend, capture, detain, hold, seize
ANTONYM release

arrive at
VERB
*I will **arrive at** your house at noon.*
▷ appear at, reach
ANTONYM depart

arrogant
ADJECTIVE
*The **arrogant** boy thinks he knows more than his classmates.*
▷ conceited, haughty, overbearing, pompous
ANTONYM modest

article
NOUN
1 *Did you read that **article** in today's newspaper?*
▷ feature, item, piece, story
2 *I do not have space for one more **article** in my desk.*
▷ item, object, thing

artificial
ADJECTIVE
*She likes to wear her **artificial** fur coat.*
▷ fake, faux, imitation, synthetic

ascend
VERB
*We watched the hikers **ascend** the hill.*
▷ climb, mount, scale
ANTONYM descend

ashamed
ADJECTIVE
*He felt **ashamed** that he had forgotten my birthday.*
▷ embarrassed, guilty, humiliated, regretful, sorry
ANTONYM proud

ask
VERB
1 ***Ask** at the desk if this is the correct place.*
▷ inquire, query, question
ANTONYM answer
2 *I will **ask** for permission to go.*
▷ appeal, beg, implore, plead

assault
VERB
*The rebels plan to **assault** the town tonight.*
▷ attack, charge, invade
ANTONYM defend

assemble
VERB
1 *The students will **assemble** in the gym.*
▷ collect, congregate, gather, meet
2 *Do you really know how to **assemble** the scooter?*
▷ build, construct, erect

assent to
VERB
*I **assent to** your request.*
▷ agree to, approve, consent to
ANTONYM refuse

assert
VERB
*They still **assert** that you were wrong.*
▷ claim, declare, insist, maintain, pronounce, state
ANTONYM deny

assess
VERB
*The builder will have to **assess** the water damage.*
▷ appraise, consider, estimate, evaluate, judge, review

assist
VERB
*Would you like me to **assist** you?*
▷ aid, help, support
ANTONYM hinder

assistant
NOUN
*Her **assistant** helped to organize the meeting.*
▷ aide, colleague, deputy, helper

associate
VERB
1 *Doctors **associate** poor eating habits with poor health.*
▷ connect, identify, link
2 *I like to **associate** with other musicians.*
▷ mingle, mix, socialize
NOUN
*My **associate** ordered our tickets online.*
▷ colleague, co-worker

association
NOUN
1 *Our school voted to form some kind of **association** with the other schools in the area.*
▷ body, club, company, confederation, group, institution, league, society, syndicate, union
2 *Is your fitness group enjoying its **association** with the gymnastics club?*
▷ affiliation, attachment, bond, connection, relationship, tie

assortment
NOUN
*I have an **assortment** of photos beside my bed.*
▷ arrangement, collection, range, variety

assume
VERB
1 *I **assume** the baseball game will be cancelled due to rain.*
▷ believe, guess, imagine, suppose, think
2 *Our neighbours will **assume** the care of the cat while we are away.*
▷ accept, undertake

assure
VERB
*I **assure** you that I will be on time.*
▷ guarantee, promise

astonish
VERB
*He continues to **astonish** us with his guitar playing.*
▷ amaze, astound, startle, surprise

astound
VERB
*I will **astound** the audience with my juggling tricks.*
▷ amaze, stagger, stupefy

astute
ADJECTIVE
*The **astute** detective solved the mystery.*
▷ alert, clever, keen, perceptive, quick, sharp, shrewd, smart

athlete
NOUN
See picture on next page.

attach
VERB
*You must **attach** the two pieces together.*
▷ connect, couple, fasten, join, link, tie, unite
ANTONYM separate

attachment
NOUN
1 *My dog and I have a great **attachment**.*
▷ affection, bond, fondness, liking, love
2 *Every **attachment** for the bicycle was in the box.*
▷ accessory, component, fitting, fixture, part

attack
VERB
1 *The pirates planned to **attack** the treasure ship at dawn.*
▷ assault, charge, invade, raid, storm
2 *Do not **attack** my decision until you know the facts.*
▷ censure, criticize
NOUN
*The enemy surrendered after our successful **attack**.*
▷ assault, charge, offensive, onslaught, raid

attempt
VERB
*I will **attempt** to set a high-jump record.*
▷ endeavour, seek, strive, try
NOUN
*Will he make another **attempt** to break the record?*
▷ bid, try

attentive
ADJECTIVE
*She is **attentive** in class, and asks a lot of questions.*
▷ alert, observant

attitude
NOUN
*I like your positive **attitude**.*
▷ outlook, perspective, point of view, viewpoint

attract
VERB
*The new science exhibit will **attract** many visitors.*
▷ appeal to, draw, entice, lure, tempt
ANTONYM repel

attractive
ADJECTIVE
*You don't have to be beautiful to be **attractive**.*
▷ appealing, charming, lovely

available
ADJECTIVE
*If I need help, are you **available**?*
▷ accessible, free, on hand

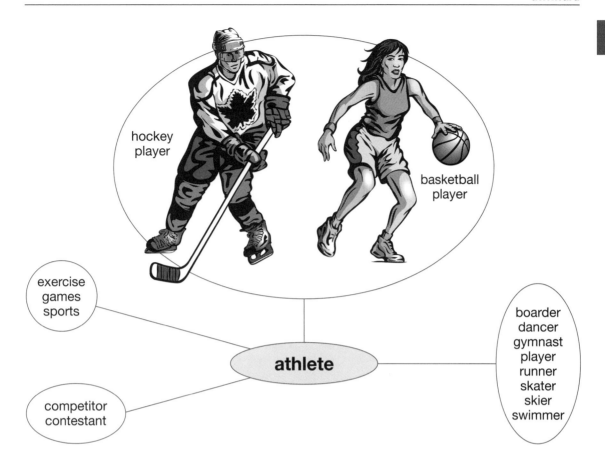

exercise
games
sports

hockey
player

basketball
player

boarder
dancer
gymnast
player
runner
skater
skier
swimmer

athlete

competitor
contestant

average

ADJECTIVE

That is the average price for a cellphone.

▷ normal, regular, standard, typical, usual

avid

ADJECTIVE

I am an avid reader.

▷ eager, enthusiastic, keen

avoid

VERB

We avoid eating junk food.

▷ dodge, evade, refrain from, sidestep

award

VERB

The king himself will award the medal.

▷ give, grant, present

aware of

ADJECTIVE

I was aware of the argument going on in the next room.

▷ conscious of, familiar with

awesome

ADJECTIVE

The Canadian Rockies are an awesome sight.

▷ amazing, impressive, terrific, wonderful

awful

ADJECTIVE

We watched the awful rioting on TV.

▷ appalling, dreadful, frightful, horrendous, horrible, terrible

awkward

ADJECTIVE

1 *The boy was nervous, and that made him awkward.*

▷ clumsy, graceless

ANTONYM graceful

2 *After she stopped yelling, there was an awkward silence.*

▷ embarrassing, uncomfortable

B b

babble

NOUN

We got bored listening to their babble.

▷ chatter, jabber, prattle

baby

NOUN

The baby is just two weeks old.

▷ child, infant

back

NOUN

Please sit at the back of the train.

▷ end, rear

ANTONYM front

VERB

I will back you if you run for class president.

▷ endorse, promote, support, uphold

ANTONYM oppose

MAKE IT MORE FORMAL

back away or **back off** retreat

back out withdraw

bad

ADJECTIVE

See box at foot of this page.

badger

VERB

I will badger you until you clean your room.

▷ hassle, nag, pester

baffle

VERB

My new card trick will baffle everyone.

▷ bewilder, mystify, perplex, puzzle

bait

NOUN

The bait to get him to help us was a chocolate bar.

▷ bribe, inducement, lure, temptation

balance

VERB

Can you balance yourself on the narrow beam?

▷ equalize, level, stabilize, steady

REPLACE AN OVERUSED WORD: BAD

The adjective **bad** is used so often that it has lost a lot of its strength. Try using one of these words instead.

- **a bad effect**

  Junk food is damaging to your health.

  Burning fossil fuels has a destructive effect on the ozone layer.

  Air pollution has a harmful effect on your lungs.

  Illnesses can be caused by an unhealthy diet.

- **feeling bad**

  I forced myself to watch the distressing images on TV.

  Reading that story brings painful memories.

  The death of a pet is a traumatic experience.

  Being a witness to an accident is upsetting.

- **a bad pain**

  She had an acute attack of appendicitis.

  I did not go swimming because my shoulder was painful.

  Since he was a child, he has had serious knee problems.

  I have a terrible cold.

- **badly made**

  The computer monitor must be defective, because it has never worked properly.

  All faulty items must be returned to the manufacturer.

  These pants are made of inferior material.

  My old snowboard had a very poor finish on it.

- **badly done**

  I had to admit my work was imperfect.

  Your essay is inadequate.

  That's a pathetic excuse!

  I liked the movie, even though the ending was unsatisfactory.

- **a bad character**

  People suffer under a corrupt leader.

  Who is the most evil person in history?

  He is very good at playing villainous characters.

  The TV show tells of a good girl and her wicked twin sister.

- **bad food**

  The cake looked good, but it was inedible.

  There is nothing to eat but a piece of mouldy bread.

  There must be a rotten apple in the basket.

  The soup was tasteless.

ball
NOUN
*She shaped the piece of clay into a tiny **ball**.*
▷ globe, pellet, sphere

ballot
NOUN
*The result of the **ballot** was 13 votes for, and 8 votes against.*
▷ election, poll, vote

ban
VERB
*The committee will **ban** Olympic athletes who break the rules.*
▷ bar, disqualify, exclude, prohibit
ANTONYM allow

band
NOUN
*A **band** of circus performers came to our town.*
▷ bunch, company, group, party, troupe

bandit
NOUN
*Did the **bandit** steal the watch?*
▷ crook, outlaw, robber, thief

bang
VERB
*He likes to **bang** his toy cars together.*
▷ beat, crash, hammer, hit, knock, pound, slam, thump
NOUN
1 *The firework went off with a loud **bang**.*
▷ blast, boom, crack, detonation, explosion, thump
2 *I got a **bang** on the head when the book fell off the shelf.*
▷ blow, knock, thump, whack

MAKE IT MORE FORMAL

bang for your buck value for your money
bang into hit
bang on exactly correct
with a bang with great success

---

banish
VERB
*The government is going to **banish** the criminal from Canada.*
▷ deport, eject, evict, exile, expel

bank
NOUN
1 *Our community keeps a **bank** of food supplies in case of emergencies.*
▷ fund, hoard, reserve, stock, store

2 *Willow trees are growing on the **bank** of the river.*
▷ brink, edge, side

banter
VERB
*The children often **banter** with their uncle.*
▷ joke, kid, rib, tease

bar
NOUN
*Nail the **bar** across the window.*
▷ pole, rail, rod, shaft
VERB
*We plan to **bar** everyone from leaving by that exit.*
▷ ban, block, obstruct, prevent, prohibit

bare
ADJECTIVE
1 *In winter, the tiles on the bathroom floor are cold on my **bare** feet.*
▷ exposed, naked, uncovered
ANTONYM covered
2 *The **bare** room had a rug, but no furniture at all.*
▷ empty, spartan, vacant

barely
ADVERB
*He **barely** comes up to his dad's shoulder.*
▷ almost, hardly, just, scarcely

bark
VERB
*We heard a dog **bark**, but nobody was home.*
▷ bay, growl, yap

barren
ADJECTIVE
*The wheat fields became **barren** after the wind blew the soil away.*
▷ arid, desolate, dry, empty, unfertile
ANTONYM fertile

barrier
NOUN
*We got inside by climbing over a **barrier**.*
▷ barricade, fence, obstacle, obstruction, wall

barter
VERB
*People expect to **barter** goods at a flea market.*
▷ exchange, swap, trade

base
NOUN
*The **base** of the statue was damaged when a truck backed into it.*
▷ bottom, foot, foundation
ANTONYM top
VERB
***Base** your story on something you did yesterday.*
▷ build, derive, found, ground

B

B

bashful
ADJECTIVE
The bashful child hid behind his mother.
▷ modest, shy, timid
ANTONYM bold

basic
ADJECTIVE
You must have some basic knowledge of computers.
▷ elementary, essential, key, necessary

batch
NOUN
Do you have the batch of keys I gave you?
▷ bunch, group, lot, set

battle
NOUN
The fierce battle went on for two days.
▷ clash, combat, conflict, fight

bawl
VERB
The hungry child started to bawl.
▷ cry, howl, shout, sob, wail

bay
NOUN
The shallow bay was a safe place to swim.
▷ cove, gulf, inlet, sound
VERB
We heard the injured coyote bay.
▷ bark, cry, howl, yelp

beach
NOUN
We camped near the beach on Prince Edward Island.
▷ coast, sands, seashore, seaside, shore

beacon
NOUN
Can you see the beacon shining in the darkness?
▷ light, lighthouse, signal

bear
VERB
1 *The wooden bridge would not bear the weight of a car.*
▷ carry, support, take
2 *I cannot bear listening to that song again.*
▷ endure, stomach, suffer, tolerate

MAKE IT MORE FORMAL
bear a resemblance to resemble
bear in mind consider
bear out confirm

bearing
NOUN
His bearing is pleasing to others.
▷ appearance, attitude, behaviour, manner, posture

beat
VERB
1 *The waves beat on the shore.*
▷ batter, buffet, hit, pound, strike, thrash
2 *In this game, you must beat the evil ruler if you want to save the kingdom.*
▷ defeat, outdo, outstrip, overcome, overwhelm, vanquish
NOUN
I like the beat of the drums.
▷ pulse, rhythm, throb

beautiful
ADJECTIVE
We took many beautiful photographs of Tofino on Vancouver Island.
▷ attractive, delightful, exquisite, fine, gorgeous, lovely, pleasing
ANTONYM ugly

because
CONJUNCTION
I liked the book because it is about the future.
▷ as, since

beckon
VERB
Beckon me if you need help.
▷ call, invite, signal, summon

before
ADVERB
I lived on a farm before, but now I live in Moncton.
▷ earlier, formerly, previously
ANTONYM after

beg
VERB
We beg you to help us.
▷ appeal to, ask, entreat, implore, petition, plead with

begin
VERB
We will begin the school food bank drive tomorrow.
▷ commence, initiate, open, originate, start
ANTONYM end

beginner
NOUN
I am still a beginner in the St. John Ambulance training course.
▷ apprentice, learner, novice, trainee
ANTONYM expert

beginning
NOUN
The beginning of the book is exciting, but the rest is disappointing.
▷ opening, start
ANTONYM end

behave

VERB

Do not expect people to behave like machines.

▷ act, function, operate, perform, work

behaviour

NOUN

Your behaviour has made everyone in your family feel proud.

▷ attitude, conduct, demeanour, manner

belief

NOUN

She has a strong belief that her plan will work.

▷ conviction, judgment, opinion, view

believe

VERB

I believe that you are telling me the truth.

▷ accept, assume, presume, suppose, think, trust

ANTONYM doubt

bellow

VERB

I heard you; there's no need to bellow!

▷ bawl, roar, shout

below

PREPOSITION

Write your address on these three lines below your name.

▷ beneath, lower than, under

ANTONYM above

bend

VERB

1 *If you force it, the metal will bend out of shape.*

▷ buckle, curve, turn, twist, warp

2 *Bend down and touch the floor.*

▷ arch, bow, crouch, lean, stoop

benefit

NOUN

Clean air is a benefit for everyone.

▷ advantage, asset, boon, gain

ANTONYM disadvantage

VERB

Eating slowly is supposed to benefit your digestive system.

▷ aid, assist, enhance, further, help

ANTONYM harm

beside

PREPOSITION

I like to sit beside my brother on the school bus.

▷ adjacent to, alongside, close to, near, next to

best

ADJECTIVE

See box at foot of this page.

betray

VERB

The traitor planned to betray his friends.

▷ deceive, double-cross, dupe, inform on

bewilder

VERB

His bad behaviour continued to bewilder everyone.

▷ baffle, confuse, mystify, puzzle

beyond

PREPOSITION

I live one kilometre beyond the bridge.

▷ farther than, over, past

REPLACE AN OVERUSED WORD: BETTER/BEST

There are a number of substitutes for the adjectives **better/best** that can make your writing more interesting.

- **best quality**

  *Our family doctor provides the **finest** health care.*

  *The last concert was the **greatest** they ever did.*

  *My cousins wanted to see all the **principal** tourist attractions.*

  *This painting is the **supreme** achievement of her career.*

- **better quality**

  *Can you think of a **finer** place to live?*

  *Your attitude is much **improved**.*

  *How can you tell if one novel is **superior** to another?*

  *I'd rather work for a **worthier** cause.*

- **best in achievement**

  *Who was the **foremost** writer of that generation?*

  *Name the person you think is the **leading** movie actor today.*

  *All of Canada's **top** swimmers qualified for the Olympics.*

  *His time for the waterski slalom is **unbeaten**.*

- **better health**

  *I am a lot **fitter** than I was last year.*

  *Eating more fruit and vegetables makes me feel **healthier**.*

  *He is becoming **stronger** every day.*

  *I hope you will soon feel **well** again.*

B

bias
NOUN
*I think that the coach showed **bias** by choosing only tall players.*
▷ favouritism, prejudice

biased
ADJECTIVE
*The **biased** newspaper article did not give enough information.*
▷ one-sided, prejudiced, slanted
ANTONYM neutral

big
ADJECTIVE
See box at foot of this page.

bill
NOUN
*I will pay the **bill** for the broken window.*
▷ account, charge, invoice, statement

bind
VERB
***Bind** the two pieces of wood together with string.*
▷ attach, fasten, tie
ANTONYM untie

birth
NOUN
*Do you remember the **birth** of our friendship?*
▷ beginning, creation, origin, source
ANTONYM death

bit
NOUN
*There is only a **bit** of one cookie left.*
▷ crumb, fragment, morsel, part, piece, scrap, speck

bite
VERB
*We watched the chipmunk **bite** the peanut.*
▷ gnaw, nibble, nip

MAKE IT MORE FORMAL

bite off more than you can chew attempt something too difficult
bite someone's head off be sharply angry with someone
bite your tongue keep from saying something
put the bite on demand money from
take a bite out of use up a large part of
What's biting you? What's annoying you?

bitter
ADJECTIVE
1 *She was **bitter** because she was not allowed to go to the movie.*
▷ acrimonious, embittered, rancorous, resentful, sour
2 *The grapes had a **bitter** flavour.*
▷ acid, acrid, sharp, sour, tart
ANTONYM sweet

bizarre
ADJECTIVE
*I saw a **bizarre** painting at the art show.*
▷ curious, eccentric, extraordinary, odd, outlandish, peculiar, queer, strange, weird
ANTONYM ordinary

black
ADJECTIVE
*Our Newfoundland dog has thick **black** fur.*
▷ ebony, inky, jet, jet black, pitch black, raven

REPLACE AN OVERUSED WORD: BIG

There are an enormous number of substitutes for the adjective **big** that will make your writing livelier.

- **big in size**
  *A **colossal** statue stands at the entrance to the park.*
  *The blue whale is a **gigantic** animal.*
  *The pillars at the front of the museum are **massive**.*
  *The **vast** new stadium can hold almost 100 000 spectators.*

- **big in society**
  *He had **important** news for us.*

*Dennis Lee is one of Canada's **leading** poets.*
*I have a **major** role in the school play.*
*The villain in the movie is a **powerful** politician.*

- **big in importance**
  *He was exhausted before the race, and so was at a **grave** disadvantage.*
  *The prime minister has to make a **momentous** decision today.*
  *This is a **serious** problem.*
  *I have an **urgent** need for a drink of water.*

blame
VERB
Who should I blame for the broken lamp?
▷ accuse, charge, condemn, hold responsible

bland
ADJECTIVE
The food is bland and not spicy at all.
▷ boring, dull, mild, tasteless

blank
ADJECTIVE
1 *All we saw was a blank computer screen.*
▷ bare, clean, clear, empty, plain, unmarked
2 *Her blank stare told us she did not recognize us.*
▷ dull, empty, vacant

blast
NOUN
We heard a loud noise and then felt a blast of hot air.
▷ blow, burst, discharge, explosion

blaze
VERB
She threw sticks on the bonfire and made it blaze again.
▷ burn, flare, glow

bleak
ADJECTIVE
He had a bleak view from his apartment window.
▷ bare, barren, desolate, dreary, dismal

blemish
NOUN
The tabletop was perfect, except for a small blemish on one corner.
▷ defect, fault, flaw, mark, spot, stain

blend
VERB
Blend the blue and yellow paints to get green.
▷ combine, merge, mingle, mix
ANTONYM separate
NOUN
The radio station plays a blend of reggae and pop music.
▷ combination, compound, mix, mixture

blessing
NOUN
It was a blessing that they remembered to take the first-aid kit.
▷ benefit, boon, help
ANTONYM disadvantage

blight
NOUN
The blight killed all our roses.
▷ disease, pest, plague

bliss
NOUN
It was pure bliss to finally get home.
▷ ecstasy, happiness, joy, rapture

block
NOUN
We bought a large block of cheese at the farmers' market.
▷ chunk, lump, mass, piece
VERB
1 *Those leaves might block the sewer if you rake them onto the street.*
▷ choke, clog, obstruct, plug
2 *The town council plans to block the construction of another mall.*
▷ bar, check, halt, obstruct, stop, thwart

bloom
VERB
Those flowers bloom only in September.
▷ blossom, flourish, flower, thrive

blow
VERB
The wind continued to blow the leaves around.
▷ buffet, drive, sweep, waft, whirl
NOUN
1 *A big icicle broke off and gave me a blow on my head.*
▷ bang, knock, smack, thump, whack
2 *It was a blow to have our field day postponed due to rain.*
▷ loss, misfortune, setback, shock, upset

MAKE IT MORE FORMAL
blow away astonish
blow off reject advances
blow over pass by; be forgotten
blow up explode
blow your mind amaze you

blue
ADJECTIVE
My sister and I both have blue eyes.
▷ aquamarine, azure, cobalt, cyan, robin's-egg blue, electric blue, gentian, indigo, midnight blue, navy, peacock blue, periwinkle, royal blue, sapphire, sky blue, teal, turquoise

blunder
NOUN
I made a stupid blunder on my math test.
▷ error, mistake, oversight, slip

blunt
ADJECTIVE
1 *The blunt knife could not cut the vegetables.*
▷ dull, rounded, unsharpened
ANTONYM sharp
2 *Mom was blunt and just said we couldn't go.*
▷ brusque, forthright, frank, outspoken, straightforward
ANTONYM tactful

blush
VERB
*I always **blush** when my grandpa teases me.*
▷ flush, redden

board
NOUN
*The **board** decided to close down the pool.*
▷ committee, council, management

boast
VERB
*I like to **boast** about my clever sister.*
▷ brag, crow, show off

boat
NOUN
See picture below.

body
NOUN
1 *He has the **body** of an athlete.*
▷ figure, form, frame, physique, shape
2 *The **body** of the moose lay by the side of the road.*
▷ carcass, corpse, remains

body of water
NOUN
See picture on next page.

bogus
ADJECTIVE
*The **bogus** money showed up in several stores.*
▷ counterfeit, fake, false, imitation, phony, sham
ANTONYM genuine

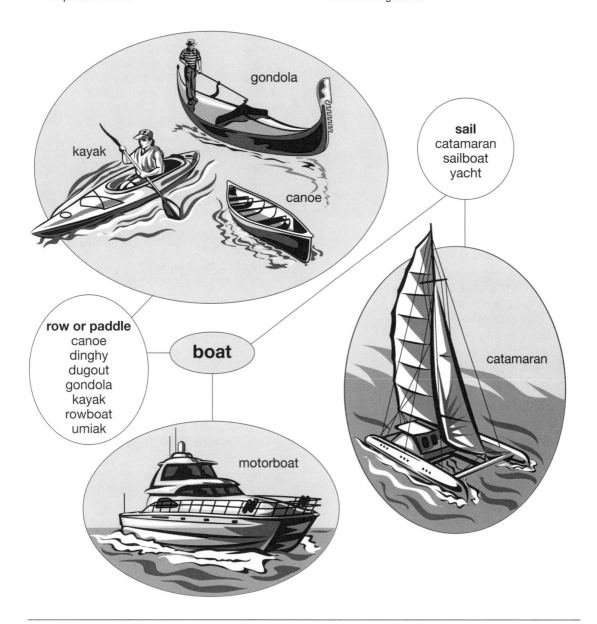

gondola

kayak

canoe

sail
catamaran
sailboat
yacht

row or paddle
canoe
dinghy
dugout
gondola
kayak
rowboat
umiak

boat

catamaran

motorboat

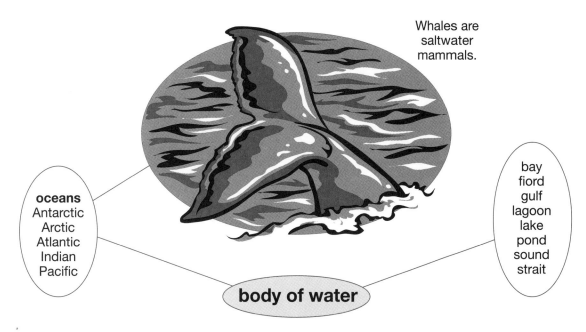

Whales are saltwater mammals.

oceans
Antarctic
Arctic
Atlantic
Indian
Pacific

bay
fiord
gulf
lagoon
lake
pond
sound
strait

body of water

boil
VERB
The liquid in the pot got hotter and hotter and then began to boil.
▷ bubble, fizz, foam, froth, steam

MAKE IT MORE FORMAL
boil down reduce to essentials
boil over let excitement or anger show

boisterous
ADJECTIVE
The boisterous children could not keep quiet.
▷ loud, noisy, rowdy, unruly, wild

bold
ADJECTIVE
1 *I am shocked by your bold behaviour.*
▷ brash, brazen, cheeky, impudent
ANTONYM shy
2 *The bold knight slew the dragon.*
▷ adventurous, brave, courageous, daring, fearless, intrepid, valiant
ANTONYM cowardly
3 *I like your ski jacket with its bold stripes.*
▷ bright, eye-catching, flashy, loud, striking, strong, vivid
ANTONYM dull

bolt
VERB
The dog tried to bolt through the gate.
▷ dash, escape, flee, fly, run away, run off, rush

bond
NOUN
1 *Most twins have a strong bond with one another.*
▷ attachment, connection, link, relationship, tie, union
2 *She broke her bond to mow the lawn every week.*
▷ agreement, contract, obligation, pledge, promise, word
VERB
Bond the pieces of wood with strong glue.
▷ bind, fasten, fuse, glue, paste

bonus
NOUN
There was a bonus given for perfect attendance.
▷ award, benefit, extra, prize, reward

book
NOUN
Every book in the library is listed in the computer.
▷ anthology, atlas, autobiography, biography, dictionary, directory, encyclopedia, glossary, guidebook, handbook, manual, novel, phrasebook, publication, textbook, thesaurus, title, volume, work
VERB
My mom is going to book our flight.
▷ arrange, charter, organize, reserve, schedule

MAKE IT MORE FORMAL
by the book according to the rules
in my book in my opinion
throw the book at punish as severely as the law allows

B

boom

NOUN

*The loud **boom** you heard was caused by an explosion at the factory.*

▷ bang, roar, rumble, thunder

boost

VERB

*We want to **boost** the number of singers in our choir.*

▷ increase, lift, raise, strengthen

border

NOUN

1 *The **border** between Canada and the United States stretches from the Atlantic Ocean to the Pacific Ocean.*

▷ boundary, frontier

2 *The backyard has flowers around the **border**.*

▷ edge, fringe, margin, rim

VERB

*The farmer built a fence to **border** her property.*

▷ edge, fringe, rim

bore

VERB

*Did I **bore** you with all my complaints?*

▷ fatigue, tire, weary

ANTONYM interest

bored

ADJECTIVE

*The **bored** fans left before the end of the game.*

▷ fed up, tired, uninterested, wearied

ANTONYM interested

boredom

NOUN

*The **boredom** of the movie made us sleepy.*

▷ dullness, flatness, monotony, tedium, weariness

ANTONYM interest

boring

ADJECTIVE

*They had all heard her **boring** story several times.*

▷ dull, flat, humdrum, monotonous, tedious, tiresome

ANTONYM interesting

boss

NOUN

*The **boss** has the only key to the safe.*

▷ chief, director, employer, head, leader, manager, supervisor

bossy

ADJECTIVE

*My **bossy** brother is always telling me what to do.*

▷ authoritarian, domineering, overbearing

bother

VERB

*Don't **bother** me when I'm studying.*

▷ annoy, disturb, irritate, pester, trouble, worry

NOUN

*We had some **bother** with raccoons getting into our garbage.*

▷ annoyance, difficulty, inconvenience, irritation, trouble, worry

bounce

VERB

*Do not **bounce** on the bed.*

▷ bound, jump, leap, spring

boundary

NOUN

*We painted a line to mark the **boundary** of our baseball game.*

▷ barrier, border, bounds, limits, perimeter

bow

VERB

*The knights must **bow** when the queen arrives.*

▷ bend, incline, kneel, stoop

box

NOUN

*Put the old magazines into the **box**.*

▷ carton, case, chest, container, trunk

boy

NOUN

*The **boy** grew much taller during the summer.*

▷ lad, youth

brag

VERB

*We are tired of hearing her **brag** about her rich uncle.*

▷ boast, crow, flaunt, gloat

brand

NOUN

*This is the **brand** of honey that I like best.*

▷ kind, make, sort, type

brandish

VERB

*The actor began to **brandish** his sword.*

▷ flourish, shake, wave

brash

ADJECTIVE

*The **brash** girl pushed her way to the front of the line.*

▷ bold, brazen, cocky, insolent, rude

brave

ADJECTIVE

*The **brave** firefighter ran into the burning building.*

▷ bold, courageous, daring, fearless, heroic, intrepid, plucky, valiant

ANTONYM cowardly

bread

NOUN

*I ate a piece of **bread** with my meal.*

▷ bannock, brioche, chapati, croissant, fry bread, pita, nan, roti, tortilla

B

REPLACE AN OVERUSED WORD: BREAK

Instead of using the verb **break**, choose a word that gives information about the way that something breaks.

- If you **crack** something, it doesn't fall apart.
  I did not know the glass would crack if I filled it with hot water.

- If you **crumble** something, it breaks into small pieces.
  The old brick began to crumble into pieces in my hand.

- If you **fracture** something, it gets a small crack in it.
  A fall could fracture your leg, or even break it.

- If you **smash** something, it breaks into many tiny pieces.
  Did you drop the plate, or did it smash all by itself?

- If you **snap** something, it breaks into two pieces.
  I watched the tree branch bend under the weight of snow, then I saw it snap.

- If you **split** something, it usually breaks into two parts lengthwise.
  Split that piece of wood down the middle.

break
VERB
See box at top of this page.

break
NOUN
There was a break after the band had played for an hour.
▷ interlude, intermission, interval, pause, recess, respite, rest

MAKE IT MORE FORMAL

break down stop functioning
break even gain nothing and lose nothing
break free escape
break off stop suddenly
break out escape
break the ice help peple begin to start talking and get acquainted
break up disintegrate; separate

breed
NOUN
What breed of tropical fish do you have?
▷ kind, species, stock, strain, type, variety
VERB
1 *My aunt wants to breed chickens in her backyard.*
▷ cultivate, develop, keep, nurture, raise, rear
2 *Mosquitoes breed best in wet weather.*
▷ multiply, produce, propagate, reproduce

bribe
VERB
The dishonest developer tried to bribe the mayor.
▷ buy off, corrupt

bridge
NOUN
See picture on next page.

brief
ADJECTIVE
We had a brief conversation, then I hung up.
▷ fleeting, little, momentary, quick, short, swift
ANTONYM lengthy

bright
ADJECTIVE
1 *The evening star was very bright tonight.*
▷ brilliant, dazzling, luminous, radiant, vivid
ANTONYM dull
2 *The bright child could read when he was two years old.*
▷ brainy, brilliant, clever, intelligent, smart
ANTONYM stupid

brilliant
ADJECTIVE
1 *After he polished it, the silver trophy was brilliant.*
▷ bright, dazzling, gleaming, luminous, sparkling, vivid
ANTONYM dull
2 *She gave a brilliant performance in the play.*
▷ acute, bright, clever, intelligent, perceptive, sharp, smart
ANTONYM stupid

bring
VERB
I will bring your book back tomorrow.
▷ carry, deliver, take, transport
ANTONYM take

MAKE IT MORE FORMAL

bring down overthrow
bring in earn
bring out produce
bring to light reveal
bring up raise

B

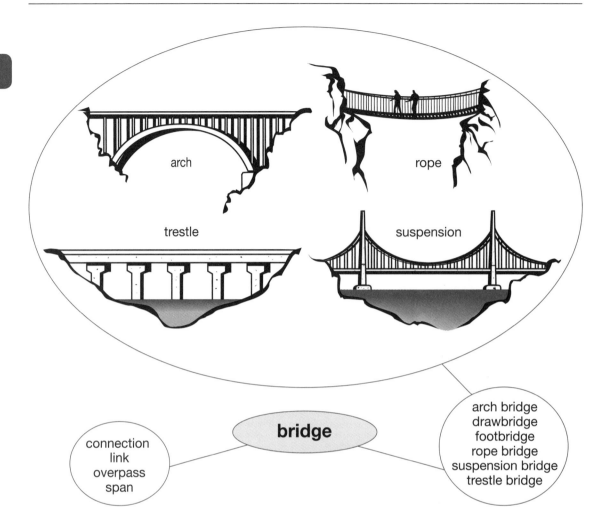

arch

rope

trestle

suspension

bridge

connection
link
overpass
span

arch bridge
drawbridge
footbridge
rope bridge
suspension bridge
trestle bridge

brisk
ADJECTIVE
*She swept the porch in a **brisk** way.*
▷ active, energetic, quick
ANTONYM sluggish

broad
ADJECTIVE
1 *The park has a **broad** flower garden along one side of the pathway.*
▷ expansive, extensive, large, thick, wide
ANTONYM narrow
2 *Our teacher has a **broad** knowledge of computer programming.*
▷ comprehensive, extensive, general, wide
ANTONYM narrow

brood
VERB
*I decided not to **brood** about my poor mark in English this year.*
▷ fret, ponder, worry

brown
ADJECTIVE
*The rug is **brown**, with a white border.*
▷ beige, bronze, chestnut, chocolate, coffee, fawn, hazel, mahogany, mocha, oatmeal, russet, rust, sandy, tan, taupe

brutal
ADJECTIVE
*Yesterday we saw a **brutal** dog attack a small child.*
▷ cruel, fierce, mean, savage, violent

budge
VERB
*I was not able to **budge** the huge rock.*
▷ move, push, shift, slide

build
VERB
*My mom and I are going to **build** a treehouse.*
▷ assemble, construct, erect, fabricate, make
ANTONYM dismantle

bulge
NOUN
*He has a huge **bulge** on his forehead where the icy snowball hit him.*
▷ bump, lump, swelling

bulky
ADJECTIVE
*Will you help me carry this **bulky** package?*
▷ big, cumbersome, huge, massive

bully
NOUN
*If a **bully** teases you, tell an adult.*
▷ oppressor, persecutor, tormentor
VERB
*The girl was caught trying to **bully** the younger children.*
▷ intimidate, oppress, persecute, tease, torment

bump
VERB
*The car seemed to **bump** the curb before it stopped.*
▷ bang, collide with, hit, knock, strike
NOUN
*Put some ice on that **bump** on your head.*
▷ bulge, hump, knob, lump, swelling

bunch
NOUN
1 *A noisy **bunch** of students stood waiting for the bus.*
▷ band, crowd, gaggle, gang, group, lot
2 *Are there more carrots in that **bunch**?*
▷ batch, bundle, cluster, heap, load, pile

bungle
VERB
*I hope I do not **bungle** the job.*
▷ botch, mess up, ruin, spoil

burden
NOUN
1 *A sack of potatoes is a heavy **burden** for a small child.*
▷ load, weight
2 *I have the **burden** of caring for my sick cat.*
▷ anxiety, care, strain, stress, trouble, worry

burly
ADJECTIVE
*The **burly** workers easily lifted the injured man.*
▷ beefy, big, brawny, hefty, muscular, stocky, strong

burn
VERB
*The sparks from the fire caused the rug to **burn**.*
▷ blaze, char, incinerate, scorch, singe

burst
VERB
*This bag will **burst** if I add one more item to it.*
▷ break, crack, explode, rupture, split

business
NOUN
*My mother owns her own catering **business**.*
▷ company, corporation, enterprise, establishment, firm, organization

busy
ADJECTIVE
1 *He is **busy** online right now.*
▷ active, engaged, engrossed, occupied, working
ANTONYM idle
2 *Summer is a very **busy** time for her.*
▷ active, full, hectic, lively

but
CONJUNCTION
*She enjoyed the tacos, **but** the sauce was too spicy.*
▷ although, though, while, yet
PREPOSITION
*We liked all the pies **but** one.*
▷ except, except for, other than, save

buy
VERB
*Where can I **buy** a cheap pair of boots?*
▷ acquire, obtain, purchase
ANTONYM sell

C c

cabin
NOUN
They stayed in a small cabin by a lake.
▷ chalet, cottage, hut, shack

calamity
NOUN
The collapse of the bridge is a calamity.
▷ catastrophe, disaster, misfortune

calculate
VERB
Please calculate what I owe you.
▷ compute, count, figure, reckon

call
VERB
See box at foot of this page.

MAKE IT MORE FORMAL
call off cancel
call on visit

callous
ADJECTIVE
Her callous remark made me cry.
▷ cold, heartless, insensitive
ANTONYM caring

calm
ADJECTIVE
1 *His calm manner made us feel better.*
▷ collected, composed, cool, relaxed
ANTONYM worried
2 *The lake was so calm, it looked as smooth as glass.*
▷ peaceful, quiet, serene, still, tranquil
ANTONYM rough
VERB
The nurse was able to calm the worried mother.
▷ comfort, ease, pacify, relax, soothe

cancel
VERB
We are not going to cancel our plans.
▷ abandon, call off

candid
ADJECTIVE
The movie star gave candid answers to the reporter.
▷ frank, open, truthful

capable
ADJECTIVE
A capable babysitter is always in demand.
▷ able, competent, efficient
ANTONYM incompetent

REPLACE AN OVERUSED WORD: CALL

Depending on which sense of **call** you are thinking of, there are a number of other verbs that you can use to make your language more colourful.

- **to give a name to**
  *The United Nations decided to **designate** Alberta's Dinosaur Provincial Park a World Heritage Site.*
  *"I **dub** thee knight," said the king.*
  *Just because I forgot to phone you yesterday, there's no need to **label** me absent-minded.*
  *What did they **name** their new baby?*

- **to describe as**
  *Do you **consider** yourself a musician?*
  *He's not what you'd **describe as** a sports lover.*
  *I **judge** that contestant the best.*
  *We don't know her well, but we **term** her intelligent.*

- **to telephone**
  Contact me immediately.

  *As soon as you get home, **phone** me.*
  *I'll **ring** you later.*
  *You should **telephone** to make an appointment.*

- **to speak loudly**
  *We all heard him **announce** the name of the winner.*
  *"Run like the wind!" she would **cry**.*
  *If you **shout**, they should hear you.*
  *I have apologized, so there's no need to **yell** at me.*

- **to bring together**
  ***Assemble** the school for the graduation ceremony.*
  *Who will **convene** a council of elders?*
  *I'd like to **gather** all of you together more often.*
  *He e-mailed to **summon** us to the meeting.*

C

capacity
NOUN
1 *What is the capacity of the measuring cup?*
▷ size, volume
2 *She does not have a great capacity for concentration.*
▷ ability, capability

captain
NOUN
She is the captain of our group.
▷ chief, commander, head, leader

capture
VERB
The police are confident they will capture the car thief.
▷ apprehend, arrest, catch
ANTONYM release

car
NOUN
We travelled by car to the Laurentian Mountains.
▷ automobile, limo, vehicle

carcass
NOUN
The students dissected the carcass of a frog.
▷ body, corpse

care
VERB
We care about global warming.
▷ be bothered, be concerned
NOUN
They left for vacation without a care.
▷ anxiety, concern, stress, trouble, worry

careful
ADJECTIVE
1 *Be careful when you cross the street.*
▷ cautious, prudent, wary
ANTONYM careless
2 *Setting up an experiment needs careful preparation.*
▷ meticulous, painstaking, precise, thorough
ANTONYM careless

careless
ADJECTIVE
The careless children lost their mittens.
▷ irresponsible, neglectful, thoughtless
ANTONYM careful

carry
VERB
Please carry the trash out to the curb.
▷ bring, convey, take, transport

MAKE IT MORE FORMAL
carry on continue
carry out perform

carton
NOUN
I need a carton so I can pack my books.
▷ box, case, container, crate

carve
VERB
Do not carve your initials into the desk.
▷ chisel, cut, engrave, inscribe

case
NOUN
1 *My glasses are kept in a plastic case.*
▷ box, container
2 *The case was dropped due to lack of evidence.*
▷ action, lawsuit, proceedings, trial

cash
NOUN
We don't keep much cash at home.
▷ bills, coins, money

cast
VERB
Try to cast the Frisbee over the trees.
▷ fling, pitch, throw, toss

casual
ADJECTIVE
He gave a casual wave from the car.
▷ careless, informal, offhand

catch
VERB
Were the police able to catch the burglar?
▷ apprehend, arrest, capture, snare, trap

MAKE IT MORE FORMAL
catch it be scolded or punished
catch on understand; be popular

cause
NOUN
1 *What was the cause of all the noise?*
▷ origin, root, source
2 *I support this worthy cause.*
▷ aim, movement
VERB
The accident will definitely cause a traffic problem.
▷ create, generate, produce

caution
NOUN
Use caution when you are rock climbing.
▷ care, prudence, wariness

cautious
ADJECTIVE
She has a cautious nature.
▷ careful, guarded, tentative, wary
ANTONYM daring

C

cease
VERB
Cease that racket immediately!
▷ discontinue, end, finish, stop, terminate
ANTONYM start

celebration
NOUN
Our town's fall celebration is in October.
▷ festival, festivity, gala, party

censor
VERB
Will the radio station censor that song?
▷ ban, cut, suppress

censure
VERB
Do not censure him for his ideas.
▷ blame, condemn, criticize, disapprove, reprimand
ANTONYM praise

centre
NOUN
The environment will be the centre of the discussion.
▷ core, focus, heart
VERB
Centre your attention on planning the party.
▷ concentrate, focus

ceremony
NOUN
There was a Remembrance Day ceremony in the gym.
▷ observance, rite, ritual

certain
ADJECTIVE
1 *Is it certain that the exam is on Monday?*
▷ definite, established, guaranteed, known, sure, undeniable
ANTONYM doubtful
2 *I am not certain that I can get there early.*
▷ confident, convinced, definite, sure, positive
ANTONYM unsure

certainly
ADVERB
She is certainly a trustworthy person.
▷ definitely, undeniably, undoubtedly, unquestionably, without doubt

certificate
NOUN
My certificate shows that I completed the course.
▷ deed, diploma, document

chain
VERB
Chain the vicious dog to the post.
▷ bind, shackle, tie

challenge
VERB
1 *I challenge you to sing alone!*
▷ dare, defy
2 *The opposition will challenge the government on every issue.*
▷ dispute, question

champion
NOUN
He is the yo-yo champion.
▷ hero, title holder, victor, winner

chance
NOUN
1 *There is a chance of snow tomorrow.*
▷ likelihood, possibility, probability
2 *I did not get a chance to call you.*
▷ occasion, opening, opportunity
3 *It was by chance that we spotted the little kitten in the tree.*
▷ accident, coincidence, fortune, luck

change
NOUN
He would not agree to the change in the club rules.
▷ alteration, difference, modification
VERB
1 *I am going to change my eating habits.*
▷ alter, convert, moderate, modify, reform, transform
2 *Change this pillow for a softer one.*
▷ exchange, replace, substitute, swap, trade

chaos
NOUN
The chaos in the schoolyard upset him.
▷ confusion, disorder, muddle, turmoil

character
NOUN
1 *She has an agreeable character.*
▷ nature, personality, temperament
2 *The boy showed character when he decided to defy the bullies.*
▷ honour, integrity, strength

characteristic
NOUN
The flatness of the land is its main characteristic.
▷ attribute, feature, property, quality, trait

charge
VERB
Why did the crowd charge onto the stage?
▷ dash, rush, stampede, storm
NOUN
There is a charge to deliver the pizza.
▷ cost, fee, price

charm

NOUN

*His **charm** is an asset in his sales job.*

▷ allure, appeal, attraction, fascination, magnetism

VERB

*She is able to **charm** almost everyone.*

▷ bewitch, captivate, delight, entrance

charming

ADJECTIVE

*The **charming** child was well-behaved.*

▷ appealing, delightful, lovable, pleasant

chase

VERB

*We had to **chase** the bouncing ball.*

▷ pursue, track

chat

VERB

*He liked to **chat** with the neighbours.*

▷ gossip, talk

cheap

ADJECTIVE

1 *I love shopping for **cheap** shoes.*

▷ bargain, economical, inexpensive, reasonable

ANTONYM expensive

2 *My **cheap** hair dryer broke.*

▷ inferior, second-rate, tacky

cheat

VERB

*They tried to **cheat** the old man, but he was too clever for them.*

▷ deceive, defraud, dupe, fleece, swindle

check

VERB

1 ***Check** the air in your bicycle tires.*

▷ examine, inspect, monitor, test

2 *Wash your hands to **check** the spread of germs.*

▷ control, curb, halt, inhibit, restrain, stop

cheer

VERB

*I tried to **cheer** her when her canary died.*

▷ comfort, console, hearten

cheerful

ADJECTIVE

*Try to be **cheerful** in spite of the rain.*

▷ bright, buoyant, glad, happy, jaunty, jolly, light-hearted, merry

ANTONYM miserable

cherish

VERB

*I **cherish** the bracelet you gave me.*

▷ appreciate, prize, treasure, value

ANTONYM neglect

chew

VERB

*Our dog Rover likes to **chew** on bones.*

▷ bite, chomp, crunch, gnaw, munch

MAKE IT MORE FORMAL

chew out scold

chew the fat chat

chief

NOUN

*She was the **chief** of the organization for years.*

▷ boss, director, head, leader, manager

ADJECTIVE

*The **chief** reason we went was to see our relatives.*

▷ foremost, key, leading, main, primary, prime, principal

child

NOUN

*Which **child** is your sister?*

▷ baby, infant, juvenile, toddler, tot, youngster

ANTONYM adult

childish

ADJECTIVE

*Making faces is a **childish** thing to do.*

▷ immature, infantile, juvenile

ANTONYM mature

chilly

ADJECTIVE

*I was **chilly**, so I put my sweater on.*

▷ cold, cool

chirp

VERB

*We heard the birds **chirp**.*

▷ cheep, trill, twitter, warble

choice

NOUN

1 *That store has a wide **choice** of skis.*

▷ range, selection, variety

2 *Do we have any **choice** in the matter?*

▷ alternative, option, say

choke

VERB

*Thick smoke can **choke** you.*

▷ gag, smother, strangle

choose

VERB

*Which one did you **choose**?*

▷ decide on, elect, pick, prefer, select, take

chop

VERB

*She began to **chop** the top off the bush.*

▷ cut, hack, lop

C

chubby
ADJECTIVE
See box at fat.

chunk
NOUN
He cut a chunk of cheese for himself.
▷ block, lump, piece, portion, slab

circle
NOUN
1 *The brooch was a simple circle of gold.*
▷ band, circuit, hoop, loop, ring
2 *She did not want to join their circle.*
▷ clique, crowd, gang, group

circulate
VERB
Please circulate the bake-sale flyers.
▷ distribute, publicize, spread

cite
VERB
You must cite the source of your information.
▷ mention, name, quote, refer to

city
NOUN
Our city has good schools.
▷ metropolis, municipality, town

civil
ADJECTIVE
I expect you to be civil to our visitors.
▷ courteous, polite

claim
VERB
Do you still claim that the dog ate your homework?
▷ allege, assert, hold, insist, maintain

clap
VERB
Please clap if you enjoyed the show.
▷ applaud, cheer

clash
VERB
My opinions and hers often clash.
▷ conflict, contradict, differ, disagree, jar
NOUN
The clash began when they bumped into each other.
▷ argument, battle, conflict, confrontation, dispute, fight, quarrel, skirmish, struggle

clasp
VERB
She reached down to clasp the child.
▷ clutch, embrace, grasp, grip, hold
NOUN
The clasp on her backpack was broken.
▷ buckle, catch, clip, fastener, fastening

class
NOUN
Into which class would you place these items?
▷ category, genre, group, kind, set, sort, type

classify
VERB
Classify the books according to subject.
▷ arrange, categorize, grade, group, rank, sort

clean
ADJECTIVE
I was impressed by how clean her room was.
▷ immaculate, impeccable, spotless
ANTONYM dirty
VERB
He tried to clean the paint from his shirt.
▷ cleanse, scour, wash, wipe

clear
ADJECTIVE
1 *It is clear that we do not have enough players.*
▷ apparent, evident, explicit, obvious, plain
2 *The clear tape let the address show through.*
▷ glassy, translucent, transparent
ANTONYM cloudy

cleft
NOUN
There was a cleft in the rock.
▷ cranny, crack, crevice, slit, split

clever
ADJECTIVE
My clever budgie has learned to say several words.
▷ bright, intelligent, shrewd, smart

cliff
NOUN
The cliff rose twenty metres above the beach.
▷ bluff, crag, height, precipice

climax
NOUN
The car race was the climax of the movie.
▷ highlight, high point, peak

climb
VERB
We climb the rock face every weekend.
▷ ascend, clamber up, mount, scale

cling
VERB
The young monkey tried to cling on to the branch.
▷ adhere, attach, clutch, grasp, stick

clip
VERB
Dad told me to clip the hedge.
▷ cut, prune, snip, trim

C

clog
VERB
The weeds will eventually clog the stream.
▷ block, choke, fill, plug

close
VERB
1 *Please close the window.*
▷ secure, shut
ANTONYM open
2 *They had to close the entrance to the building.*
▷ bar, block, obstruct, seal
ADJECTIVE
See box at foot of this page.

cloth
NOUN
The pillow is made from silky cloth.
▷ fabric, material

clothes
NOUN
I want to show you my new winter clothes.
▷ attire, clothing, costume, garments, outfit

clothing
NOUN
See picture on next page.

cloud
NOUN
The sun was just coming out from behind the cloud.
▷ fog, haze, mist, vapour

cloudy
ADJECTIVE
1 *The day was cloudy, so they stayed indoors.*
▷ dull, gloomy, leaden, overcast
2 *I decided not to drink the cloudy water.*
▷ muddy, murky, opaque
ANTONYM clear

club
NOUN
1 *Our club meets once a week.*
▷ association, circle, group, guild, society, union
2 *You can use my club if you break yours.*
▷ bat, stick

clue
NOUN
The clue to the missing pie was the crumbs on her face.
▷ evidence, hint, indication, sign

clumsy
ADJECTIVE
The clumsy child tripped over the box.
▷ awkward, gawky, uncoordinated, ungainly
ANTONYM graceful

clutch
VERB
Clutch onto the side of the boat!
▷ clasp, cling, grab, grasp, grip, seize

clutter
NOUN
He cleaned up the clutter in the living room.
▷ disorder, jumble, litter, mess

coach
NOUN
Their swimming coach is very patient.
▷ instructor, teacher, trainer, tutor

coarse
ADJECTIVE
1 *The surface of the wood was coarse.*
▷ rough, uneven, unpolished
ANTONYM smooth
2 *It is unacceptable to use coarse language.*
▷ crude, offensive, vulgar
ANTONYM polite

REPLACE AN OVERUSED WORD: CLOSE

If you are talking about people or things that are **close** in distance or in time, or you are describing the closeness of personal relationships, you can use various other adjectives as substitutes.

- **close in distance**
  *My cousins live in the apartment building **adjacent** to this one.*
  *Keep a dictionary **handy** when you are writing.*
  *My home is very **near** to my school.*
  *We like to go swimming in a **nearby** lake.*

- **close in time**
  *Isn't your birthday **approaching**?*
  *We knew the storm was **at hand**.*

  *The end of term is **imminent**, and then I go on holiday.*
  *Can animals sense an **impending** earthquake?*

- **close in relationship**
  *My sister and I are very **attached** to one another.*
  *Her cat was a **dear** companion to her.*
  *The three students gradually became very **friendly** with each other.*
  *The two of them formed a **loving** relationship.*

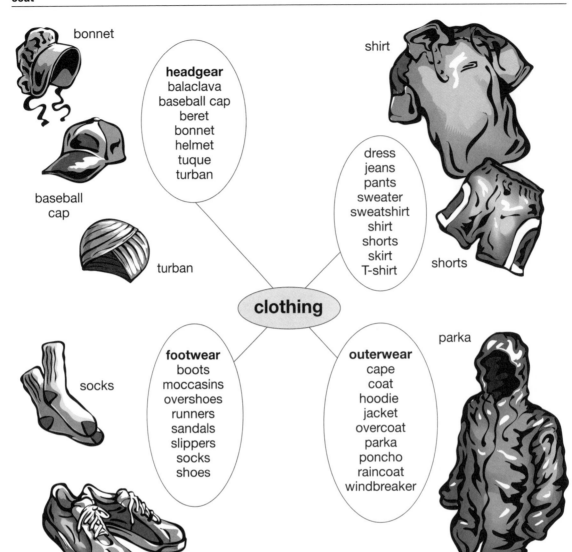

bonnet

headgear
balaclava
baseball cap
beret
bonnet
helmet
tuque
turban

baseball
cap

turban

shirt

dress
jeans
pants
sweater
sweatshirt
shirt
shorts
skirt
T-shirt

shorts

clothing

socks

footwear
boots
moccasins
overshoes
runners
sandals
slippers
socks
shoes

outerwear
cape
coat
hoodie
jacket
overcoat
parka
poncho
raincoat
windbreaker

parka

runners

coat
NOUN
The goat's coat was a dirty white colour.
▷ fleece, fur, hair, hide, pelt

coating
NOUN
She put a thin coating of paint on the paper.
▷ coat, covering, layer

coax
VERB
We had to coax him to play the guitar.
▷ cajole, persuade, urge
ANTONYM dissuade

coil
VERB
Ask her to coil the rope neatly.
▷ curl, loop, spiral, twine, twist, wind

cold
ADJECTIVE
1 *The cold weather lasted for two weeks.*
▷ arctic, biting, bitter, bleak, chilly, freezing, frigid, frosty, frozen, icy, wintry
ANTONYM hot
2 *He gave us a cold look and then ignored us.*
▷ aloof, cool, distant, reserved, stony, unfriendly
ANTONYM warm

MAKE IT MORE FORMAL
cold feet loss of courage
out cold unconscious
out in the cold neglected
break out in a cold sweat sweat from fear
catch cold become sick with a cold
cold cash money

collapse

VERB

*We watched the children's sandcastle **collapse** as the tide came in.*

▷ disintegrate, fall, topple

colleague

NOUN

*My brother and his **colleague** decorated the gym.*

▷ associate, partner, workmate

collect

VERB

***Collect** as many people as you can to help.*

▷ accumulate, assemble, gather

ANTONYM scatter

collection

NOUN

*My sister has a huge **collection** of toys.*

▷ assortment, heap, hoard, mass

collective noun

NOUN

See picture at foot of this page.

collide

VERB

*Did you see the two hockey players **collide**?*

▷ bump, crash, hit, strike

colossal

ADJECTIVE

*The **colossal** jet took off with a roar.*

▷ enormous, giant, gigantic, huge, immense, mammoth, massive, vast

ANTONYM tiny

colourful

ADJECTIVE

*The **colourful** balloons drifted across the sky.*

▷ bright, brilliant, intense, rich, vibrant, vivid

ANTONYM dull

column

NOUN

*The porch has a **column** at each end.*

▷ pillar, post

combat

VERB

*The health department has a plan to **combat** the spread of disease.*

▷ battle, fight, oppose, resist

combine

VERB

*The teachers will **combine** the two classes for Music.*

▷ blend, fuse, integrate, join, merge, mix, unite

ANTONYM separate

a colony of seals

birds, fish, and insects
a swarm of bees
a flock of birds
a cloud of blackflies
a brood of chicks
a shoal of fish
a gaggle of geese
or
a skein of geese

collective noun

mammals
a herd of cattle
a litter of kittens
a pride of lions
a troop of monkeys
a colony of seals
a flock of sheep
a pod of whales
or
a school of whales
a pack of wolves

come

VERB

I will come early to help you get ready.

▷ appear, arrive, enter, materialize

MAKE IT MORE FORMAL

come about happen
come across discover
come after follow
come apart split
come back return
come between divide
come first win
come out appear
come to total; wake
come up with invent

---

comfort

NOUN

1 *I enjoyed the comfort of the soft chair.*

▷ ease, luxury

2 *The nurse gave her patients some comfort.*

▷ help, relief, support

VERB

I tried to comfort the lost child.

▷ cheer, console, reassure, soothe

comfortable

ADJECTIVE

1 *This room is very comfortable.*

▷ cozy, easy, homey, relaxing, restful

2 *Will you feel comfortable here?*

▷ at ease, contented, happy, relaxed

ANTONYM uneasy

command

VERB

1 *He will command the elephant to pick up the log.*

▷ demand, direct, order

2 *Who is going to command the troops?*

▷ control, head, lead, manage, supervise

commence

VERB

The race will commence at the main entrance.

▷ begin, originate, start

ANTONYM finish

comment

NOUN

My comment on the TV program was ignored.

▷ observation, remark, statement

comment on

VERB

She expected them to comment on her new bike.

▷ mention, note, observe, remark on

commit

VERB

He refused to commit the crime.

▷ carry out, perform, perpetrate

common

ADJECTIVE

1 *White is a common choice for kitchen walls.*

▷ general, popular, universal, widespread

ANTONYM rare

2 *This style is quite common now.*

▷ average, commonplace, everyday, ordinary, standard, usual

commotion

NOUN

What caused the commotion?

▷ disturbance, excitement, fuss, noise, racket, stir, uproar

communicate

VERB

Did you communicate the problem to her?

▷ express, relate, report, reveal

companion

NOUN

My companion intends to come with me.

▷ associate, comrade, crony, friend, pal, partner

company

NOUN

1 *She works for a large company.*

▷ business, corporation, establishment, firm, outfit

2 *The plan is to add twenty people to the company.*

▷ assembly, band, circle, community, crowd, ensemble, group, party, troupe

compare

VERB

Compare the two plans and choose the better one.

▷ contrast, match, weigh

compassion

NOUN

The family appreciated his compassion.

▷ kindness, mercy, pity, sympathy

compel

VERB

How will you compel her to go with you?

▷ force, make, require

compensate

VERB

1 *The courier will compensate you for the lost package.*

▷ repay, reward

2 *The speed of the players will compensate for their smaller size.*

▷ balance, counteract, offset

C

compete
VERB
I intend to compete for a place on the team.
▷ contend, contest, fight, vie

competent
ADJECTIVE
The competent assistant corrected the error.
▷ able, capable, efficient, skilful
ANTONYM incompetent

competition
NOUN
Did you watch the skateboarding competition?
▷ championship, contest, event, tournament

complain
VERB
Why do you complain about school so much?
▷ grouse, grumble, moan, whine

complete
ADJECTIVE
1 *Our science experiment was a complete success.*
▷ absolute, perfect, thorough, total, utter
2 *The teacher asked for their complete attention.*
▷ entire, full, undivided, whole
VERB
Complete your homework before you go out.
▷ conclude, finish

complex
ADJECTIVE
He was not able to do the complex puzzle.
▷ complicated, difficult, intricate, involved
ANTONYM simple

complicated
ADJECTIVE
She made up a complicated game.
▷ complex, elaborate, intricate, involved
ANTONYM simple

compliment
VERB
I want to compliment you on your success.
▷ congratulate, praise, honour

compose
VERB
Did it take long to compose the poem?
▷ create, devise, produce, write

composed
ADJECTIVE
The girl was composed enough to help the injured child.
▷ calm, confident, cool
ANTONYM excited

compound
NOUN
Steel is a compound of iron and carbon.
▷ alloy, blend, mixture

comprehend
VERB
The boy finally began to comprehend the problem.
▷ appreciate, grasp, understand

compress
VERB
Compress your essay but keep all the facts.
▷ abbreviate, condense, reduce

compulsory
ADJECTIVE
They must go to the compulsory class.
▷ mandatory, obligatory, required
ANTONYM voluntary

con
VERB
The salesperson tried to con us.
▷ cheat, deceive, mislead, swindle, trick

conceal
VERB
Try to conceal your anger.
▷ cover, hide, mask
ANTONYM reveal

conceited
ADJECTIVE
The conceited girl ignored us.
▷ arrogant, egotistical, proud, smug, vain
ANTONYM modest

conceive
VERB
Try to conceive a better idea.
▷ create, devise, imagine, invent

concentrate on
VERB
Concentrate on becoming a better reader.
▷ focus on, ponder

concept
NOUN
He had difficulty explaining his concept.
▷ idea, theory, view, vision

concern
NOUN
1 *My concern is that we will be late.*
▷ anxiety, apprehension, disquiet, worry
2 *Your problems are not her concern.*
▷ affair, business, responsibility
VERB
1 *He did not concern himself about the future.*
▷ bother, distress, disturb, trouble, worry
2 *Will this decision concern anyone else?*
▷ affect, involve

concerning
PREPOSITION
Concerning the plan, please give us some information.
▷ about, regarding, respecting

C

concise

ADJECTIVE

He wrote a concise account of his trip.

▷ brief, compact, condensed, short

ANTONYM long

conclude

VERB

1 *I did conclude that the e-mail was a joke.*

▷ decide, deduce, infer, judge, reason

2 *They will conclude the concert with O Canada.*

▷ close, end, finish

ANTONYM begin

conclusion

NOUN

1 *Her conclusion was that she had made a mistake.*

▷ deduction, judgment, verdict

2 *The story's conclusion left us puzzled.*

▷ close, end, ending, finish

ANTONYM beginning

concoct

VERB

Why did you concoct such a silly excuse?

▷ devise, hatch, invent

concrete

ADJECTIVE

We appreciated his concrete suggestions.

▷ actual, real, solid

ANTONYM abstract

concur

VERB

Does your opinion concur with their view?

▷ agree, coincide, correspond

ANTONYM disagree

condemn

VERB

They were quick to condemn the unpopular boy.

▷ blame, censure, criticize

condense

VERB

Condense your speech to two minutes only.

▷ abridge, compress, concentrate, cut, shorten

condition

NOUN

The old painting is in fine condition.

▷ form, shape

condone

VERB

The league will not condone biased refereeing.

▷ allow, excuse, forgive, overlook

conduct

NOUN

Her conduct is always satisfactory.

▷ attitude, behaviour, manners

conference

NOUN

The topic of the conference was healthy eating.

▷ convention, discussion, forum, meeting

confess to

VERB

Did he confess to his part in the crime?

▷ acknowledge, admit to, declare

ANTONYM deny

confidence

NOUN

1 *I have confidence in her.*

▷ belief, faith, reliance, trust

ANTONYM distrust

2 *He has great confidence when speaking in public.*

▷ assurance, boldness, firmness

ANTONYM shyness

confident

ADJECTIVE

She speaks in a confident way.

▷ assured, self-possessed

ANTONYM shy

confine

VERB

1 *Please confine your speech to your topic.*

▷ limit, restrict

2 *The judge had to confine the young offender.*

▷ detain, imprison, restrict

confirm

VERB

Can anyone confirm that information?

▷ validate, verify

confiscate

VERB

The police will confiscate all the stolen goods.

▷ impound, seize

conflict

NOUN

1 *There was conflict within the team.*

▷ disagreement, discord, friction, hostility

2 *The conflict was widely reported in the media.*

▷ battle, combat, fighting, strife, war

VERB

His actions seem to conflict with his ideas.

▷ clash, differ, disagree

conform to

VERB

Students are expected to conform to school rules.

▷ comply with, follow

confront

VERB

Did you confront the bully?

▷ defy, face, oppose

confuse
VERB
*She did not mean to **confuse** you.*
▷ baffle, bewilder, muddle, mystify, puzzle

confusion
NOUN
*The school renovations caused much **confusion**.*
▷ chaos, disarray, disorder, disorganization, mess
ANTONYM order

congenial
ADJECTIVE
*The new student is very **congenial**.*
▷ agreeable, companionable, friendly
ANTONYM disagreeable

congested
ADJECTIVE
*The **congested** roads made everyone late for school.*
▷ clogged, crowded, jammed, packed

congratulate
VERB
*I **congratulate** you on your good grades.*
▷ commend, compliment, praise

congregate
VERB
*Do not **congregate** in the hallways.*
▷ assemble, crowd, gather, meet

connect
VERB
***Connect** the cable to the television.*
▷ attach, fasten, join, link
ANTONYM separate

connection
NOUN
1 *There is a **connection** between studying and good marks.*
▷ association, correlation, correspondence, link, relationship
2 *The broken **connection** caused a power failure.*
▷ fastening, junction, link

conquer
VERB
*He tried to **conquer** his fear of heights.*
▷ beat, defeat, overcome, overpower, vanquish

conscience
NOUN
*Her **conscience** would not let her cheat.*
▷ principles, scruples

conscientious
ADJECTIVE
*The boy cleared the snow from the path in a **conscientious** way.*
▷ careful, industrious, scrupulous

conscious
ADJECTIVE
*Did you make a **conscious** decision to be late?*
▷ deliberate, intentional

consent to
VERB
*Please **consent to** his request.*
▷ agree to, assent to, permit
ANTONYM oppose

conserve
VERB
*Make a plan to **conserve** energy this year.*
▷ preserve, protect, save
ANTONYM waste

consider
VERB
*Will you **consider** going to Prince Edward Island in the summer?*
▷ contemplate, examine, ponder

considerable
ADJECTIVE
*She has saved a **considerable** amount of money by walking to school instead of taking the bus.*
▷ abundant, ample, great, significant
ANTONYM insignificant

consistent
ADJECTIVE
*He has been a **consistent** goal scorer all season.*
▷ regular, steady, unchanging
ANTONYM inconsistent

console
VERB
*We tried to **console** her, but she was heartbroken.*
▷ comfort, soothe, sympathize with

conspicuous
ADJECTIVE
*Leave the note in a **conspicuous** place so she will be sure to see it.*
▷ noticeable, obvious, prominent
ANTONYM inconspicuous

conspire
VERB
*Did the team members **conspire** to make their captain look bad?*
▷ intrigue, plot, scheme

constant
ADJECTIVE
1 *Many celebrities receive **constant** attention.*
▷ continuous, nonstop, perpetual, relentless
2 *The temperature stayed **constant** at 20 degrees all day.*
▷ fixed, stable, steady, uniform
ANTONYM variable

C

construct
VERB
What would it cost to construct a new stadium behind the school?
▷ assemble, build, create, erect
ANTONYM demolish

consult
VERB
Consult your doctor if you still feel unwell.
▷ ask, confer with, refer to

consume
VERB
The hikers expect to consume a lot of food.
▷ devour, eat, use up

contact
NOUN
He stays in contact with his friend by texting.
▷ communication, touch
VERB
My mother had to contact the gas company.
▷ approach, communicate with

contain
VERB
1 *Does your paragraph contain enough facts?*
▷ comprise, include
2 *He found it difficult to contain his joy.*
▷ control, curb, repress, restrain, stifle

contaminate
VERB
Do not contaminate the lake with garbage.
▷ pollute, spoil, taint

contemplate
VERB
I must contemplate my future.
▷ consider, examine, reflect on

contempt
NOUN
She allowed her contempt to show by the look on her face.
▷ disdain, disrespect, scorn
ANTONYM respect

content
ADJECTIVE
Are you content with the result of the vote?
▷ happy, satisfied

contest
NOUN
My friend entered an arm-wrestling contest.
▷ competition, game, match, tournament
VERB
The loser is going to contest the judge's decision.
▷ challenge, dispute, oppose, question
ANTONYM accept

continue
VERB
They expect the storm to continue all night.
▷ last, persist, remain

contract
NOUN
A contract is not legal until it is signed.
▷ agreement, pact, understanding
VERB
Metal will contract in cold weather.
▷ decrease, diminish, shrink

contradict
VERB
He likes to contradict everyone's statements.
▷ deny, dispute, oppose

contrary
ADJECTIVE
Your opinion is contrary to mine.
▷ adverse, counter, opposite

contrast
VERB
Do you like colours that match or colours that contrast?
▷ differ, oppose

contribute
VERB
Thank you for your offer to contribute to our fundraiser.
▷ assist in, donate, give, help with

control
NOUN
The control of the club was shared by two people.
▷ authority, command, direction, government, management
VERB
1 *He will control the organization very well.*
▷ administer, command, direct, govern, manage, rule
2 *Try to control your spending.*
▷ curb, regulate, restrain

convenient
ADJECTIVE
Having a map of Edmonton was convenient for walking around the city.
▷ handy, helpful, useful
ANTONYM inconvenient

conversation
NOUN
The conversation was about blogs.
▷ chat, discussion, talk

convert
VERB
Do you know where we can convert our Canadian dollars into euros?
▷ change, transform, turn

C

convey
VERB
I will convey your message to my brother when I see him.
▷ communicate, express, relate, relay

convince
VERB
Please try to convince me that you know what you are doing.
▷ assure, persuade, satisfy

cook
VERB
Are you going to cook the food right now?
▷ bake, barbecue, boil, fry, grill, microwave, poach, roast, sauté, steam, stew, stir-fry

cool
ADJECTIVE
1 *We were hot and tired, and so we really enjoyed the cool lemonade.*
▷ chilled, cold, refreshing
ANTONYM warm
2 *The actor kept cool in spite of the delay.*
▷ calm, collected, composed, relaxed, serene
ANTONYM nervous

co-operate
VERB
Will they want to co-operate on the project?
▷ collaborate, join forces, unite

copy
NOUN
He made a copy of the painting.
▷ duplicate, imitation, replica, reproduction
VERB
Children copy adult behaviour.
▷ ape, emulate, imitate, mimic

cordial
ADJECTIVE
The meeting was cordial.
▷ friendly, warm
ANTONYM hostile

core
NOUN
They finally got to the core of the problem.
▷ basis, centre, essence, heart

corner
NOUN
Meet me at the corner of the street.
▷ angle, bend

corpse
NOUN
Do we know that a corpse was buried in this pyramid?
▷ body, carcass

correct
ADJECTIVE
What's the correct time?
▷ accurate, exact, precise
ANTONYM wrong
VERB
Can you correct this mistake?
▷ amend, improve, rectify, reform, remedy

correspond
VERB
Your feelings and mine must correspond.
▷ agree, coincide, fit, match, tally

corrupt
ADJECTIVE
The corrupt manager was fired.
▷ crooked, dishonest, fraudulent, unscrupulous
ANTONYM honest
VERB
Do violent video games corrupt young people?
▷ deprave, pervert

cost
NOUN
What is the cost for a new cellphone?
▷ charge, expense, payment, price, rate

costly
ADJECTIVE
The burglar stole several things, including a costly camera.
▷ expensive, valuable

council
NOUN
The council voted against changing the bylaw.
▷ assembly, board, committee

counsel
VERB
Who will counsel the students?
▷ advise, guide

count
VERB
1 *Count the number of books on the shelf.*
▷ calculate, compute, tally
2 *Computer knowledge will count highly in that job.*
▷ matter, rate, signify

MAKE IT MORE FORMAL

count for be worth
count on rely on
count up add

counterfeit
ADJECTIVE
That coin is counterfeit.
▷ bogus, fake, false, forged, fraudulent

C

country
NOUN
The story takes place in a distant country.
▷ kingdom, land, nation, state

couple
NOUN
They make a handsome couple.
▷ pair, twosome

courage
NOUN
Firefighters show courage in their job.
▷ bravery, daring, grit, heroism, nerve, valour
ANTONYM cowardice

courageous
ADJECTIVE
That was a courageous thing to do.
▷ bold, brave, valiant

course
NOUN
If you change your course you may get lost.
▷ direction, path, route

courteous
ADJECTIVE
She is always courteous.
▷ considerate, gracious, polite
ANTONYM discourteous

courtesy
NOUN
His courtesy is an example to others.
▷ civility, gallantry, graciousness, manners, politeness

cover
VERB
Cover the stain and no one will notice it.
▷ cloak, conceal, hide, mask, obscure, screen, shade
ANTONYM reveal
NOUN
We need some kind of cover to keep dirt off.
▷ canopy, case, lid, roof

cowardly
ADJECTIVE
Do you remember the cowardly lion?
▷ faint-hearted, fearful, spineless, timid
ANTONYM brave

cower
VERB
Don't ever cower if a bully comes near you.
▷ cringe, shrink

cozy
ADJECTIVE
I wrapped myself in a cozy blanket.
▷ comfortable, snug, warm

crack
VERB
The plate might crack if you bang it.
▷ break, fracture, snap
NOUN
She tripped on the crack in the sidewalk.
▷ break, cleft, crevice, fracture, split

MAKE IT MORE FORMAL
crack down impose stricter discipline
crack up laugh; suffer a breakdown
get cracking hurry up

crafty
ADJECTIVE
The crafty fox slipped into the henhouse.
▷ cunning, devious, scheming, sly, wily

cram
VERB
Do not cram too much into your backpack.
▷ jam, pack, squeeze, stuff

crash
VERB
The car was about to crash into the wall.
▷ bump, slam, smash

crave
VERB
Do you ever crave peppermint?
▷ desire, long for, want

crawl
VERB
He had to crawl under the fence to escape.
▷ creep, slither, wriggle

craze
NOUN
What new craze is she following now?
▷ fad, fashion, trend, vogue

crazy
ADJECTIVE
1 *I think bungee jumping is crazy.*
▷ foolish, ridiculous, wild, zany
ANTONYM sensible
2 *I'm crazy about the band's new singer.*
▷ fanatical, obsessed, passionate
ANTONYM uninterested

crease
NOUN
Smooth out the crease in the paper.
▷ fold, line, pucker

create
VERB
He plans to create a new software program.
▷ devise, invent, originate

C

creation
NOUN
We are impressed with your original creation.
▷ handiwork, invention, production

creature
NOUN
The noisy creature we heard was just a skunk.
▷ animal, beast

credible
ADJECTIVE
Her strange story is not credible.
▷ believable, convincing, likely

creep
VERB
We watched the baby creep across the floor.
▷ crawl, slither, wriggle

creepy
ADJECTIVE
The dark cave was creepy.
▷ disturbing, eerie, scary

crest
NOUN
He jogged to the crest of the hill.
▷ crown, height, peak, top

crevice
NOUN
My ring fell into a crevice in the sidewalk, but I managed to get it out.
▷ cleft, crack, gap, split

crew
NOUN
The ship's crew looked for the missing dog.
▷ company, gang, staff, team

crime
NOUN
She was accused of a crime.
▷ felony, misdemeanour, offence, violation

criminal
NOUN
The criminal showed no regret.
▷ culprit, offender, villain
ADJECTIVE
His criminal behaviour surprised everyone.
▷ corrupt, crooked, illegal, illicit, unlawful

cringe
VERB
I cringe every time he tells that joke.
▷ cower, flinch, squirm, wince

cripple
VERB
The accident was serious enough to cripple the dog.
▷ disable, maim, paralyze

crisis
NOUN
How will you react if there is a crisis?
▷ catastrophe, emergency

critical
ADJECTIVE
1 *The prime minister must make a critical decision today.*
▷ crucial, vital
ANTONYM unimportant
2 *The patient is in critical condition.*
▷ grave, serious
3 *Your critical comments are hurtful.*
▷ disapproving, negative
ANTONYM complimentary

criticize
VERB
The opposition will usually criticize the government.
▷ censure, condemn
ANTONYM praise

crook
NOUN
A crook took my money.
▷ cheat, rogue, swindler, thief, villain

crooked
ADJECTIVE
1 *The old tree has many crooked branches.*
▷ bent, deformed, distorted, twisted, warped
ANTONYM straight
2 *His crooked activities landed him in jail.*
▷ corrupt, criminal, dishonest, fraudulent, illegal
ANTONYM honest

cross
VERB
A suspended walkway will cross the river.
▷ bridge, ford, span, traverse
ADJECTIVE
Mom was cross when a squirrel dug up the tulip bulbs that she had planted.
▷ angry, annoyed, fretful, grumpy

MAKE IT MORE FORMAL
cross out delete
cross your mind occur to you

crouch
VERB
Crouch and then stretch your arms out.
▷ bend down, squat, stoop

crow
VERB
He likes to crow about his athletic skill.
▷ boast, brag, gloat

C

crowd
NOUN
The crowd gathered around the rock star.
▷ horde, mass, mob, multitude, swarm, throng

crowded
ADJECTIVE
Our living room is crowded, but very cozy.
▷ full, overflowing, packed

crucial
ADJECTIVE
This is a crucial time in her life.
▷ critical, decisive, key, momentous, pivotal, vital

crude
ADJECTIVE
1 *We made a crude bench from the log.*
▷ primitive, rough, simple
2 *Your crude remarks disgust me.*
▷ coarse, indecent, obscene, tasteless, vulgar
ANTONYM refined

cruel
ADJECTIVE
In the story, the cruel giant climbed down the beanstalk.
▷ barbarous, brutal, callous, cold-blooded, heartless, inhumane, sadistic, vicious
ANTONYM kind

crumb
NOUN
The dog begged for a crumb of bread.
▷ bit, morsel, scrap, shred

crumble
VERB
Many of these old statues are starting to crumble, and should be repaired.
▷ decay, decompose, disintegrate

crumple
VERB
Crumple the paper and stuff it in the box.
▷ crease, crush, wrinkle
ANTONYM fold

crunch
VERB
We like to crunch on celery and carrots.
▷ chew, chomp, munch

crush
VERB
1 *Crush the boxes before you recycle them.*
▷ crumble, crumple, mash, squash
2 *We intend to crush the other lacrosse team.*
▷ conquer, vanquish

cry
VERB
See box at foot of this page.
NOUN
His loud cry attracted our attention.
▷ call, exclamation, shout, yell

cuddle
VERB
I like to cuddle puppies.
▷ caress, embrace, hug, snuggle

cue
NOUN
My nod was her cue to leave the room.
▷ hint, sign, signal

cunning
ADJECTIVE
That was a cunning trick.
▷ artful, crafty, devious, sly, wily
ANTONYM open

REPLACE AN OVERUSED WORD: CRY

There are a number of verbs that you can use instead of **cry**, if you want to say a little more about how someone cries.

- If you **bawl**, you cry very loudly.
  The door banged shut, and one of the little kids began to bawl.

- If you **blubber**, you cry noisily and your nose may run.
  He began to blubber, then reached for the box of tissues.

- If you **howl**, you cry with a loud noise.
  Don't howl like that, you're not really hurt.

- If you **snivel**, you cry in a whining way.
  She pushed out her lip and began to snivel.

- If you **sob**, you cry in a noisy way, with short breaths.
  We tried to calm her, but she continued to sob.

- If you **wail**, you cry with a long noise.
  The child fell, and immediately started to wail.

- If you **weep**, you cry. This is quite a formal word.
  The ending is so sad that it will make you weep.

- If you **whimper**, you make a soft sound as if you are about to cry.
  He wanted to call for help, but could only whimper.

---

curb

VERB

*I am trying to **curb** my temper.*
▷ check, contain, control, limit, restrain, suppress

cure

NOUN

*The doctor suggested a **cure** for the rash.*
▷ medicine, remedy, treatment

curious

ADJECTIVE

1 *He has a **curious** mind, and is always asking questions.*
▷ inquiring, inquisitive, interested
2 *No one knows what that **curious** old object is.*
▷ bizarre, extraordinary, odd, peculiar, singular, strange, unusual
ANTONYM ordinary

curl

VERB

*Smoke began to **curl** up from the bonfire.*
▷ coil, curve, twist, wind

currency

NOUN

See picture of the currency of some countries at foot of this page.

current

ADJECTIVE

*Which of the **current** styles do you prefer?*
▷ contemporary, fashionable, present
ANTONYM out of date

curt

ADJECTIVE

*Her **curt** answer made me feel embarrassed.*
▷ abrupt, impatient, terse

currency

balboa: Panama
birr: Ethiopia
bolivar: Venezuela
cedi: Ghana
colon: Costa Rica
dinar: Algeria
dollar: Canada
dram: Armenia
euro: Europe
kuna: Croatia
ek: Albania
lev: Bulgaria
naira: Nigeria
peso: Argentina
pound: Egypt
rand: South Africa
real: Brazil
ruble: Belarus
rupee: India
sucre: Ecuador
taka: Bangladesh
yen: Japan
yuan: China

C

curve

NOUN

*Look at the **curve** of the rainbow!*

▷ arc, bend

custom

NOUN

1 *The **custom** is to sing Canada's national anthem before public events.*

▷ convention, practice, ritual, tradition

2 *His **custom** is to exercise every day.*

▷ habit, practice, routine

customer

NOUN

*The **customer** waited her turn.*

▷ buyer, client, consumer, patron, purchaser, shopper

cut

VERB

See box at foot of this page.

MAKE IT MORE FORMAL

cut back cut

cut down to size humiliate

cut it fine leave no room for error

cut it out stop it

cut short halt

make the cut be one of a number selected

cute

ADJECTIVE

*The **cute** child did a little dance.*

▷ adorable, appealing, attractive, charming

REPLACE AN OVERUSED WORD: CUT

Different words can be used for the verb **cut**, depending on what is being cut, what is doing the cutting, and how deep the cut is.

- If you **carve** an object, you cut it out of wood or stone.
  *To **carve** a statue out of marble takes great skill.*

- If you **chop** something, you cut it into pieces with downward movements of a knife or axe.
  *Please **chop** the vegetables into small pieces.*

- If you **clip** something, you cut around it with scissors or shears.
  *Will you **clip** out this newspaper article for me?*

- If you **divide** something, you cut it into parts.
  ***Divide** the pizza into six equal parts.*

- If you **hack** something, you cut it using rough strokes.
  *The firefighter had to **hack** through a door to save the child.*

- If you **lop** something off, you cut it off with one quick stroke.
  *Someone was mean enough to **lop** the heads off all the tulips.*

- If you **mow** grass, you cut it with a lawn mower.
  *One of my jobs is to **mow** the lawn.*

- If you **nick** something, you make a small cut on its surface.
  *Be careful or you will **nick** your finger on the broken glass.*

- If you **pare** something, you peel the skin off it.
  *If you want to help, **pare** the potatoes.*

- If you **pierce** something, you make a hole in it.
  *Why did you **pierce** the skin of the potato with a fork?*

- If you **prune** a tree or bush, you cut off some of its branches.
  *Should we **prune** that bush in spring?*

- If you **saw** something, you cut it with a saw.
  *It will take two people to **saw** down that tree.*

- If you **sever** something, you cut right through it.
  *When I broke my leg, I was lucky not to **sever** any muscles.*

- If you **slash** something, you make a long, deep cut in it.
  *How did you manage to **slash** your thumb?*

- If you **slice** something, you cut it into thin pieces.
  *Will you **slice** the tomatoes very thinly, please?*

- If you **slit** something, you make a long, narrow cut in it.
  *I used a paper knife to **slit** the envelope open.*

- If you **snip** something, you cut it with scissors or shears.
  *She had to **snip** the chewing gum out of her hair.*

- If you **trim** something, you cut off small amounts to make it look neater.
  *I really must **trim** my nails.*

D d

dab
VERB
Dab the cream on your nose.
▷ daub, pat, smear

daily
ADJECTIVE
We made our daily trip to the mall.
▷ everyday, normal, ordinary, routine, usual

dainty
ADJECTIVE
That is a dainty piece of lace.
▷ delicate, fine, fragile

damage
VERB
Did the heavy rain damage the fruit trees?
▷ harm, hurt, mar, ruin, spoil, wreck

damp
ADJECTIVE
The sleeping bags always seemed damp on that camping trip.
▷ clammy, dank, moist, soggy, wet
ANTONYM dry

dance
NOUN
See picture below.

danger
NOUN
Foolishly, he ignored the danger.
▷ jeopardy, peril, risk, threat
ANTONYM safety

dangerous
ADJECTIVE
Stay away from the dangerous tide.
▷ hazardous, perilous, unsafe
ANTONYM safe

dangle
VERB
She likes to wear earrings that dangle.
▷ hang, sway, swing

dank
ADJECTIVE
It was a dank morning, but the sun shone in the afternoon.
▷ damp, moist, soggy

daring
ADJECTIVE
Climbing alone is a daring (and foolish) thing to do.
▷ adventurous, bold, reckless
ANTONYM cautious

D

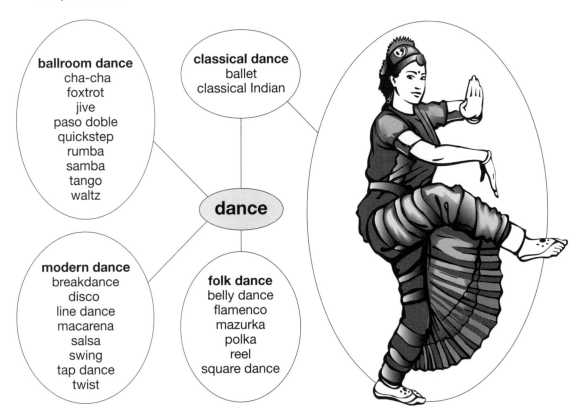

ballroom dance
cha-cha
foxtrot
jive
paso doble
quickstep
rumba
samba
tango
waltz

classical dance
ballet
classical Indian

dance

modern dance
breakdance
disco
line dance
macarena
salsa
swing
tap dance
twist

folk dance
belly dance
flamenco
mazurka
polka
reel
square dance

dark
ADJECTIVE
The long, dark hall was scary.
▷ dim, dull, murky, shadowy, shady
ANTONYM light

> ### MAKE IT MORE FORMAL
>
> **in the dark** not knowing or not understanding
> **keep dark** keep secret

darling
NOUN
Darling, will you be my valentine?
▷ honey, love, pet, sweetheart

darn
VERB
Does anyone darn socks anymore?
▷ mend, patch, repair, sew

dart
VERB
She said she saw a mouse dart across the floor.
▷ dash, scamper, scurry, scuttle

dash
VERB
1 *I must dash or I'll be late.*
▷ bolt, charge, race, rush, sprint, tear
2 *He had to dash his son's hope for a pet.*
▷ crush, destroy, shatter
NOUN
1 *My dash around the block took six minutes.*
▷ bolt, race, rush, sprint
2 *Add a dash of vanilla for flavour.*
▷ drop, pinch, splash, sprinkling, touch

dawn
NOUN
1 *They got up at dawn to go fishing.*
▷ daybreak, sunrise, sunup
ANTONYM dusk
2 *That happened before the dawn of the computer age.*
▷ beginning, birth, rise
ANTONYM end

dead
ADJECTIVE
The squirrel was dead when we found it.
▷ deceased, departed, gone, lifeless
ANTONYM alive

> ### MAKE IT MORE FORMAL
>
> **dead in the water** totally defeated
> **dead to the world** deeply asleep
> **over my dead body** I will resist to the end.
> **wouldn't be caught dead** be extremely
>   unwilling to do

deaden
VERB
Deaden the sound of the drums, please.
▷ muffle, stifle, suppress

deadly
ADJECTIVE
That gas is deadly if you inhale it.
▷ fatal, lethal

deal
VERB
Can you deal with the extra work?
▷ cope, handle, manage

dealer
NOUN
That dealer sells only organic fruit.
▷ merchant, retailer, trader, vendor

dear
ADJECTIVE
1 *My dear aunt is ninety-two.*
▷ beloved, cherished, esteemed, precious, prized, treasured
2 *She thought the watch was too dear.*
▷ costly, expensive, high-priced, valuable
ANTONYM cheap

death
NOUN
His death was reported in the newspaper.
▷ decease, demise, passing
ANTONYM life

debate
VERB
Are you going to debate this all day?
▷ argue about, discuss, dispute, question

decay
VERB
The lettuce has already begun to decay.
▷ decompose, deteriorate, disintegrate, rot, spoil

deceive
VERB
The magician's job is to deceive the audience.
▷ con, delude, dupe, fool, mislead, trick

decent
ADJECTIVE
1 *I received a decent grade in Math.*
▷ adequate, passable, reasonable, respectable, satisfactory, tolerable
2 *The decent thing to do is to tell the truth.*
▷ ethical, fair, moral, proper, respectable
ANTONYM improper

decide
VERB
Did you decide what to do?
▷ choose, elect, resolve

D

decision

NOUN
The judge's decision is final.
▷ conclusion, finding, judgment, ruling, verdict

declare

VERB
She likes to declare that she is a computer expert.
▷ announce, assert, proclaim, state

decline

VERB
1 *Will the cost of oil ever decline?*
▷ decrease, diminish, drop, reduce
ANTONYM increase
2 *Should I decline her invitation?*
▷ refuse, reject
ANTONYM accept
NOUN
We expect a decline in cellphone sales.
▷ decrease, downturn, drop, fall
ANTONYM increase

decorate

VERB
They decorate their home with flags on Canada Day.
▷ adorn, deck, embellish

decrease

VERB
The group's CD sales are expected to decrease.
▷ decline, diminish, drop, dwindle, lessen, reduce, shrink
ANTONYM increase
NOUN
There was a decrease in the temperature overnight.
▷ decline, drop, reduction
ANTONYM increase

deduce

VERB
What did you deduce from the clues?
▷ conclude, draw, infer

deduct

VERB
Deduct your expenses from the total.
▷ remove, subtract, withdraw
ANTONYM add

deed

NOUN
She was rewarded for her brave deed.
▷ accomplishment, act, exploit, feat, undertaking

deep

ADJECTIVE
He gets deep enjoyment from reading.
▷ great, intense, profound, serious
ANTONYM superficial

deface

VERB
Why would anyone deface a painting?
▷ mutilate, spoil, vandalize

defeat

VERB
We were able to defeat last year's champions.
▷ beat, conquer, overcome, overthrow, overwhelm, rout, subdue, trounce, vanquish

defect

NOUN
Her quick temper is a defect in her character.
▷ fault, flaw, imperfection, weakness

defence

NOUN
His defence is that his watch stopped.
▷ excuse, explanation, justification

defend

VERB
How can we defend ourselves against the flu?
▷ guard, protect, safeguard, shield

defender

NOUN
She is a great defender of animal rights.
▷ advocate, champion, supporter

defer

VERB
We had to defer the picnic because of rain.
▷ delay, postpone

deficient

ADJECTIVE
His hockey skills are deficient.
▷ imperfect, inadequate, lacking, wanting

definite

ADJECTIVE
He would not give a definite answer.
▷ clear, explicit, precise, sure
ANTONYM vague

deformed

ADJECTIVE
The trees looked deformed and quite eerie in the moonlight.
▷ contorted, distorted, misshapen

defraud

VERB
They tried to defraud the insurance company.
▷ deceive, swindle, trick

defy

VERB
She's stubborn, and continues to defy any authority.
▷ challenge, disobey, disregard, resist
ANTONYM obey

D

D

degree

NOUN

*I believe your story, up to a **degree**.*

▷ level, point, stage

delay

VERB

1 *I would like to **delay** our trip for a week.*

▷ defer, postpone, suspend

2 *Who would want to **delay** our progress?*

▷ hinder, impede, obstruct

deliberate

ADJECTIVE

*We made a **deliberate** decision to avoid a fight.*

▷ intentional, planned, premeditated

ANTONYM accidental

delicious

ADJECTIVE

*She passed around a plate of **delicious** cookies.*

▷ appetizing, mouth-watering, scrumptious, tasty

delight

NOUN

*Their **delight** at my gift made me glad.*

▷ glee, happiness, joy, satisfaction

ANTONYM misery

delightful

ADJECTIVE

*Our visit to Louisburg in Nova Scotia was **delightful**.*

▷ enchanting, enjoyable, entertaining, pleasurable

delude

VERB

*He tried to **delude** me by telling a lie.*

▷ con, dupe, hoodwink, misguide, mislead, trick

deluge

NOUN

*The umbrella was no help during the **deluge**.*

▷ downpour, flood, torrent

demand

VERB

*I **demand** that you apologize to me.*

▷ ask, insist, request

demolish

VERB

*They hired two boys to **demolish** the old shed.*

▷ destroy, smash, wreck

ANTONYM build

den

NOUN

*The children found some animal's **den**.*

▷ cave, lair, nest

dense

ADJECTIVE

1 *There was a **dense** crowd outside the stadium.*

▷ solid, thick

ANTONYM sparse

2 *She seemed **dense**, but she was just tired.*

▷ dull, foolish, ignorant, stupid

ANTONYM clever

dent

NOUN

*The corner of the desk has made a **dent** in the wall.*

▷ chip, depression, hollow, indentation, notch

deny

VERB

*Please do not **deny** my request.*

▷ decline, refuse, reject

ANTONYM allow

dependable

ADJECTIVE

*I'm a **dependable** babysitter.*

▷ faithful, loyal, reliable, responsible, trustworthy

depict

VERB

***Depict** your idea in a storyboard.*

▷ describe, outline, portray, represent, sketch

deplorable

ADJECTIVE

*The kitchen was a **deplorable** mess.*

▷ disgraceful, dreadful, horrible, shameful

deport

VERB

*The government will **deport** criminals.*

▷ banish, expel

depraved

ADJECTIVE

*He played a **depraved** character in the movie.*

▷ corrupt, evil, immoral

ANTONYM upright

depressed

ADJECTIVE

*She became **depressed** when her cat disappeared.*

▷ blue, dejected, downcast, melancholy

ANTONYM cheerful

derelict

ADJECTIVE

*The **derelict** house has been empty for years.*

▷ abandoned, deserted, dilapidated, ruined

deride

VERB

*I become upset when you **deride** my ideas.*

▷ belittle, mock, ridicule

ANTONYM praise

descend
VERB
He watched the kite descend into a tree.
▷ drop, fall, plummet, plunge, sink
ANTONYM ascend

describe
VERB
Can you describe how you feel about music?
▷ define, explain, report, tell

desert
NOUN
Lack of rain turned the farmland into a desert.
▷ wasteland, wilderness
ADJECTIVE
There are few trees, if any, in a desert region.
▷ arid, barren, desolate
VERB
Do not desert a friend in need.
▷ abandon, forsake, leave

deserve
VERB
I think I deserve the award.
▷ be entitled to, be worthy of, merit, warrant

design
NOUN
1 *The poster design needs to be improved.*
▷ draft, drawing, model, outline, plan
2 *He drew a complicated design on the paper.*
▷ form, pattern, shape

desire
VERB
What do you desire most in all the world?
▷ crave, wish for, yearn for
NOUN
He has a desire to travel around the world.
▷ longing, urge, yearning

desolate
ADJECTIVE
I could not live in such a desolate place.
▷ barren, bleak, empty, forlorn, isolated, lonely

despair
NOUN
His despair caused him to ask for help.
▷ depression, gloom, hopelessness, misery, sorrow
ANTONYM hope

desperate
ADJECTIVE
The situation was desperate—people were dying from hunger.
▷ critical, urgent

despicable
ADJECTIVE
Cruelty to animals is despicable.
▷ contemptible, detestable
ANTONYM noble

despise
VERB
I despise bullies.
▷ abhor, detest, hate, loathe
ANTONYM love

despondent
ADJECTIVE
They were despondent over the loss of their pet.
▷ depressed, forlorn, miserable, unhappy
ANTONYM cheerful

destitute
ADJECTIVE
She was destitute after her business failed.
▷ bankrupt, penniless, poverty-stricken
ANTONYM wealthy

destroy
VERB
Did the storm destroy many trees?
▷ demolish, obliterate, wreck

destruction
NOUN
Fire caused the destruction of the whole area.
▷ annihilation, devastation, obliteration, ruin

detach
VERB
Please detach the trailer from the car.
▷ disconnect, separate, split, unfasten
ANTONYM attach

detain
VERB
The police will detain the suspect.
▷ arrest, confine, imprison, jail
ANTONYM release

detect
VERB
Did you detect anything unusual in the room?
▷ discover, find, notice, observe, perceive, spot
ANTONYM miss

deter
VERB
I will try to deter her from going.
▷ discourage, dissuade, prevent, stop
ANTONYM encourage

determine
VERB
Fingerprints may determine who stole the cellphone.
▷ establish, identify, verify

D

detest
VERB
I detest violence.
▷ abhor, despise, hate, loathe
ANTONYM adore

devastate
VERB
Locusts can devastate a farmer's crop.
▷ annihilate, demolish, destroy, ruin

develop
VERB
We watched the seed develop into a bean plant.
▷ evolve, grow, mature, ripen

device
NOUN
I have a device for getting lids off jars.
▷ appliance, gadget, instrument, machine, tool

devious
ADJECTIVE
She can be devious if she really wants something.
▷ calculating, crafty, cunning, scheming, sly, sneaky, wily

devise
VERB
Can you devise a better plan?
▷ conceive, create, design, fashion, form, invent

devote
VERB
I must devote some time to research on the Internet.
▷ allocate, allot, assign, dedicate

devoted
ADJECTIVE
He is a devoted hockey fan.
▷ dedicated, faithful, loyal, true
ANTONYM indifferent

devour
VERB
Do not devour your food so quickly.
▷ consume, gobble, gulp, wolf down

diagram
NOUN
Prepare a diagram to illustrate weather patterns.
▷ chart, drawing, outline, plan, sketch

die
VERB
Did the driver die at the scene of the accident?
▷ expire, pass away, pass on, perish
ANTONYM live

difference
NOUN
What's the difference between the two DVD players?
▷ discrepancy, disparity, distinction, variation
ANTONYM similarity

different
ADJECTIVE
1 *Their opinions are different.*
▷ contrasting, dissimilar, divergent, opposed, unlike
ANTONYM similar
2 *She has a different painting style.*
▷ distinctive, original, special, unique, unusual
ANTONYM undistinguished

difficult
ADJECTIVE
That is a difficult problem to solve.
▷ baffling, complex, complicated, demanding, hard
ANTONYM easy

difficulty
NOUN
There may be a difficulty with our field trip.
▷ complication, obstacle, problem, snag

dig
VERB
Dig a fork into your baked potato.
▷ jab, poke, thrust

digit
NOUN
I can't remember the last digit of her phone number.
▷ figure, number

dignified
ADJECTIVE
My grandfather walks in a dignified way.
▷ distinguished, grand, lofty, majestic, noble, stately

dilapidated
ADJECTIVE
The dilapidated house is being fixed up.
▷ crumbling, decayed, neglected, rundown, shabby

dilemma
NOUN
I can't choose, so will you please help me with my dilemma?
▷ jam, plight, predicament, quandary

dim
ADJECTIVE
She has only a dim memory of her cousins.
▷ faint, hazy, indistinct, vague
ANTONYM clear

dingy
ADJECTIVE
He painted the walls a dingy shade of brown.
▷ drab, dull, gloomy, faded
ANTONYM bright

dip

VERB

Dip your hands into the soapy water.
▷ immerse, plunge, submerge

dire

ADJECTIVE

The icy roads were in a dire state.
▷ alarming, awful, terrible

direct

ADJECTIVE

1 *Take the direct route to the park.*
▷ shortest, straight, uninterrupted
ANTONYM indirect
2 *My mother can be very direct sometimes.*
▷ blunt, candid, forthright, frank, straightforward
ANTONYM devious

VERB

1 *Can you direct me to the CN Tower?*
▷ point, show
2 *A good leader is able to direct others.*
▷ command, control, guide, manage, order, oversee, run, supervise

direction

NOUN

The direction he took led him back to the lake.
▷ path, route, way

dirt

NOUN

1 *The cabin floor was covered with dirt.*
▷ filth, grime, muck, mud
2 *Plant the flowers in the dirt by the fence.*
▷ earth, ground, soil

dirty

ADJECTIVE

1 *I cannot get the stains off that dirty shirt!*
▷ filthy, grimy, grubby, soiled
ANTONYM clean
2 *Politicians who take bribes are dirty.*
▷ corrupt, crooked
ANTONYM honest
3 *He refused to tell a dirty joke.*
▷ filthy, indecent, obscene, rude, vulgar

disadvantage

NOUN

Living a long way from the bus stop is a disadvantage.
▷ drawback, inconvenience, obstacle

disagree

VERB

They often disagree, but they are still friends.
▷ argue, differ, dispute

disagree with

VERB

We disagree with the decision.
▷ object to, oppose

disagreeable

ADJECTIVE

A disagreeable smell came from the drain.
▷ horrible, horrid, nasty, objectionable, offensive, unpleasant

disagreement

NOUN

We had a disagreement over which movie to watch.
▷ argument, dispute, quarrel, row, squabble, tiff

disappear

VERB

1 *They saw the ship disappear in the fog.*
▷ fade, recede, vanish
2 *Your stomach upset will disappear in a day.*
▷ cease, pass, vanish

disapprove of

VERB

She is likely to disapprove of our actions.
▷ condemn, criticize, object to, oppose

disaster

NOUN

The train crash was a horrible disaster.
▷ accident, calamity, catastrophe, misfortune, tragedy

discard

VERB

Discard your old files from the computer.
▷ dispose of, dump, eliminate, scrap
ANTONYM keep

discern

VERB

Can you discern how the magician does the trick?
▷ detect, distinguish, notice, observe, perceive, spot

discharge

VERB

1 *Did the city discharge raw sewage into the river?*
▷ emit, expel, release
2 *Why did the manager discharge the employee?*
▷ dismiss, expel, fire

disclose

VERB

Do not disclose the contents of this e-mail.
▷ divulge, reveal, show
ANTONYM conceal

disconcert

VERB

Having to give a speech will disconcert most people.
▷ confound, confuse, embarrass, upset

disconnect

VERB

Disconnect the wire at the back.
▷ cut off, detach, disengage, separate, sever

D

discontented

ADJECTIVE

*The **discontented** child cried for more ice cream.*

▷ disgruntled, displeased, dissatisfied, unhappy

discord

NOUN

*There was **discord** among the team members.*

▷ conflict, disagreement

ANTONYM agreement

discourage

VERB

1 *Rejection of his idea will **discourage** him.*

▷ depress, dishearten, dismay, dispirit

2 *We should **discourage** her from going alone.*

▷ deter, dissuade, prevent

ANTONYM encourage

discuss

VERB

*Please **discuss** the problem in a group.*

▷ confer about, consider, debate

disease

NOUN

*The **disease** spread quickly through the population.*

▷ illness, infection, sickness

disgrace

NOUN

*She brought **disgrace** on herself by cheating.*

▷ dishonour, scandal, shame

ANTONYM honour

disgraceful

ADJECTIVE

*That was a **disgraceful** way to act.*

▷ scandalous, shameful, shocking

disguise

VERB

*He found it hard to **disguise** his disgust.*

▷ conceal, cover up, hide, mask

disgust

NOUN

*They showed their **disgust** by leaving the room.*

▷ aversion, distaste, loathing, repulsion, revulsion

VERB

*Such a violent movie will **disgust** you.*

▷ offend, repel, revolt, sicken

disgusting

ADJECTIVE

*That smell is **disgusting**.*

▷ foul, gross, repellent, revolting, sickening, unpleasant, vile

dishonest

ADJECTIVE

*The **dishonest** employee cheated the company.*

▷ corrupt, crooked, deceitful

disintegrate

VERB

*Acid rain causes some materials to **disintegrate**.*

▷ crumble, deteriorate, erode

dislike

VERB

*I **dislike** loudmouthed people.*

▷ abhor, despise, detest, loathe

NOUN

*He tried to hide his **dislike**, but it was obvious.*

▷ animosity, aversion, distaste, hostility, loathing

ANTONYM liking

dismal

ADJECTIVE

*The day was dark and **dismal**.*

▷ cheerless, depressing, dreary, gloomy

ANTONYM cheerful

dismiss

VERB

*She said she could not **dismiss** the class early.*

▷ discharge, release

disobey

VERB

*Do not **disobey** school rules.*

▷ break, defy, flout, ignore, infringe, violate

disorder

NOUN

1 *I was surprised at the **disorder** in her locker.*

▷ clutter, disarray, muddle

2 *To prevent **disorder**, do not run during the fire drill.*

▷ chaos, confusion, disarray, mayhem, turmoil

3 *His **disorder** gave him headaches.*

▷ affliction, ailment, disease, illness

display

VERB

*We will **display** the art on the classroom walls.*

▷ exhibit, present, show

ANTONYM hide

displease

VERB

*Her rude remarks **displease** her friends.*

▷ anger, annoy, irritate, offend

dispose of

VERB

*How will you **dispose of** your garbage?*

▷ discard, dump, eliminate, jettison

ANTONYM keep

disprove

VERB

*New evidence may **disprove** the result of the trial.*

▷ discredit, invalidate, refute

dispute
NOUN
What was your dispute about?
▷ argument, clash, conflict, disagreement, feud, quarrel, row
VERB
We dispute the result of the vote.
▷ challenge, contest, query, question
ANTONYM accept

disregard
VERB
Do not disregard my advice.
▷ ignore, neglect, overlook

disrespectful
ADJECTIVE
The child did not mean to be disrespectful, so she apologized for her actions.
▷ impertinent, impudent, insolent, rude

dissimilar
ADJECTIVE
The twins look alike, but their personalities are dissimilar.
▷ different, diverse, unlike

dissolve
VERB
1 *The sugar will dissolve in the hot tea.*
▷ liquefy, melt
2 *The two countries plan to dissolve their alliance.*
▷ discontinue, end, terminate

dissuade
VERB
I could not dissuade him from leaving.
▷ deter, discourage
ANTONYM persuade

distance
NOUN
The distance from the building to the fence is six metres.
▷ expanse, length, span, stretch

distant
ADJECTIVE
1 *The heroine was shipwrecked on a distant island.*
▷ faraway, out-of-the-way, remote
ANTONYM close
2 *She seems distant but she is really shy.*
▷ aloof, cold, detached, reserved, unsociable, withdrawn
ANTONYM friendly

distinguished
ADJECTIVE
He is a distinguished guitar player.
▷ eminent, famed, notable
ANTONYM ordinary

distort
VERB
1 *An old mirror may distort a reflection.*
▷ bend, buckle, deform, warp
2 *The witness is trying to distort the facts.*
▷ falsify, misrepresent, twist

distress
NOUN
1 *What is the cause of his distress?*
▷ heartache, pain, sorrow, suffering
2 *The fallen skier seems to be in distress.*
▷ difficulty, need, trouble
VERB
The bad news will distress them.
▷ disturb, pain, sadden, trouble, upset, worry

district
NOUN
Our district held a tree-planting day last week.
▷ area, community, neighbourhood, region, territory

distrust
VERB
Do you distrust me?
▷ doubt, question, suspect

distrustful
ADJECTIVE
Are you distrustful of strangers?
▷ cynical, suspicious, wary

disturb
VERB
1 *Please do not disturb me while I am reading.*
▷ bother, interrupt
2 *This news may disturb them.*
▷ agitate, distress, trouble, unsettle, upset
ANTONYM calm

dive
VERB
The swimmers prepared to dive into the pool.
▷ jump, leap, plunge

diverse
ADJECTIVE
The city is home to people of diverse cultures.
▷ different, dissimilar, mixed, numerous, various
ANTONYM identical

divert
VERB
She tried to divert his attention.
▷ alter, change, deflect, turn

divide
VERB
Divide the cake for all to share.
▷ cut up, distribute, split

division

NOUN

That division of the company sells computers.

▷ branch, department, section, sector, unit

divulge

VERB

The principal will divulge the winner of the essay contest tomorrow.

▷ announce, broadcast, disclose, tell

dizzy

ADJECTIVE

She got dizzy running around in circles.

▷ faint, giddy, lightheaded, shaky, unsteady

do

VERB

1 *How will you do the math problem?*

▷ carry out, execute, perform, undertake

2 *One piece of cake will do for me, thank you.*

▷ be adequate, be sufficient, serve, suffice

3 *He promises to do better next term.*

▷ get on, manage, perform

docile

ADJECTIVE

The pet pig was quite docile.

▷ gentle, meek, obedient, passive, submissive, tame

Newfoundland

Working dog
Doberman
Great Dane
husky
mastiff
Newfoundland
Rottweiler
Saint Bernard

Non-sporting dog
bulldog
chow
Dalmatian
poodle
Shar-Pei

bulldog

Hound
Afghan
basset
beagle
bloodhound
borzoi
dachshund
greyhound
Saluki

beagle

Toy
Chihuahua
Pekingese
poodle
pug
Yorkshire terrier

Chihuahua

dog

Sporting dog
pointer
retriever
setter
spaniel

Terrier
Airedale
bull terrier
fox terrier
Jack Russell

Herding dog
collie
corgi
German shepherd
sheepdog

retriever

Airedale

collie

dodge
VERB
*She tried to **dodge** her chores.*
▷ avoid, evade, shirk, sidestep

dog
NOUN
See picture on previous page.

dominant
ADJECTIVE
*He is the **dominant** member of the group.*
▷ controlling, leading
ANTONYM subordinate

dominate
VERB
*The leader will **dominate** the meeting.*
▷ command, control, direct, rule

donation
NOUN
*Thank you for your **donation** to the food bank.*
▷ contribution, gift, present

doom
NOUN
*The fearless knight rode out to meet his **doom**.*
▷ destiny, fate

door
NOUN
*The **door** on the left leads to the street.*
▷ doorway, entrance, exit

doubt
NOUN
*I have a tiny **doubt** about his excuse.*
▷ misgiving, suspicion, uncertainty
ANTONYM certainty
VERB
*They **doubt** her word and do not believe her.*
▷ distrust, question, suspect
ANTONYM believe

doubtful
ADJECTIVE
*It is **doubtful** that my relatives will visit us this year.*
▷ debatable, questionable, uncertain
ANTONYM certain

down
ADJECTIVE
*Why are you so **down**?*
▷ dejected, depressed, glum, miserable, unhappy

MAKE IT MORE FORMAL

come down with get sick with (a short-term illness)
down on critical of

downfall
NOUN
*The **downfall** of the company left many people jobless.*
▷ collapse, defeat, failure, fall, ruin

downright
ADJECTIVE
1 *He was always **downright**, but never rude.*
▷ blunt, candid, forthright
2 *She is a **downright** genius.*
▷ absolute, complete, positive, total, utter

down-to-earth
ADJECTIVE
*My aunt is a **down-to-earth** person.*
▷ practical, realistic, sensible

doze
VERB
*I sometimes **doze** in front of the TV.*
▷ drowse, nap, sleep, slumber, snooze

drab
ADJECTIVE
*Why do you wear such **drab** clothes?*
▷ colourless, dingy, dismal, dreary
ANTONYM bright

draft
VERB
***Draft** your essay and I will check it.*
▷ outline, plan

drag
VERB
*Horses were once used to **drag** logs out of the forest.*
▷ haul, lug, pull, tow

MAKE IT MORE FORMAL

drag in bring something irrelevant into a discussion
drag on be boringly long
drag your feet act slowly on purpose

drain
VERB
1 ***Drain** the water from the barrel.*
▷ empty, pump
2 *We cannot allow sewage to **drain** into the lake.*
▷ discharge, empty, seep
3 *The heavy work will **drain** him.*
▷ exhaust, sap, tax, tire

dramatic
ADJECTIVE
*Saskatchewan has a lot of **dramatic** scenery.*
▷ exciting, remarkable, sensational, spectacular, surprising
ANTONYM ordinary

D

D

drastic

ADJECTIVE
*Her mood swings are **drastic**.*
▷ extreme, harsh, severe
ANTONYM mild

draw

VERB
1 *Can you **draw** a cow?*
▷ depict, illustrate, paint, sketch
2 *Pioneers used oxen to **draw** rocks from the fields.*
▷ drag, haul, pull

> ### MAKE IT MORE FORMAL
>
> **beat to the draw** manage to do something before someone else
> **draw a blank** fail to figure out or remember
> **draw out** extend too much
> **draw up** write out in a certain form; come to a stop
> **draw the line** set a limit

drawback

NOUN
*One **drawback** for me is that I get carsick.*
▷ difficulty, disadvantage, downside, hitch, problem
ANTONYM advantage

dread

NOUN
*He lived in **dread** of snakes.*
▷ fear, horror, terror

dreadful

ADJECTIVE
*There was a **dreadful** accident on the highway.*
▷ appalling, atrocious, awful, frightful, ghastly, horrendous, terrible
ANTONYM wonderful

dream

NOUN
1 *Was it a **dream** or was it real?*
▷ fantasy, hallucination, illusion, vision
2 *Her **dream** is to become an astronaut.*
▷ ambition, aspiration, desire, hope

> ### MAKE IT MORE FORMAL
>
> **a dream come true** exactly what you would have wanted
> **dream up** have an idea, especially an unusual one
> **like a dream** perfectly
> **not dream of** never consider at all

dreary

ADJECTIVE
1 *He spent a **dreary** day with nothing to do.*
▷ dull, humdrum, monotonous, tedious, uneventful
ANTONYM exciting
2 *The weather was wet and **dreary** all week.*
▷ cheerless, dismal, dull, gloomy
ANTONYM bright

dress

VERB
***Dress** the child in a warm snowsuit.*
▷ attire, clothe

drift

VERB
*The crowd began to **drift** toward the exit.*
▷ float, flow, stray, wander

drink

VERB
***Drink** your juice.*
▷ gulp, sip, swallow

drip

VERB
*We watched the rain **drip** off the roof.*
▷ dribble, splash, trickle
NOUN
*There's a tiny **drip** of ketchup on your chin.*
▷ bead, drop, droplet

drive

VERB
1 *My older sister can **drive** a tractor.*
▷ handle, operate, steer
2 *A desire for wealth can **drive** a person to work harder.*
▷ compel, force, lead, motivate, prompt, push, spur
3 ***Drive** the fence post into the ground.*
▷ hammer, knock, ram, sink, thrust
NOUN
1 *We were promised a **drive** to the lake.*
▷ excursion, jaunt, journey, ride, spin, trip
2 *Her **drive** to do well in school is admirable.*
▷ ambition, determination, initiative, motivation

> ### MAKE IT MORE FORMAL
>
> **drive into** crash
> **drive off** repel
> **drive someone up the wall** pester

drizzle

NOUN
*The light **drizzle** turned into a thunderstorm.*
▷ rain, shower, spit, sprinkle

droop

VERB

Lack of water made the flowers droop.
▷ bend, sag, wilt, wither

drop

VERB

1 *The temperature is likely to drop tonight.*
▷ decrease, fall, plummet, plunge, sink, tumble
ANTONYM rise
2 *He had to drop his plan to go skateboarding.*
▷ abandon, discard, discontinue, ditch, scrap, shelve

NOUN

There was a drop of oil on the floor.
▷ bead, drip, droplet

MAKE IT MORE FORMAL

a drop in the bucket a comparatively small amount
at the drop of a hat willingly and at once
drop by visit briefly
drop out leave school without finishing courses
drop out of sight disappear
drop the ball make a mess of what one is doing

drown

VERB

Do not drown the plants with water.
▷ flood, immerse, submerge, swamp

drowsy

ADJECTIVE

A big meal makes me drowsy.
▷ sleepy, tired
ANTONYM alert

dry

ADJECTIVE

1 *Without rain, the soil became quite dry.*
▷ arid, dried-up, parched
ANTONYM wet
2 *We thought the discussion was dry.*
▷ boring, dull, monotonous, tedious, uninteresting

dubious

ADJECTIVE

The diamond is of dubious quality.
▷ questionable, suspect, suspicious, unreliable

duck

VERB

Please do not duck my questions.
▷ avoid, dodge, evade

due

ADJECTIVE

1 *Payment of this account is due at the end of the month.*
▷ needed, owing, payable
2 *The meeting is due to take place on Monday.*
▷ expected, scheduled

duel

NOUN

The debaters had a duel with words.
▷ battle, clash, contest, fight

dull

ADJECTIVE

1 *The book was good, but the movie was dull.*
▷ boring, humdrum, monotonous, tedious, uninteresting
ANTONYM interesting
2 *I don't like dull colours.*
▷ drab, muted, subdued
ANTONYM bright
3 *The sky was dull all weekend.*
▷ cloudy, leaden, murky, overcast

dumb

ADJECTIVE

1 *We were dumb with surprise.*
▷ mute, silent, speechless
2 *He was just pretending to be dumb.*
▷ foolish, stupid

dump

VERB

Do not dump garbage by the side of the road.
▷ abandon, dispose of, discard, ditch, throw away, throw out, unload

dupe

VERB

It is easy to dupe a greedy person.
▷ cheat, con, deceive, fool, trick

duplicate

NOUN

The assistant kept a duplicate of the file.
▷ copy, facsimile, replica, reproduction

durable

ADJECTIVE

Marble is a durable material.
▷ enduring, lasting, resilient, solid, sturdy, tough
ANTONYM fragile

dusk

NOUN

Some birds feed at dusk.
▷ evening, nightfall, twilight
ANTONYM dawn

dusty

ADJECTIVE

*The **dusty** room needed to be cleaned.*
▷ dirty, filthy, gritty, grubby

duty

NOUN

1 *It is your **duty** to report the crime.*
▷ obligation, responsibility
2 *Each team member had a **duty**.*
▷ assignment, job, responsibility, role, obligation
3 *You pay the **duty** at Canada's border.*
▷ excise, levy, tariff, tax

MAKE IT MORE FORMAL

above and beyond the call of duty more or
further than required
duty bound morally compelled to do something

---

dwell

VERB

1 *He wanted to **dwell** a bit longer by the river.*
▷ linger, rest, stay
2 *Nomads do not **dwell** for long in one place.*
▷ inhabit, live, occupy, reside
3 *I try not to **dwell** on unhappy events.*
▷ brood, meditate, reflect

dwindle

VERB

*Your emergency supplies will **dwindle** if you keep using
them.*
▷ decrease, diminish, shrink
ANTONYM increase

dye

NOUN

*Spread the **dye** evenly over the material.*
▷ colour, pigment, stain, tint

E e

eager
ADJECTIVE
She is eager to learn to ski.
▷ ardent, avid, enthusiastic, keen

early
ADVERB
Why did you leave early?
▷ ahead of time, beforehand, in advance, prematurely

MAKE IT MORE FORMAL
early on at an early stage
early bird someone who arrives early

earn
VERB
1 *He plans to earn money by cutting lawns.*
▷ bring in, make, obtain
2 *I work hard to earn top grades.*
▷ acquire, merit, win

earnest
ADJECTIVE
She is earnest, but has a sense of humour.
▷ intense, serious, sincere, solemn

earth
NOUN
1 *People used to think the earth was flat.*
▷ globe, planet, world
2 *Loosen the earth before you plant the bush.*
▷ clay, dirt, ground, soil

ease
VERB
The pain seems to ease when I put ice on my ankle.
▷ abate, slacken

easy
ADJECTIVE
1 *Your directions were easy to follow.*
▷ effortless, painless, simple, straightforward
ANTONYM difficult
2 *He had an easy time over the summer.*
▷ carefree, comfortable, quiet, relaxed

MAKE IT MORE FORMAL
easy does it act gently
take it easy relax

eat
VERB
See box below.

REPLACE AN OVERUSED WORD: EAT

There are a number of more descriptive verbs that you can use instead of **eat**, to say something about the way a person eats.

- If you **chew** something, you break it up with your teeth so that it is easier to swallow.
  Chew your food well, and it will be easier for you to digest it.

- If you **consume** something, you eat it. This is a formal word.
  Employees may not consume meals at their workstations.

- If you **devour** something, you eat it quickly and eagerly.
  He seemed ready to devour the whole cake.

- If you **dine**, you eat a formal meal, usually in the evening.
  The queen and her guests will dine at eight.

- When animals **feed on** something, they eat it.
  Raccoons seem to like to feed on garbage.

- If you **gobble** food, you eat it quickly.
  I got up late this morning, and had to gobble my breakfast.

- If you **guzzle** food, you eat it quickly and greedily. This is an informal word.
  If you guzzle the whole pie, you'll be sick.

- If you **munch** food, you eat it by chewing it noisily.
  Apples are good to munch.

- If you **nibble** food, you eat it by biting very small pieces of it.
  She wasn't hungry, but she did nibble a cookie.

- If you **snack**, you eat things between meals.
  Why do you snack on potato chips all the time?

- If you **stuff** yourself, you eat a lot of food.
  I shouldn't stuff myself with candy before supper.

- If you **swallow** something, you make it go from your mouth into your stomach.
  Do not swallow food without chewing it.

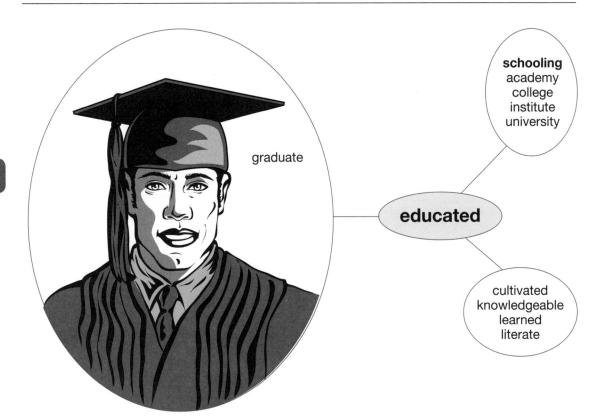

graduate

schooling
academy
college
institute
university

educated

cultivated
knowledgeable
learned
literate

eccentric
ADJECTIVE
Her eccentric behaviour is a worry.
▷ bizarre, erratic, odd, strange, unusual

echo
VERB
I wish you would not echo everything I say.
▷ imitate, mimic, repeat

economical
ADJECTIVE
He is not economical, so he is always short of money.
▷ frugal, prudent, thrifty
ANTONYM extravagant

ecstasy
NOUN
Her ecstasy showed on her face.
▷ bliss, delight, elation, joy, rapture
ANTONYM misery

edge
NOUN
Draw a design around the edge of the paper.
▷ border, boundary, fringe, margin, perimeter
ANTONYM centre

MAKE IT MORE FORMAL
on edge tense
take the edge off take away the sharpness of

edit
VERB
Your partner will help you to edit your writing.
▷ check, correct, revise

educate
VERB
Schools exist to educate young people.
▷ instruct, teach, train

educated
ADJECTIVE
See picture at top of this page.

eerie
ADJECTIVE
We sat around the campfire, telling eerie stories.
▷ creepy, mysterious, scary, spooky

effect
NOUN
Eating too much can have a bad effect on your health.
▷ consequence, end, outcome, result

MAKE IT MORE FORMAL
for effect as a way to impress others
put into effect put into operation
take effect begin to operate

E

effective
ADJECTIVE
Our new team is very effective.
▷ competent, efficient, productive

efficient
ADJECTIVE
I am now more efficient when doing research.
▷ capable, competent, effective, organized
ANTONYM inefficient

effort
NOUN
1 *I put a lot of effort into that project.*
▷ energy, trouble, work
2 *Her effort to make the team was successful.*
▷ attempt, bid

eject
VERB
The ushers had to eject some rowdy fans.
▷ expel, evict, oust, remove

elaborate
ADJECTIVE
1 *He made up an elaborate excuse for being late.*
▷ complex, complicated, detailed, intricate, involved
ANTONYM simple
2 *The artist drew an elaborate design.*
▷ complex, detailed, fancy, ornate

elaborate on
VERB
She began to elaborate on her original idea.
▷ develop, enlarge on, expand

elated
ADJECTIVE
I was elated when my friend came to visit.
▷ delighted, ecstatic, excited, overjoyed

elect
VERB
Who should we elect to chair the meeting?
▷ choose, decide on, pick, select

elegant
ADJECTIVE
Dancers have an elegant way of walking.
▷ exquisite, graceful, refined

elementary
ADJECTIVE
There are four elementary questions, and one that is more difficult.
▷ basic, easy, simple, straightforward

elevate
VERB
Elevate your hands to shoulder level.
▷ hoist, lift, raise
ANTONYM lower

eliminate
VERB
Try to eliminate spelling errors.
▷ delete, eradicate, erase, remove

elude
VERB
The criminal could not elude the police for long.
▷ avoid, dodge, escape, evade

embarrass
VERB
Please do not embarrass me in front of my friends.
▷ disconcert, fluster, humiliate, shame

emblem
NOUN
Who designed the school emblem?
▷ badge, crest, logo, sign, symbol

embrace
VERB
She held out her arms to embrace her friend.
▷ clasp, hold, hug

eminent
ADJECTIVE
We invited the eminent scientist to speak to our class.
▷ famous, important, leading, prominent
ANTONYM unknown

emotion
NOUN
He put a lot of emotion into his farewell speech.
▷ feeling, passion, sentiment

emotional
ADJECTIVE
I am a very emotional person.
▷ passionate, sensitive

emphasis
NOUN
Give more emphasis to your main topic.
▷ importance, prominence, weight

emphasize
VERB
It's important to emphasize the need for exercise.
▷ accentuate, highlight, stress, underline

employ
VERB
He would like to employ you, but you're too young.
▷ appoint, engage, hire

empty
ADJECTIVE
1 *The streets were empty at that time in the morning.*
▷ bare, deserted, uninhabited, vacant
ANTONYM full
2 *She felt her life was empty.*
▷ meaningless, worthless

enchant
VERB
The school musical will enchant everyone.
▷ charm, delight, enthral, fascinate

enclose
VERB
We built a fence to enclose the vegetable garden.
▷ encircle, surround

encounter
VERB
I hope we do not encounter any opposition.
▷ confront, experience, face, meet

encourage
VERB
Fans should encourage the team with applause.
▷ hearten, inspire, motivate, reassure
ANTONYM discourage

end
NOUN
See box at foot of this page.
VERB
I would like to end this discussion now.
▷ cease, conclude, finish, stop, terminate
ANTONYM begin

MAKE IT MORE FORMAL

at loose ends not doing anything in particular
end up do (*or* be) eventually
jump (*or* **go**) **off the deep end** act rashly
make both ends meet spend no more than you have
no end very much (*or* very many)

endanger
VERB
Ignoring road safety rules will endanger your life.
▷ imperil, jeopardize, threaten

endeavour
VERB
I endeavour to get good marks.
▷ attempt, strive, try

endure
VERB
1 *How can you endure the long bus ride every day?*
▷ bear, stand, suffer, tolerate
2 *Our friendship will endure.*
▷ last, persist, remain, survive

enemy
NOUN
She smiled at her enemy across the chessboard.
▷ adversary, antagonist, foe, opponent
ANTONYM friend

energetic
ADJECTIVE
We like having energetic people in our group.
▷ dynamic, tireless, vigorous, vital

energy
NOUN
I do not have the energy to run today.
▷ drive, strength, vigour, vitality

enforce
VERB
Someone will have to enforce the rules.
▷ administer, apply, impose

REPLACE AN OVERUSED WORD: END

End is an overused noun. You can use the following substitutes to add some variety to your writing.

- **the end of a period of time**

  Our team had only four wins by the close of last season.

  June marks the ending of the school year.

  An election will be held at the expiry of the mayor's term of office.

  The baseball season is nearing its finish.

- **the end of an event**

  There was a parade to mark the close of the Olympic Games.

  I was disappointed by the conclusion of the story.

  There were fireworks for the grand finale of the Canada Day celebrations.

  I arrived late and missed the exciting finish of the race.

- **the farthest end of something**

  They camped near the southern boundary of the park.

  Don't stand too near the edge of the stage.

  There's a safe beach at the western extremity of the island.

  Students who live outside the city limits will travel by school bus.

engrave
VERB
Engrave your name on your sculpture.
▷ carve, chisel

engrossed
ADJECTIVE
He was engrossed in the game, and did not hear me.
▷ absorbed, enthralled, fascinated, preoccupied

enhance
VERB
You can enhance your vocabulary by reading.
▷ enrich, improve, increase, strengthen
ANTONYM decrease

enigma
NOUN
The disappearance of the book is an enigma.
▷ mystery, puzzle

enjoy
VERB
Did you enjoy the CD I gave you?
▷ appreciate, like, relish, savour

enjoyable
ADJECTIVE
Our dinner in the restaurant was enjoyable.
▷ agreeable, likeable, pleasant
ANTONYM disagreeable

enlarge
VERB
The city plans to enlarge the size of the sports complex.
▷ broaden, expand, extend, increase
ANTONYM shrink

enlighten
VERB
The teacher will enlighten us on the proper use of the equipment.
▷ educate, inform, instruct

enlist
VERB
We need to enlist more help to tidy the classroom.
▷ employ, engage, recruit

enormous
ADJECTIVE
Some of these boulders are enormous.
▷ colossal, gigantic, huge, immense, massive, tremendous, vast
ANTONYM tiny

enough
ADJECTIVE
Is five dollars enough for lunch?
▷ adequate, sufficient
ANTONYM insufficient

enrage
VERB
Do not enrage the bull by teasing him.
▷ anger, infuriate, provoke
ANTONYM soothe

enrich
VERB
We can enrich our lives by reading.
▷ enhance, improve
ANTONYM impoverish

enrol in
VERB
He intends to enrol in a French class.
▷ join, register in

entertain
VERB
The clown went to entertain the sick children.
▷ amuse, charm, delight, enthral

enthusiasm
NOUN
Speak your lines with more enthusiasm.
▷ eagerness, excitement, warmth

enthusiastic
ADJECTIVE
The boy is enthusiastic about his new hobby.
▷ excited, keen, passionate

entice
VERB
I tried to entice the stray cat with some fish.
▷ attract, tempt

entire
ADJECTIVE
The entire class went on the trip.
▷ complete, full, total, whole
ANTONYM partial

entirely
ADVERB
The accident was entirely my fault.
▷ absolutely, completely, utterly, wholly

entrance
NOUN
Which school entrance should visitors use?
▷ door, doorway, entry, gate
VERB
A puppy always seems to entrance people.
▷ bewitch, captivate, charm, delight, enthral, fascinate

entry
NOUN
The entry was decorated with flowers.
▷ door, doorway, entrance, gate

E

envious
ADJECTIVE
Try not to be envious of their success.
▷ jealous, resentful

environmental
ADJECTIVE
The environmental group spoke about air quality.
▷ conservationist, ecological, green

envy
NOUN
She had trouble hiding her envy.
▷ jealousy, resentment
VERB
It is useless to envy the success of others.
▷ begrudge, resent

episode
NOUN
That was an unhappy episode in his life.
▷ event, experience, incident

equal
ADJECTIVE
The competitors are almost equal in skill.
▷ equivalent, identical

equip
VERB
Equip yourself with a good dictionary.
▷ furnish, provide, supply

equipment
NOUN
Our camping equipment is piled at the door.
▷ apparatus, gear, supplies

equivalent
ADJECTIVE
The two prizes are equivalent in value.
▷ comparable, equal, same
ANTONYM unlike

erase
VERB
Erase all your old files from the computer.
▷ delete, eliminate, remove

erect
VERB
The children used the blocks to erect bridges.
▷ assemble, build, construct
ANTONYM demolish
ADJECTIVE
Keep an erect stance, and don't look down.
▷ upright, vertical

err
VERB
If you err while adding, your total will be wrong.
▷ blunder, miscalculate

erratic
ADJECTIVE
His behaviour is erratic.
▷ changeable, eccentric, irregular

erroneous
ADJECTIVE
The newspaper printed erroneous information.
▷ false, inaccurate, incorrect, untrue, wrong
ANTONYM accurate

error
NOUN
You will make an error if you rush your work.
▷ blunder, fault, mistake, slip

erupt
VERB
The discussion is going to erupt into an argument.
▷ burst, explode

escape
VERB
He tried to escape from his captors.
▷ break away, break free, elude, evade
NOUN
She jogs as an escape from her worries.
▷ distraction, diversion, relief

escort
VERB
I will escort you around Charlottetown.
▷ accompany, guide

essential
ADJECTIVE
1 *Smoke alarms are essential in homes.*
▷ crucial, indispensable, vital
2 *Follow the essential rules for good grammar.*
▷ basic, fundamental, necessary

establish
VERB
I want to establish a karate club at school.
▷ begin, form, organize, start

estate
NOUN
The rich family left its estate to the town.
▷ grounds, land, property

esteem
NOUN
His classmates have great esteem for him.
▷ admiration, estimation, regard, respect

estimate
NOUN
My estimate is that the work will take two hours.
▷ assessment, estimation, guess

evacuate
VERB
We were told to evacuate the building.
▷ empty, leave, vacate

evade

VERB

The thieves could not evade capture forever.

▷ avoid, escape

evaporate

VERB

The puddle began to evaporate in the heat.

▷ disappear, vanish, vaporize

even

ADJECTIVE

1 *The new steps are not quite even.*

▷ flat, horizontal, level

2 *She could hear the even ticking of the clock.*

▷ constant, regular, smooth, steady, uniform

3 *He cut the pie into even pieces.*

▷ equal, identical, uniform

MAKE IT MORE FORMAL

break even have equal gains and losses
even out become more level
even though in spite of
get even take revenge

event

NOUN

We witnessed the unfortunate event.

▷ affair, episode, incident, occurrence

everlasting

ADJECTIVE

I am tired of their everlasting arguments.

▷ endless, eternal, infinite

everyday

ADJECTIVE

The campers had to do everyday chores.

▷ common, ordinary, routine

evidence

NOUN

Is there any evidence to show who took your pen?

▷ proof, sign, trace

evident

ADJECTIVE

Her joy was evident when she won the prize.

▷ apparent, clear, conspicuous, noticeable, obvious, plain

evil

ADJECTIVE

At the end of the movie, the evil tyrant dies.

▷ bad, malevolent, vile, wicked

ANTONYM good

exact

ADJECTIVE

He made an exact copy of the painting.

▷ accurate, faithful, faultless, precise, true

ANTONYM approximate

exaggerate

VERB

Do not exaggerate the amount of work to be done.

▷ inflate, overestimate, overstate

examine

VERB

Examine your work before you hand it in.

▷ analyze, check, inspect, study

example

NOUN

1 *She gave me an example of her art.*

▷ illustration, sample, specimen

2 *His honesty is an example we can all follow.*

▷ ideal, model

exasperate

VERB

Children often exasperate their parents.

▷ aggravate, annoy, irritate

exceed

VERB

How many points do you need to exceed the record?

▷ beat, pass, surpass

excellent

ADJECTIVE

Listen to this excellent CD.

▷ brilliant, exceptional, first-class, great, outstanding, superb

ANTONYM terrible

except

PREPOSITION

I like all fruit except bananas.

▷ apart from, barring, excluding, other than, with the exception of

exceptional

ADJECTIVE

1 *This exceptional story was written by a student.*

▷ excellent, outstanding, remarkable

ANTONYM mediocre

2 *The snowstorm was exceptional for April.*

▷ extraordinary, rare, special, uncommon, unusual

ANTONYM common

excess

NOUN

We grew an excess of beans and gave some away.

▷ glut, overabundance, surfeit, surplus

ANTONYM shortage

ADJECTIVE

She had excess food at lunchtime, and shared it with me.

▷ extra, surplus

exchange

VERB

Could I exchange my watch for yours?

▷ swap, switch, trade

excited

ADJECTIVE

Our family is excited about going to Nunavut.

▷ ecstatic, enthusiastic, thrilled

ANTONYM bored

exciting

ADJECTIVE

We watched an exciting mystery on TV.

▷ dramatic, electrifying, exhilarating, rousing, stimulating, thrilling

ANTONYM boring

exclaim

VERB

They heard the woman exclaim as she fell.

▷ call out, shout, yell

exclude

VERB

1 *Do not exclude the other items on the agenda.*

▷ eliminate, ignore, omit, rule out

ANTONYM include

2 *Contest rules exclude employees.*

▷ ban, bar, prohibit

ANTONYM welcome

excuse

NOUN

His excuse seems really weak.

▷ explanation, justification

VERB

Please excuse my carelessness.

▷ forgive, overlook, pardon

execute

VERB

Can she execute the difficult skating routine?

▷ accomplish, achieve, perform

exempt

ADJECTIVE

The imported radio was exempt from tax.

▷ excused, immune

exercise

NOUN

For me, exercise consists of running and skipping.

▷ activity, exertion, training

exhaust

VERB

1 *Did they exhaust themselves by training too hard?*

▷ drain, fatigue, tire, weaken

2 *Do not exhaust our food supplies in one day.*

▷ consume, deplete, drain, use up

exhibition

NOUN

This pumpkin won first prize at the exhibition.

▷ display, fair, show

exhilarating

ADJECTIVE

We had an exhilarating time tubing on the river.

▷ exciting, invigorating, stimulating, thrilling

exile

VERB

The new government planned to exile the dictator.

▷ banish, deport, expel

exist

VERB

I cannot exist on so little money.

▷ live, survive

expand

VERB

She intends to expand her business.

▷ enlarge, extend, increase, spread

ANTONYM decrease

expand on

VERB

Will you please expand on your plan?

▷ develop, elaborate on, enlarge on

expect

VERB

I expect that he will need help.

▷ anticipate, assume, presume, suppose

expedition

NOUN

The expedition ended when two people died.

▷ exploration, journey, quest

expensive

ADJECTIVE

Why are CDs so expensive?

▷ costly, dear, pricey

ANTONYM inexpensive

experience

NOUN

1 *She has computer experience.*

▷ expertise, know-how, knowledge, training

2 *Our experience during the snowstorm was scary.*

▷ adventure, incident, ordeal

VERB

I always experience difficulty with the key.

▷ encounter, undergo

expert

NOUN

He is a cooking expert.

▷ authority, guru, professional, specialist

ANTONYM beginner

explain

VERB

She tried to explain her meaning.

▷ clarify, define, describe

explanation

NOUN

We need an explanation of that rule.

▷ clarification, definition, description

explode

VERB

The accident caused the tanker to explode.

▷ blow up, burst, detonate, erupt

exploit

VERB

Do not exploit my generous nature.

▷ abuse, manipulate, take advantage of

NOUN

That was a bold exploit!

▷ act, deed, feat

expose

VERB

1 *If you remove that wall, you will expose the old fireplace.*

▷ reveal, show, uncover

2 *Her lies helped to expose her bad character.*

▷ reveal, show, uncover

express

VERB

We went to the meeting to express our views.

▷ communicate, declare, voice

ADJECTIVE

They use an express courier for their parcels.

▷ direct, fast, high-speed, non-stop, speedy, swift

expression

NOUN

1 *Her delighted expression made us happy.*

▷ countenance, face

2 *He used a rude expression to show his anger.*

▷ idiom, phrase, remark

extend

VERB

The building will extend to the lakefront.

▷ reach, spread, stretch

extent

NOUN

We did not realize the extent of his plan.

▷ range, scale, size

exterior

NOUN

It is time to paint the exterior of the building.

▷ front, outside

ANTONYM interior

extract

NOUN

The magazine printed an extract from the book.

▷ excerpt, passage, section

extraordinary

ADJECTIVE

1 *What an extraordinary thing to say!*

▷ bizarre, curious, incredible, strange, surprising, unusual, weird

ANTONYM everyday

2 *We had an extraordinary vacation kayaking in the Northwest Territories.*

▷ exceptional, remarkable

ANTONYM ordinary

extravagant

ADJECTIVE

My extravagant ways get me into trouble.

▷ lavish, spendthrift, wasteful

extreme

ADJECTIVE

1 *The extreme heat made us very uncomfortable.*

▷ acute, great, intense, profound, severe

2 *His extreme behaviour was unusual.*

▷ excessive, extravagant, radical

E

F f

fabric
NOUN
I would like one metre of fabric, please.
▷ cloth, material, textile

face
NOUN
1 *Her serious face told me something was wrong.*
▷ countenance, features
2 *The face of the building is brick.*
▷ exterior, front, surface

MAKE IT MORE FORMAL

face down (*or* **up**) with the main side down (*or* up)
face someone down successfully confront someone
face to face in person
face up to meet bravely
face with present with a problem
get in your face confront you
in the face of in the presence of; in spite of
on the face of it going by appearances
pull a long face look sad or disapproving
put a good face on it make the best of the situation
to someone's face in someone's presence

fact
NOUN
It is a fact that we must leave soon.
▷ certainty, reality, truth
ANTONYM fiction

factual
ADJECTIVE
She wrote a factual account of her trip.
▷ actual, real, true
ANTONYM imaginary

fad
NOUN
You do not have to follow the latest fad.
▷ craze, fashion, whim

fade
VERB
At six o'clock daylight began to fade.
▷ disappear, vanish

fail
VERB
1 *You might fail at the competition if you don't practise every day.*
▷ be defeated, be unsuccessful
ANTONYM succeed
2 *Our enthusiasm for the project has begun to fail.*
▷ decline, sink, weaken

failure
NOUN
The experiment was a failure.
▷ disaster, fiasco, flop
ANTONYM success

faint
ADJECTIVE
She has only faint memories of her grandparents.
▷ dim, indistinct, vague, weak
ANTONYM strong
VERB
The bad news made me faint.
▷ collapse, pass out, swoon

fair
ADJECTIVE
1 *The accused complained that the trial was not fair.*
▷ impartial, just, proper
2 *The movie was only fair.*
▷ average, mediocre, moderate
3 *The weather for the picnic was fair.*
▷ beautiful, clear, dry, sunny

faith
NOUN
1 *We have great faith in his ability.*
▷ confidence, trust
2 *He and I are not of the same faith.*
▷ belief, creed

faithful
ADJECTIVE
1 *She is a faithful friend.*
▷ devoted, loyal, staunch, true
2 *Is this a faithful copy of the original?*
▷ accurate, exact, true
ANTONYM inaccurate

faithless
ADJECTIVE
He was betrayed by his faithless friend.
▷ disloyal, false, treacherous
ANTONYM faithful

fake
NOUN
This five-dollar bill is a fake.
▷ copy, forgery, fraud, imitation, reproduction, sham
ADJECTIVE
Everyone was fooled by the fake diamond.
▷ artificial, bogus, counterfeit, false, imitation, mock
ANTONYM genuine
VERB
She decided to fake a headache to avoid going.
▷ feign, pretend, simulate

fall

VERB

1 *I knew the books would fall off the shelf.*
▷ drop, plunge, topple
ANTONYM rise

2 *The price of skateboards will fall later in the year.*
▷ decline, decrease, diminish, dwindle, plummet, subside
ANTONYM increase

MAKE IT MORE FORMAL

fall all over yourself be extremely eager
fall apart (*or* **to pieces**) disintegrate
fall behind lag
fall down collapse
fall for be fooled by; fall in love with
fall off decline
fall out quarrel
fall through fail

false

ADJECTIVE

1 *Four of the five multiple-choice answers are false.*
▷ fictitious, incorrect, untrue, wrong
ANTONYM true

2 *The smuggler had a false passport.*
▷ bogus, fake, forged
ANTONYM genuine

falsehood

NOUN

I told a falsehood, and blushed bright red.
▷ fabrication, fib, lie, untruth
ANTONYM truth

fame

NOUN

The young actor enjoyed his fame.
▷ celebrity, glory, prominence, renown, reputation

familiar

ADJECTIVE

These are old, familiar excuses.
▷ common, frequent, well-known
ANTONYM rare

famished

ADJECTIVE

They came home famished.
▷ hungry, ravenous, starving

famous

ADJECTIVE

The Okanagan Valley is famous for its apples.
▷ celebrated, legendary, noted, renowned, well-known
ANTONYM unknown

fan

NOUN

She is a fan of that country singer.
▷ admirer, follower, supporter

fanatic

NOUN

He is a fanatic about recycling.
▷ activist, devotee, extremist, militant, zealot

fancy

ADJECTIVE

We put the photograph in a fancy frame.
▷ elaborate, intricate, ornate
ANTONYM plain

fantastic

ADJECTIVE

We had a fantastic time travelling in Nova Scotia.
▷ excellent, glorious, great, marvellous, wonderful

fascinate

VERB

The Museum of Civilization in Ottawa will fascinate the tourists.
▷ captivate, enthral, intrigue

fashion

NOUN

I like to follow the latest fashion.
▷ craze, fad, style, trend, vogue

fashionable

ADJECTIVE

Are jeans always fashionable?
▷ current, popular, trendy

fast

ADJECTIVE

Dad made a fast trip to the grocery store.
▷ accelerated, hurried, quick, rapid, speedy, swift
ANTONYM slow

fasten

VERB

Fasten the name tag to your jacket.
▷ attach, fix, join, secure, tie

fat

NOUN

See box on next page.

fatal

ADJECTIVE

That disease is usually fatal.
▷ deadly, incurable, lethal, terminal

fate

NOUN

Many people do not believe in fate.
▷ destiny, fortune

REPLACE AN OVERUSED WORD: FAT

A person who is **fat** weighs more than is considered normal. Some words used to describe such a person can be hurtful and insulting. There are also words that are acceptable.

- If you describe a woman as **buxom**, you mean that she looks healthy and has a rounded body.
  My big sister is tall and buxom.

- A **chubby** person, usually a child, is slightly fat.
  My little brother is only two, and is chubby.

- If you describe someone as **fleshy**, you mean that they are slightly too fat.
  She is strong, but has become a bit fleshy lately.

- If you describe someone as **gross**, you mean that they are extremely fat and unattractive. This is a very insulting word to use.
  He had difficulty getting his gross body into a car.

- An **obese** person is extremely fat, to the point of being unhealthy.
  Being obese can seriously damage your health.

- If you say someone is **overweight**, you mean that they are fatter than is considered normal.
  The woman was slightly overweight just after having a baby.

- You can use the word **plump** to describe someone who is rather fat or rounded, usually when you think this is a good quality.
  The baby was plump and pretty, with lots of hair.

- A **portly** person is quite fat. This word is mostly used to describe men.
  Portly men are usually considered to be very good-natured.

- If you say someone is **pudgy**, you mean that they are slightly fat. This is an informal word.
  Dad's getting a little pudgy round his waist.

- If you describe a woman's figure as **rounded**, you mean that it is attractive because it is well-developed and not too thin.
  The heroine is a beautiful woman with a full, rounded figure.

- A **stout** person, usually an older adult, is rather fat.
  The store manager was a stout man with grey hair and a beard.

fatigue
NOUN
Her eyes closed from sheer fatigue.
▷ exhaustion, tiredness, weariness

fault
NOUN
1 *The fault was mine.*
▷ blame, blunder, liability, oversight, responsibility
2 *The company found a fault in the software.*
▷ blemish, defect, deficiency, flaw, imperfection

MAKE IT MORE FORMAL

at fault deserving the blame
find fault with criticize in a negative way
to a fault to a great degree

faulty
ADJECTIVE
Your memory of the event is faulty.
▷ defective, flawed, imperfect

favour
NOUN
1 *She looked with favour on the proposed plan.*
▷ approval, esteem, support
ANTONYM disapproval
2 *I did my sister a favour by washing the dishes.*
▷ courtesy, kindness, service

favourite
ADJECTIVE
This is my favourite dessert.
▷ best-loved, dearest, preferred

fear
NOUN
Her eyes grew big with fear.
▷ alarm, awe, dread, fright, panic, terror

fearful
ADJECTIVE
We were fearful that we would be late.
▷ afraid, anxious, worried

fearless
ADJECTIVE
They were fearless in spite of the danger.
▷ bold, brave, courageous, daring

feat
NOUN
That was an amazing feat.
▷ act, achievement, deed, exploit, performance

feature
NOUN
Good humour is his best feature.
▷ aspect, attribute, characteristic, quality
VERB
The newsletter will feature the girls' hockey team.
▷ emphasize, spotlight

fee
NOUN
The fee for ice skating at this arena is two dollars.
▷ charge, cost, payment, price, rate

feeble
ADJECTIVE
His excuse was feeble.
▷ pathetic, puny, weak

feed
VERB
Eat healthy meals to feed your body properly.
▷ nourish, sustain

feel
VERB
1 *She began to feel pains in her legs.*
▷ experience, suffer, undergo
2 *I feel that I am wrong.*
▷ believe, consider, judge, think
3 *Feel the cat's soft fur.*
▷ stroke, touch

MAKE IT MORE FORMAL
feel for sympathize with
feel like have a desire for
feel out find out about, in a cautious way

fellow
NOUN
He thinks he's such a fine fellow.
▷ guy, male, man

female
NOUN
Which female is the tallest?
▷ girl, lady, woman

fence
NOUN
We took down the fence.
▷ barricade, barrier, wall

ferocious
ADJECTIVE
There is a ferocious lion at the zoo.
▷ fierce, savage, violent, wild
ANTONYM gentle

fertile
ADJECTIVE
Wheat grows well in the fertile soil of the Prairie Provinces.
▷ fruitful, productive, rich
ANTONYM barren

fervent
ADJECTIVE
They are fervent supporters of the basketball team.
▷ ardent, committed, devout, enthusiastic, passionate

festival
NOUN
Our music festival will be held in June.
▷ carnival, celebration, entertainment, fete, gala

feud
NOUN
They have forgotten how the feud began.
▷ argument, conflict, dispute, fight, quarrel, squabble

fiasco
NOUN
The party was a fiasco.
▷ disaster, failure, scandal

fib
NOUN
Did you tell me a fib?
▷ falsehood, lie, untruth

fidget
VERB
Don't fidget so much.
▷ jiggle, squirm, twitch

field
NOUN
We saw cows and horses in the field.
▷ meadow, pasture

fierce
ADJECTIVE
1 *Grizzly bears can be fierce.*
▷ aggressive, dangerous, ferocious
ANTONYM gentle
2 *There is a fierce storm raging up north.*
▷ intense, strong, violent

fight
VERB
The fans began to fight in the street.
▷ battle, brawl, grapple, struggle
NOUN
1 *The fight in the movie looked realistic.*
▷ action, battle, bout, combat, duel, skirmish
2 *They had a big fight about who was correct.*
▷ argument, dispute, row, squabble

F

F

figure

NOUN

1 *Write down this figure.*
▷ digit, number, numeral, symbol
2 *We saw a figure hiding behind the bushes.*
▷ body, form, shape

VERB

They figure the trip will take two days.
▷ expect, guess, suppose

fill

VERB

I will fill my backpack with supplies for the hike.
▷ cram, load, pack, stock, stuff

ANTONYM empty

> **MAKE IT MORE FORMAL**
>
> **fill the bill** be just what is needed
> **fill you in** bring you up to date

filth

NOUN

The old couch was covered with filth.
▷ dirt, grime

filthy

ADJECTIVE

The filthy water was unfit to drink.
▷ dirty, foul, polluted

ANTONYM clean

final

ADJECTIVE

1 *Friday is the final day of the sale.*
▷ closing, concluding, last, ultimate

ANTONYM first

2 *Our vacation plans are now final.*
▷ absolute, conclusive, definite

finally

ADVERB

Finally, here is my decision.
▷ in conclusion, in summary, lastly

find

VERB

Did you ever find your sweater?
▷ discover, locate, track down, unearth

ANTONYM lose

> **MAKE IT MORE FORMAL**
>
> **find fault** complain
> **find fault with** criticize
> **find it in your heart** be willing (to do something)
> **find your feet** grow in ability or confidence
> **find yourself** figure out your purpose or goal
>   in life
> **find out** discover

fine

ADJECTIVE

1 *There are many fine buildings in Ottawa.*
▷ admirable, beautiful, excellent, magnificent, outstanding, splendid
2 *This cotton is so fine that it feels like silk.*
▷ delicate, lightweight

finish

VERB

He plans to finish his project tomorrow.
▷ complete, conclude, end, finalize

ANTONYM start

fire

NOUN

The fire could be seen ten kilometres away.
▷ blaze, combustion, flames, inferno

VERB

1 *The soldiers plan to fire the cannons at noon.*
▷ detonate, explode, set off, shoot
2 *The company had to fire some employees.*
▷ discharge, dismiss, sack

> **MAKE IT MORE FORMAL**
>
> **fire away** go ahead and ask
> **light a fire under someone** encourage someone
>   to act more quickly

firm

ADJECTIVE

1 *Leave the mixture in the freezer till firm.*
▷ hard, rigid, set, solid, stiff

ANTONYM soft

2 *She is firm, but fair.*
▷ determined, inflexible, resolute, staunch, unshakable

NOUN

My father liked working for that firm.
▷ business, company, corporation, enterprise, organization

first

ADJECTIVE

Our first try at solving the puzzle failed.
▷ earliest, initial, opening, original

ANTONYM last

first-rate

ADJECTIVE

We saw a first-rate movie on TV last night.
▷ excellent, exceptional, marvellous, outstanding, splendid, superb

fishy

ADJECTIVE

There is something fishy about him.
▷ doubtful, shady, suspect, suspicious

ANTONYM honest

flag

Yukon Territory

Northwest Territories

Nunavut

British Columbia

Alberta

Canada

Saskatchewan

Manitoba

Ontario

Québec

New Brunswick

Prince Edward Island

Nova Scotia

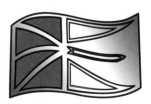
Newfoundland and Labrador

fissure
NOUN
The cold weather has caused a fissure in the road.
▷ cleft, crack, crevice, pothole

fit
ADJECTIVE
Keep fit with lots of exercise.
▷ healthy, robust, trim, well

fitting
ADJECTIVE
The applause was a fitting reward for all our work.
▷ appropriate, correct, proper, suitable

fix
VERB
Can't you fix that rip in your jeans?
▷ mend, patch up, repair
NOUN
She is in a fix because she did not finish her project.
▷ difficulty, mess, predicament

flag
NOUN
See picture on previous page.

flagrant
ADJECTIVE
There has been a flagrant disregard of the rules.
▷ blatant, obvious, outrageous, shameless

flair
NOUN
You have a real flair for writing.
▷ ability, gift, knack, talent

flashy
ADJECTIVE
That's a flashy outfit you are wearing!
▷ flamboyant, showy

flat
ADJECTIVE
1 *I like to work on a flat surface.*
▷ even, horizontal, level
2 *The first scene of the play is good, but the rest is flat.*
▷ boring, dull, insipid, monotonous

flaw
NOUN
Turn the mug around and you will see the flaw.
▷ blemish, defect, fault, imperfection

flawless
ADJECTIVE
He made a flawless dive.
▷ faultless, perfect

flee
VERB
The burglar tried to flee but was caught.
▷ escape, leave
ANTONYM stay

fleeting
ADJECTIVE
I had only a fleeting look at the car.
▷ brief, momentary, passing, short

flexible
ADJECTIVE
My muscles are very flexible.
▷ elastic, lithe, pliable, supple

flimsy
ADJECTIVE
Do not stand on that flimsy chair!
▷ fragile, rickety, weak
ANTONYM sturdy

flinch
VERB
You may flinch when you get your flu shot.
▷ cringe, shrink, wince

fling
VERB
Fling the ball to me.
▷ heave, hurl, pitch, throw, toss

float
VERB
The swan stayed still for a moment, and then began to float away.
▷ drift, glide

flood
VERB
After days of heavy rain, water began to flood the land.
▷ deluge, engulf, submerge, swamp

floor
NOUN
It was above sea level, so the floor of the cave was dry.
▷ base, bottom, ground

flop
VERB
The flowering plants started to flop over.
▷ droop, drop, fall

flourish
VERB
1 *At first, the restaurant seemed to flourish.*
▷ boom, prosper, succeed, thrive
ANTONYM fail
2 *We saw him flourish the letter in excitement.*
▷ brandish, shake, wave

flow
VERB
The liquid began to flow through the tubing.
▷ glide, gush, run, slide, stream

fluent
ADJECTIVE
The class visitor was a fluent speaker.
▷ articulate, effortless, flowing
ANTONYM hesitant

flush

VERB

Her face slowly began to flush.

▷ blush, redden

fluster

VERB

He tried to fluster me by making a face.

▷ bother, confuse, rattle, ruffle

flutter

VERB

Flags look almost alive as they flutter in the wind.

▷ blow, fly, wave

fly

VERB

1 *We watched the kite fly up into the air.*

▷ float, glide, soar

2 *I must fly or I'll be late!*

▷ dart, dash, hurry, race, rush, speed, tear

foam

NOUN

Running water quickly turned the liquid soap into foam.

▷ bubbles, froth, lather

F

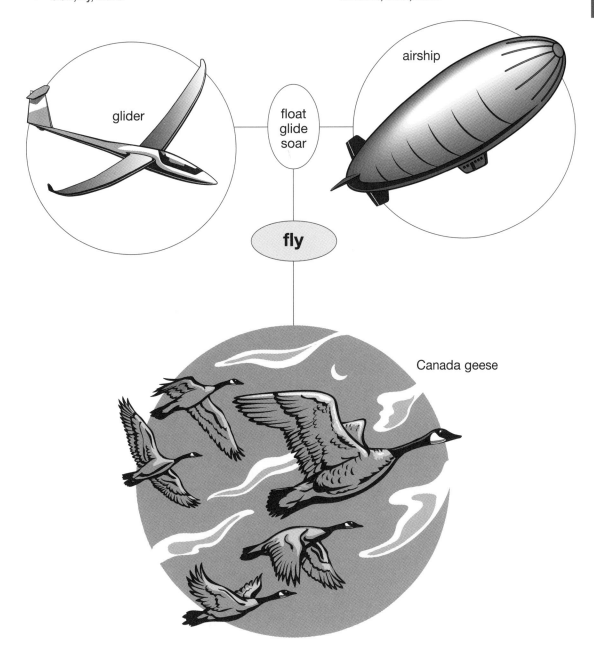

glider

float
glide
soar

airship

fly

Canada geese

F

focus

VERB

*Try to **focus** the light beam on the wall.*

▷ concentrate, direct, fix

NOUN

*The science project was the **focus** of the exhibit at the fair.*

▷ centre, focal point, hub, target

foe

NOUN

*He is my **foe** in the tournament.*

▷ adversary, enemy, opponent

ANTONYM ally

fog

NOUN

*There was no wind to blow the **fog** away.*

▷ haze, mist, murk, smog

foil

VERB

*Why did you **foil** my attempt to speak?*

▷ check, counter, frustrate, prevent, thwart

fold

VERB

***Fold** the newspaper in half.*

▷ bend, crease

NOUN

*I ironed out the **fold** in the sheet.*

▷ bend, crease, wrinkle

follow

VERB

1 *My little brother was determined to **follow** me.*

▷ chase, hound, pursue

2 *What technology will **follow** cellphones?*

▷ succeed, supersede

ANTONYM precede

3 ***Follow** the posted rules.*

▷ comply with, conform to, heed, obey, observe

MAKE IT MORE FORMAL

as follows in the following way

follow out carry out (instructions)

follow through complete whatever needs to be done

follow up make more enquiries

follow your nose do what your instinct tells you

---

fond

ADJECTIVE

*I gave my aunt a **fond** hug.*

▷ adoring, affectionate, loving

fondle

VERB

*She liked to **fondle** the dog's ears.*

▷ caress, stroke, touch

food

NOUN

*We buy most of our **food** at a supermarket.*

▷ fare, foodstuffs, nourishment, provisions

fool

NOUN

*Please do not behave like a **fool**.*

▷ clown, idiot, ignoramus, simpleton

VERB

*They didn't **fool** us.*

▷ deceive, dupe, mislead, trick

foolhardy

ADJECTIVE

*He thinks he's brave, but I think he's **foolhardy**.*

▷ impetuous, madcap, reckless

foolish

ADJECTIVE

*If there is any more **foolish** talk, I will refuse to listen.*

▷ absurd, idiotic, nonsensical, senseless, silly, unintelligent, unwise

ANTONYM wise

forbid

VERB

*Does the school **forbid** talking in the hallways?*

▷ ban, bar, prevent, prohibit, veto

ANTONYM allow

force

VERB

*I'll eat the food, but you cannot **force** me to like it!*

▷ compel, drive, oblige, pressure

NOUN

*The water gushed out with great **force**.*

▷ might, power, pressure, strength

forecast

VERB

*His job is to **forecast** the weather.*

▷ foresee, foretell, predict

foremost

ADJECTIVE

*He is the **foremost** surgeon in the hospital.*

▷ chief, greatest, leading, principal

forest

NOUN

*They searched for mushrooms in the **forest**.*

▷ bush, jungle, rainforest, woodland

forgery

NOUN

*The coin is a **forgery**.*

▷ fake, imitation

forget
VERB
Don't forget the cat food.
▷ omit, overlook
ANTONYM remember

forgive
VERB
I hope you can forgive me for what I said.
▷ excuse, pardon
ANTONYM blame

form
NOUN
1 *Haiku is one form of poetry.*
▷ class, kind, sort, type, variant, variety
2 *A basketball has a round form.*
▷ figure, outline, shape, structure
VERB
Can you form a triangle with the string?
▷ create, develop, fashion, make

formal
ADJECTIVE
My dad wore a tuxedo to the formal dinner.
▷ ceremonial, official
ANTONYM informal

former
ADJECTIVE
She is a former teacher of mine.
▷ earlier, past, previous, prior

formidable
ADJECTIVE
There was a formidable amount of snow to shovel.
▷ challenging, daunting, intimidating

forsake
VERB
I could never forsake my best friend.
▷ abandon, desert, leave

forthright
ADJECTIVE
He spoke in a forthright manner.
▷ blunt, candid, direct, frank, straightforward

fortify
VERB
Fortify yourself by eating breakfast.
▷ protect, strengthen

fortunate
ADJECTIVE
Our meeting was accidental, but fortunate.
▷ favourable, lucky

fortune
NOUN
1 *The pirates' fortune is hidden somewhere on this island.*
▷ riches, treasure, wealth
2 *It was good fortune that she found her gloves.*
▷ chance, fate, luck

foul
ADJECTIVE
What is that foul smell?
▷ disgusting, rancid, rotten, vile

found
VERB
Our community plans to found a gymnastics club.
▷ begin, establish, start

foundation
NOUN
The foundation of his hockey skill is practice.
▷ base, basis

fraction
NOUN
I took only a small fraction of the cake.
▷ fragment, part, piece, portion

fragile
ADJECTIVE
He was afraid to use the fragile cup.
▷ breakable, brittle, delicate, flimsy, frail
ANTONYM tough

fragment
NOUN
There was a fragment of dirt in my eye.
▷ bit, morsel, particle, piece

fragrance
NOUN
We enjoyed the fragrance of the flowers.
▷ aroma, perfume, scent, smell

frail
ADJECTIVE
The patient looked tired and frail.
▷ feeble, fragile, weak

frank
ADJECTIVE
She was frank in her talk with the student.
▷ candid, direct, honest, open, plain, straightforward

frantic
ADJECTIVE
The man began a frantic search for the missing money.
▷ agitated, excited, frenzied
ANTONYM calm

fraud
NOUN
1 *They were victims of Internet fraud.*
▷ deceit, deception, swindle, trickery
2 *Do not give that fraud any money.*
▷ cheater, imposter, quack

freak
ADJECTIVE
That was a freak accident.
▷ abnormal, bizarre, unusual
ANTONYM common

F

F

free
ADJECTIVE
1 *The trapped animal is now free.*
▷ at large, at liberty, loose
ANTONYM captive
2 *We used the coupon to get a free pizza.*
▷ complimentary, gratis
VERB
They plan to free the bird after its leg heals.
▷ liberate, release, set loose
ANTONYM imprison

MAKE IT MORE FORMAL
a free hand freedom to behave as you see fit
for free at no cost
free and easy with little attention to rules
there's no free lunch you can't get something
for nothing

freeze
VERB
Freeze the dessert for an hour, then serve.
▷ chill, congeal, harden
ANTONYM melt

frenzy
NOUN
He tried to control his frenzy as he searched for the lost child.
▷ agitation, fury, hysteria

frequent
ADJECTIVE
We make frequent trips to the mall.
▷ continual, habitual, recurrent, repeated
ANTONYM rare

fresh
ADJECTIVE
The group has a fresh idea for its project.
▷ new, novel, recent
ANTONYM stale

friend
NOUN
She has been my friend since we started school.
▷ buddy, chum, companion, crony, pal
ANTONYM enemy

friendly
ADJECTIVE
Our neighbours are friendly people.
▷ affectionate, amiable, genial, welcoming

friendship
NOUN
Friendship must be based on trust.
▷ affection, attachment, closeness
ANTONYM hostility

fright
NOUN
Their fright showed on their faces.
▷ alarm, fear, horror, panic

frighten
VERB
That mask may frighten the children.
▷ alarm, intimidate, scare, startle, terrify, unnerve

frightening
ADJECTIVE
The unexpected noise was frightening.
▷ alarming, intimidating, menacing, terrifying

frigid
ADJECTIVE
February was frigid.
▷ cold, chilly, frosty, icy
ANTONYM warm

fringe
NOUN
I like the red fringe on your jacket.
▷ border, edge

frivolous
ADJECTIVE
Her frivolous behaviour was boring.
▷ flippant, foolish, juvenile, silly
ANTONYM serious

frontier
NOUN
The pioneers travelled beyond the frontier.
▷ border, boundary, edge

froth
NOUN
You have froth from the hot chocolate on your nose.
▷ bubbles, foam

frown
VERB
The bus driver tends to frown at noisy children.
▷ glare, glower, scowl

frugal
ADJECTIVE
Be frugal and save part of your allowance.
▷ economical, thrifty
ANTONYM wasteful

fruitful
ADJECTIVE
The team meeting was fruitful.
▷ productive, profitable
ANTONYM barren

fruitless
ADJECTIVE
It was fruitless to run after the dog.
▷ futile, pointless

frustrate
VERB
Do not frustrate my attempt to study.
▷ block, check, spoil

fulfill
VERB
I cannot fulfill my goal without help.
▷ accomplish, achieve, meet, realize, satisfy

full
ADJECTIVE
1 *My backpack was full.*
▷ filled, loaded, packed
ANTONYM empty
2 *Can you give us a full report?*
▷ comprehensive, detailed, thorough

fun
NOUN
I must tell you about the fun we had.
▷ enjoyment, entertainment, pleasure, recreation

function
NOUN
1 *The bodyguard's function is to keep the fans away.*
▷ duty, job, purpose, responsibility, role
2 *My parents are going to a fundraising function.*
▷ gathering, party, reception
VERB
Can you get this machine to function properly?
▷ behave, operate, perform, run, work

fund
NOUN
He seems to have a huge fund of knowledge.
▷ reserve, reservoir, store
VERB
The company will fund the new arena.
▷ finance, pay for, subsidize, support

fundamental
ADJECTIVE
I have fundamental computer skills.
▷ basic, essential

funny
ADJECTIVE
1 *There is a funny smell coming from the box.*
▷ mysterious, odd, peculiar, puzzling, strange, unusual
2 *He told a funny story.*
▷ amusing, comical, hilarious, humorous, witty

furious
ADJECTIVE
They were furious at the vandalism.
▷ angry, enraged, fuming, infuriated, livid

furnish
VERB
This store can furnish us with all we need for the fishing trip.
▷ equip, provide, supply

furtive
ADJECTIVE
The raccoon made a furtive move toward the garbage.
▷ secretive, sly, stealthy
ANTONYM open

fury
NOUN
Her fury was so great that she could hardly speak.
▷ anger, frenzy, rage

fuse
VERB
He had to fuse the broken ends of the wires together.
▷ bond, combine, join, weld

fuss
NOUN
There was a lot of fuss over the spilled milk.
▷ agitation, bother, commotion, confusion, stir, uproar

fussy
ADJECTIVE
The child is very fussy about her clothes.
▷ choosy, exacting, fastidious, particular

futile
ADJECTIVE
He made a futile effort to fix the bicycle.
▷ hopeless, unsuccessful, useless, vain
ANTONYM successful

future
ADJECTIVE
Our future plans include a visit to Lake Manitoba.
▷ forthcoming, impending

F

G g

gadget
NOUN
*I have a **gadget** that shuffles cards.*
▷ contraption, device, machine, tool

gag
NOUN
*He pulled a good **gag** on his family.*
▷ joke, prank

gain
VERB
*They can **gain** respect by working hard.*
▷ acquire, attain, earn, obtain

gale
NOUN
*The **gale** blew the roof off the shed.*
▷ squall, storm, tempest, windstorm

gallant
ADJECTIVE
*Knights were taught to be **gallant**.*
▷ chivalrous, courteous

gallop
VERB
*The dogs barked excitedly, then began to **gallop** round the yard.*
▷ bolt, dash, hurry, run, rush, tear

game
NOUN
*I'm going to watch the **game** on TV.*
▷ contest, competition, match, meet

MAKE IT MORE FORMAL

ahead of the game winning rather than losing
game over final defeat
off your game not performing well
play the game follow the rules

---

gang
NOUN
*A **gang** of us gathered in the park to play soccer.*
▷ band, bunch, group, pack

gap
NOUN
*The wind whistled through the **gap** in the tent.*
▷ hole, opening

garbage
NOUN
1 *Fast food restaurants create a lot of **garbage**.*
▷ debris, junk, litter, refuse, trash, waste
2 *We thought the newspaper article was **garbage**.*
▷ drivel, gibberish, nonsense

gasp
VERB
*We all had to **gasp** for air after the race.*
▷ gulp, pant, puff

gather
VERB
1 *Let's **gather** round the table.*
▷ assemble, congregate, convene
ANTONYM scatter
2 ***Gather** your belongings, please.*
▷ accumulate, collect, pick up
3 *I **gather** that you prefer to walk.*
▷ assume, conclude, hear, understand

gathering
NOUN
*There was a **gathering** of the school staff.*
▷ assembly, get-together, meeting

gaudy
ADJECTIVE
*The clown wore a **gaudy** costume.*
▷ flashy, garish, loud

gauge
VERB
*Try to **gauge** the number of beans in the jar.*
▷ estimate, guess, judge

gaze
VERB
*Fans like to **gaze** at celebrities.*
▷ gawk, stare

gear
NOUN
*We packed our **gear** and set out on the hike.*
▷ accessories, equipment, possessions

gem
NOUN
*My favourite **gem** is the ruby.*
▷ jewel, precious stone
See picture on next page.

general
ADJECTIVE
*The new school logo received **general** approval.*
▷ across-the-board, broad, overall, widespread

generous
ADJECTIVE
1 *She has a **generous** nature.*
▷ charitable, giving, unselfish
ANTONYM selfish
2 *They picked a **generous** amount of apples.*
▷ abundant, ample, lavish, plentiful
ANTONYM meagre

genius

NOUN

He is a genius at word puzzles.

▷ whiz, wizard

gentle

ADJECTIVE

1 *The dog is gentle and likes children.*

▷ kindly, mild, placid

ANTONYM rough

2 *There was a gentle slope to the top.*

▷ gradual, moderate, slight

genuine

ADJECTIVE

1 *My wallet is genuine leather.*

▷ authentic, real

ANTONYM fake

2 *I could tell that his smile was genuine.*

▷ honest, sincere

ANTONYM false

gesture

NOUN

He made a small gesture to show me where he was sitting in the theatre.

▷ motion, sign, signal

get

VERB

1 *I will get our plane tickets for St. John's.*

▷ fetch, obtain, pick up, secure

2 *The weather will get warmer in May.*

▷ become, grow, turn

3 *It took me a while to get the joke.*

▷ catch on, comprehend, figure out, understand

MAKE IT MORE FORMAL

get across convey

get away escape

get (something) back recover (something)

get back at retaliate

get better recover

get even retaliate

get going start

get hold of contact; obtain

get in the way obstruct

get in touch with contact

get off your chest reveal

get on someone's nerves annoy someone

get out of avoid

get rid of dispose of

get through pass

get to reach

get together meet

get well recover

get your own back revenge yourself

G

gem

agate
amber
amethyst
aquamarine
bloodstone
carnelian
coral
diamond
emerald
garnet
jade
jasper
lapis lazuli
moonstone
onyx
opal
pearl
ruby
sapphire
sardonyx
topaz
tourmaline
turquoise
zircon

ghastly
ADJECTIVE
The explosion was a ghastly accident.
▷ appalling, awful, hideous, horrible, shocking, terrible

ghostly
ADJECTIVE
The trees looked ghostly through the fog.
▷ eerie, haunted, spooky, supernatural

giant
ADJECTIVE
Giant dinosaurs once roamed the earth.
▷ colossal, enormous, gigantic, immense
ANTONYM tiny

gibberish
NOUN
She was so tired that everything she said was gibberish.
▷ babble, drivel, garbage, nonsense

gift
NOUN
I would like to have her gift for singing.
▷ ability, aptitude, flair, skill, talent

gigantic
ADJECTIVE
The hot-air balloon looked gigantic from below.
▷ colossal, enormous, immense, huge

giggle
VERB
The audience began to giggle.
▷ chuckle, laugh, snicker, titter

girl
NOUN
In the story, the girl is really a princess.
▷ female, maiden, miss

give
VERB
1 *Can you give a few dollars to the charity?*
▷ contribute, donate, present
ANTONYM take
2 *The bench will give if too many people sit on it.*
▷ buckle, cave in, collapse
3 *Which cow will give the most milk?*
▷ produce, provide, supply

MAKE IT MORE FORMAL
give a talk lecture
give back return
give in surrender
give off emit
give out emit; fail
give up quit; sacrifice
give way collapse

glad
ADJECTIVE
I'm glad that you're feeling better.
▷ delighted, happy, joyful, pleased
ANTONYM sad

glance
NOUN
We got a quick glance at the new timetable.
▷ glimpse, look, peek

glare
VERB
Why did he glare at us like that?
▷ frown, glower, scowl

glass
NOUN
Drink a glass of cold milk.
▷ cup, goblet, tumbler

gleam
VERB
The silver cup will gleam if you polish it.
▷ glimmer, shimmer, sparkle, twinkle

glee
NOUN
We greeted the team's victory with glee.
▷ delight, happiness, joy, pleasure, satisfaction

glide
VERB
We watched the owl glide over the trees.
▷ float, sail, skim, soar

glimmer
NOUN
1 *They saw a glimmer of light.*
▷ flash, flicker, shimmer
2 *The good news gave us a glimmer of hope.*
▷ hint, inkling, suggestion, trace

glimpse
NOUN
Did you get a glimpse at her through the window?
▷ glance, look, peek

glint
NOUN
They saw a glint of gold from the ring on his finger.
▷ flash, gleam, glimmer

glisten
VERB
Polish the shoes until they glisten.
▷ gleam, shine, sparkle

globe
NOUN
1 *The artist formed the clay into a globe.*
▷ ball, sphere
2 *We are studying the rivers of the globe.*
▷ earth, planet, world

gloomy
ADJECTIVE
1 *We were gloomy after our team lost.*
▷ cheerless, disheartened, down, glum
ANTONYM cheerful
2 *What a gloomy picture that is!*
▷ bleak, cheerless, dark, dismal, dreary, shadowy

glorious
ADJECTIVE
The campers watched the glorious sunset.
▷ brilliant, magnificent, splendid, wonderful

glory
NOUN
1 *He had the glory of being in first place.*
▷ distinction, honour, prestige
2 *The sun rose in all its glory.*
▷ grandeur, magnificence, majesty, splendour
VERB
You can glory in a job well done.
▷ delight, relish, revel, triumph

gloss
NOUN
I like the gloss on silver jewellery.
▷ sheen, shimmer, shine

glossy
ADJECTIVE
Sunlight shone on her glossy hair.
▷ lustrous, shiny, sleek

glow
NOUN
The room looked cozy in the soft glow of the lantern.
▷ gleam, glimmer
VERB
The fireflies began to glow in the darkness.
▷ gleam, glimmer, radiate, shine

glue
NOUN
Be sure to get the correct type of glue.
▷ adhesive, epoxy, paste
VERB
Glue the pieces together.
▷ fasten, paste, stick

glum
ADJECTIVE
The losing team was glum after the game.
▷ down, miserable, sad

glut
NOUN
The hot weather produced a glut of tomatoes.
▷ abundance, excess, surplus

gnaw
VERB
Try not to gnaw your fingernails.
▷ bite, chew, nibble

go
VERB
1 *I will go at eight o'clock in the morning.*
▷ depart, leave, proceed, set off
2 *The machine will go if you restart it.*
▷ function, operate, work

MAKE IT MORE FORMAL
go against clash with
go as far as reach
go away disappear
go back return
go beyond pass
go down decline; descend
go for like
go for it make a serious attempt
go into discuss
go off explode
go on continue
go on at hassle
go over examine
go through experience
go together with accompany
go up rise
go with accompany; suit
go wrong err

goad
VERB
We can often goad him into joining us for a walk.
▷ prod, provoke, urge

goal
NOUN
Her goal is to become a better reader.
▷ aim, intention, objective, purpose

gobble
VERB
Did you gobble the whole lot?
▷ devour, swallow, wolf down

good
ADJECTIVE
See box on next page.

goodness
NOUN
Her goodness was appreciated by everyone.
▷ generosity, integrity, kindness, virtue
ANTONYM wickedness

goods
NOUN
The goods on sale were piled on a table.
▷ merchandise, products, stock, wares

G

REPLACE AN OVERUSED WORD: GOOD

Like the word **bad**, the word **good** is used in so many ways to describe so many things that it has lost a great deal of its strength. Try using one of these adjectives instead.

- **good quality**

  The food in Montréal was **excellent**.

  Our team played a **first-class** game.

  This is a **great** story, full of interesting people.

  All the actors in the school play were **superb**.

- **a good experience**

  We spent an **agreeable** afternoon sightseeing.

  My friend and I had a **delightful** time at the party.

  The weather was fine, and that made our camping trip very **enjoyable**.

  Have a **pleasant** day!

- **having a good effect**

  Eating a balanced diet is **advantageous** for your health.

  What are the **beneficial** effects of exercise?

  The wind conditions were not **favourable** for sailing.

  A **positive** attitude helps when things go wrong.

- **good in a moral way**

  Telling lies is not a **decent** thing to do.

  He's an **honest** person and wouldn't cheat.

  What is the **honourable** thing to do?

  People will help if the cause is a **worthy** one.

- **good in a kind way**

  Giving money to a charity is a **benevolent** action.

  Please be **considerate** to the other passengers.

  She was **generous** enough to admit I was the better dancer.

  It was very **thoughtful** of her to visit me when I was ill.

- **good at some skill**

  It takes years of practice to become an **accomplished** pianist.

  Even **expert** skiers fall sometimes.

  My uncle is a **skilled** carpenter.

  She was introduced as one of Canada's most **talented** writers.

- **good behaviour**

  I like dogs that are **obedient**.

  During a fire drill, **orderly** behaviour is most important.

  Please be **polite** at all times.

  The child was **well-behaved** throughout the whole performance.

- **good advice**

  He read my essay, then made some **constructive** suggestions.

  Don't you have any **helpful** suggestions?

  We need some **practical** ideas for our class project.

  You will find some **useful** information on our website.

- **a good idea**

  She thought up a **brilliant** way to solve the problem.

  Wouldn't it be **prudent** to save some money for your trip?

  I can't think of a **sensible** plan.

  You have made a **wise** decision.

- **a good quantity**

  You have had **ample** time to finish your work.

  Rock stars make a **considerable** income.

  The settlers looked for a place with a **plentiful** supply of water.

  She has saved a **substantial** amount of money.

- **a good mood**

  She does not have a **cheerful** nature.

  The travellers had eaten well, and were all in a **happy** mood.

  I feel **optimistic** about my grades this year.

  The child was in an extremely **sunny** mood.

gorge

NOUN

We followed the path down into the **gorge**.

▷ canyon, gulch, gully, ravine

gorgeous

ADJECTIVE

Which of these **gorgeous** outfits do you like best?

▷ beautiful, magnificent, stunning

gossip

NOUN

My sister says she never listens to **gossip**.

▷ hearsay, rumour

govern

VERB

It is not easy to **govern** a country.

▷ command, lead, manage, rule, reign

government
NOUN
The government will pass the law next Monday.
▷ administration, legislature

grab
VERB
He had to grab the railing to keep from falling.
▷ clutch, grasp, seize

grace
NOUN
We admired the grace of the figure skater.
▷ elegance, poise
ANTONYM clumsiness

grade
VERB
Grade the items according to size.
▷ classify, group, rank, sort

gradual
ADJECTIVE
There was a gradual increase in the price.
▷ continuous, gentle, steady
ANTONYM sudden

grain
NOUN
There was not a grain of dust on the furniture.
▷ bit, drop, particle, speck

grand
ADJECTIVE
The grand house on the corner was built 100 years ago.
▷ imposing, impressive, magnificent, majestic

grant
NOUN
He received a grant to go to college.
▷ award, bursary, scholarship
VERB
Would you please grant us more time?
▷ allow, award, bestow, give, permit
ANTONYM deny

grasp
VERB
1 *Grasp the side of the boat.*
▷ clutch, grab, grip, hold, seize
2 *I did not grasp her meaning.*
▷ comprehend, realize, understand
3 *She reached down to grasp the child's hand.*
▷ clasp, grip, hold

grateful
ADJECTIVE
We were grateful for the advice.
▷ appreciative, indebted, thankful

grate on
VERB
His jokes can grate on me at times.
▷ annoy, bother, irritate

gratify
VERB
Nothing will gratify you when you are in a bad mood.
▷ content, delight, please, satisfy

gratitude
NOUN
She sent flowers in gratitude for our help.
▷ appreciation, recognition, thanks
ANTONYM ingratitude

grave
NOUN
The author's grave is in the town cemetery.
▷ crypt, mausoleum, tomb, vault
ADJECTIVE
1 *The climbers are in a grave situation.*
▷ critical, dangerous, perilous, serious, severe
2 *His face is grave, but he has a twinkle in his eye.*
▷ dignified, sober, solemn, sombre

graze
VERB
1 *I saw the child fall and graze her knee.*
▷ scrape, scratch, skin
2 *The sheep graze in the park and keep the grass short.*
▷ browse, feed, nibble
NOUN
Dad put a bandage on the graze on my elbow.
▷ abrasion, scrape, scratch

great
ADJECTIVE
See box on next page.

greedy
ADJECTIVE
A person can be greedy in many ways.
▷ materialistic, piggish, selfish
ANTONYM unselfish

green
ADJECTIVE
Hand me the can of green paint.
▷ avocado, chartreuse, emerald, jade, khaki, lime, olive, pea green, pistachio, sage, sea green, turquoise

greet
VERB
The teacher asked me to greet our visitor.
▷ receive, welcome

grey
ADJECTIVE
I have to wear grey pants.
▷ charcoal, slate, taupe

grief
NOUN
We were overcome with grief.
▷ heartache, sadness, sorrow, unhappiness
ANTONYM happiness

G

REPLACE AN OVERUSED WORD: GREAT

There are a number of ways in which the adjective **great** can be used. But why not make your language more interesting and use one of the following instead?

- **great in size**

  The new museum is a *colossal* building.

  It must have taken years to complete this *enormous* theme park.

  The largest animal that ever lived is the *gigantic* blue whale.

  Much of northern Africa is covered by a *vast* desert.

- **great in degree**

  The movie features *extreme* violence.

  He ate a *fantastic* number of hot dogs.

  He takes *immense* pride in his work.

  It is difficult to believe the *tremendous* power of an earthquake.

- **great in fame**

  She is a *celebrated* author.

  The research was carried out by an *eminent* scientist.

  The ballet will be performed by two of the world's most *illustrious* dancers.

  This bridge was designed by a *renowned* team of engineers.

- **great in importance**

  Hockey is the *main* interest in my life.

  Protecting the environment is a *major* issue.

  Coming to live in Canada was a *momentous* event for my family.

  There is a *significant* improvement in your work.

- **great in skill**

  He's an *excellent* pitcher.

  This trick can only be done by an *expert* skateboarder.

  The special-effects team did some *outstanding* work in this film.

  The drummer is a *talented* musician.

- **great in quality**

  All of the groups gave *excellent* presentations.

  The cleanup crew did a *first-rate* job.

  We have eaten many *superb* meals at my grandmother's house.

  Thank you for a *wonderful* party.

grieve
VERB
1 *Our friends still grieve for their lost cat.*
▷ lament, mourn
ANTONYM rejoice
2 *It will grieve the child to leave her favourite toy at home.*
▷ distress, pain, sadden, upset
ANTONYM cheer

grill
VERB
1 *Grill the fish and serve it hot.*
▷ barbecue, broil, fry
2 *My friends will grill me to find out what happened.*
▷ interrogate, question, quiz

grim
ADJECTIVE
1 *His grim look worried us.*
▷ dour, forbidding, grave, serious, solemn, stern
2 *The grim news upset everyone.*
▷ awful, dreadful, horrid, terrible

grime
NOUN
Clean the grime off your boots.
▷ dirt, dust, filth, soil, soot

grin
NOUN
Take that grin off your face!
▷ smile, smirk
VERB
She had to grin, although the joke wasn't very funny.
▷ beam, smile

grip
NOUN
1 *The football player lost his grip on the ball.*
▷ grasp, hold
2 *The captain lost his grip over the team.*
▷ control, influence, power
VERB
Do not grip your pen so tightly.
▷ clutch, grasp, hold

groan
VERB
They always groan when they are asked to help.
▷ complain, gripe, grumble, moan, protest

gross
ADJECTIVE
Some of the ads in that magazine are gross.
▷ crude, disgusting, repulsive

ground
NOUN
The ground in the yard is very hard.
▷ dirt, earth, land, soil

MAKE IT MORE FORMAL

break new ground do something original
get off the ground make a successful start
lose ground give up what has been gained
run something into the ground mismanage
   something so that it fails
stand your ground refuse to give in

grounds
NOUN
1 *The students planted a garden on school grounds.*
▷ land, premises, property
2 *What grounds do you have to accuse her of theft?*
▷ basis, cause, reason

group
NOUN
The group goes swimming most summer weekends.
▷ bunch, crowd, gang, pack
VERB
Group the vegetables by colour.
▷ arrange, classify, organize, sort

grow
VERB
1 *The number of Canada geese continues to grow.*
▷ expand, increase, multiply, rise
ANTONYM shrink
2 *Which herbs will grow indoors?*
▷ flourish, flower, mature, thrive

grow up
VERB
Our bones get stronger as we grow up.
▷ age, develop, mature

growth
NOUN
The growth of the city threatens farmland.
▷ development, expansion, increase, spread

grubby
ADJECTIVE
Your grubby clothes need to be washed.
▷ dirty, filthy, messy
ANTONYM clean

gruesome
ADJECTIVE
The car accident was a gruesome sight.
▷ ghastly, grisly, horrible, shocking

gruff
ADJECTIVE
1 *Her sore throat made her voice gruff.*
▷ croaky, hoarse, husky
2 *We expected a gruff response from him.*
▷ abrupt, bad-tempered, curt, rude

grumble
VERB
Please do not grumble so much.
▷ complain, gripe, groan, moan, protest, whine
NOUN
What is your grumble about this time?
▷ complaint, objection, protest

grumpy
ADJECTIVE
I get grumpy if I haven't had enough sleep.
▷ crabby, irritable, surly

grunt
NOUN
Was that grunt meant to be an answer?
▷ growl, mutter, snort

guarantee
NOUN
Give me your guarantee that you will be there.
▷ assurance, pledge, promise, word
VERB
We guarantee that you will like this book.
▷ promise, swear

guard
VERB
1 *The dog is there to guard the building.*
▷ patrol, protect, safeguard
2 *Two police officers were there to guard the entrance.*
▷ patrol, police, supervise
NOUN
There is a guard at every entrance.
▷ sentry, warden

guess
VERB
I guess I am going to be late.
▷ imagine, reckon, suppose, suspect, think
NOUN
My answer is just a guess.
▷ assumption, feeling, speculation

guide
VERB
1 *Guide me to where you found the money.*
▷ direct, lead, steer
2 *Her parents are trying to guide her.*
▷ counsel, govern, influence

guilty
ADJECTIVE
I felt guilty for telling such a lie.
▷ ashamed, regretful, remorseful, repentant

G

gulf

NOUN

1 *We can watch whales as they swim across the **gulf**.*
▷ basin, bay, inlet
2 *The earthquake created a deep **gulf** in the ground.*
▷ abyss, chasm, opening

gullible

ADJECTIVE

*Try not to be so **gullible**.*
▷ naive, trusting
ANTONYM suspicious

gully

NOUN

*We used to find frogs in that **gully**.*
▷ channel, ditch, trench

gush

VERB

*Did a lot of oil **gush** from the pipe?*
▷ flow, pour, spurt, stream, rush

gust

NOUN

*The sudden **gust** blew the box along the street.*
▷ blast, flurry, squall, wind

gutter

NOUN

*A **gutter** was built to take the water away.*
▷ channel, ditch, drain, groove, trough

G

H h

habit
NOUN
*Make it a **habit** to have a good breakfast.*
▷ custom, practice, routine, tradition

habitat
NOUN
*Our class is studying the **habitat** of black bears.*
▷ environment, home, territory

hail
VERB
*They began to **hail** us from across the street.*
▷ call, signal

hair
NOUN
*Her curly **hair** hung to her waist.*
▷ locks, mane, tresses

hall
NOUN
*Everyone gathered in the **hall**.*
▷ entrance, foyer, lobby, vestibule

hallucination
NOUN
*He thought he was having a **hallucination**.*
▷ delusion, dream, illusion, mirage, vision

halt
VERB
*They had to **halt** construction due to rain.*
▷ cease, check, curb, end, stop, terminate
ANTONYM start

hammer
VERB
***Hammer** the nail into the wood.*
▷ bang, beat, hit, pound

hamper
VERB
*The overturned truck will **hamper** traffic for hours.*
▷ hinder, impede, obstruct, restrict

hand
NOUN
*The farmer needed one more **hand** at harvest time.*
▷ employee, labourer, worker

MAKE IT MORE FORMAL
hand down bequeath
hand in submit
hand out distribute

handicap
NOUN
*Dull hockey skates are a **handicap** in a game.*
▷ disadvantage, drawback, hindrance, obstacle

handle
VERB
1 ***Handle** the fabric with care.*
▷ feel, finger, hold, touch
2 *She will **handle** the project herself.*
▷ conduct, manage, supervise

handsome
ADJECTIVE
1 *I don't think he's **handsome**.*
▷ attractive, good-looking
ANTONYM ugly
2 *They get a **handsome** sum of money for shovelling the snow.*
▷ ample, considerable, generous, lavish, plentiful, sizable
ANTONYM small

handy
ADJECTIVE
*We keep the broom **handy** in the kitchen.*
▷ close, convenient, nearby

hang
VERB
1 *Do not let the towel **hang** out the window.*
▷ dangle, droop, sag
2 ***Hang** the picture on that wall.*
▷ attach, fasten, fix, suspend

MAKE IT MORE FORMAL
get the hang of learn how to do
hang around loiter
hang back be unwilling to go forward
hang in (there) be persistent
hang out spend time with someone or in some place
hang together be consistent
hang up end a phone conversation
hang your head be ashamed

happen
VERB
*What can **happen** in such a short time?*
▷ occur, result, take place

happiness
NOUN
***Happiness** showed on his face.*
▷ contentment, delight, ecstasy, elation, joy, satisfaction
ANTONYM sadness

happy
ADJECTIVE
See box on next page.

H

H

REPLACE AN OVERUSED WORD: HAPPY

Happy is an overused adjective. You can vary your language by choosing one of the words shown below.

- **in a happy mood**

  *We will feel more **cheerful** when the weather improves.*

  *It's good to see your **cheery** face.*

  *If someone tries to tease me, I just respond with a **merry** laugh.*

  *Everyone in that family has a **sunny** nature.*

- **feeling happy about something**

  *Mom was **delighted** with the flowers I gave her.*

  *The player who scored the last goal had the most **ecstatic** grin on her face.*

  *He stayed **elated** for days after making the swim team.*

  *I am **overjoyed** to see you.*

- **causing happiness**

  *He said he'd spent an **agreeable** evening chatting with some friends.*

  *Let me tell you about the **blissful** dream I had.*

  *Birthday parties are supposed to be **joyful** events.*

  *Does soaking in a hot bath give you a **pleasurable** feeling?*

- **happy to do something**

  *I don't want to play—I'm **content** to watch the game.*

  *He seemed **glad** that I called.*

  *She said she'd be **pleased** to show us her work.*

  *I'd be **willing** to go with you.*

harass
VERB
She loves to harass her older brother.
▷ annoy, bother, hassle, pester

hard
ADJECTIVE
1 *We need a hard surface for cutting the material.*
▷ firm, rigid, solid, stiff, tough
ANTONYM soft
2 *He did 30 minutes hard exercise every day.*
▷ exhausting, strenuous, tough
ANTONYM easy
3 *This math problem is hard.*
▷ baffling, complicated, difficult, puzzling
ANTONYM simple

hardly
ADVERB
We hardly had time to eat lunch today.
▷ barely, just, scarcely

hardship
NOUN
The pioneers' lives were full of hardship.
▷ difficulty, misfortune, suffering, trouble, want

hardy
ADJECTIVE
The hardy campers ignored the bad weather.
▷ robust, strong, sturdy, tough

harm
VERB
She is gentle, and would not harm anyone.
▷ abuse, hurt, ill-treat

harmful
ADJECTIVE
The termite is a harmful insect.
▷ damaging, destructive, detrimental
ANTONYM harmless

harmless
ADJECTIVE
This harmless chemical will not pollute the water.
▷ nontoxic, safe
ANTONYM harmful

harmony
NOUN
There was harmony among the team members.
▷ accord, agreement, unity
ANTONYM discord

harsh
ADJECTIVE
Saskatchewan has harsh winters.
▷ cruel, hard, ruthless, severe
ANTONYM mild

harvest
VERB
Harvest herbs in the early morning.
▷ gather, pick, reap

hassle
NOUN
Carrying the bike up the stairs was a hassle.
▷ bother, effort, inconvenience, trouble
VERB
Do not hassle the referee.
▷ bother, harass, nag, pester

haste
NOUN
In my haste, I forgot my lunch.
▷ hurry, rush, swiftness

hasty
ADJECTIVE
He made a hasty exit from the room.
▷ abrupt, fast, hurried, rapid, swift, sudden

hate
VERB
I hate people who tell lies.
▷ abhor, despise, detest, loathe
ANTONYM love

hateful
ADJECTIVE
That was a hateful thing to do!
▷ despicable, horrible, loathsome, obnoxious, offensive

haughty
ADJECTIVE
I get tired of her haughty behaviour.
▷ arrogant, conceited, proud, snobbish
ANTONYM humble

haul
VERB
Please haul the bags of leaves to the curb.
▷ drag, draw, pull, tug

have
VERB
1 *I would like to have a bicycle.*
▷ keep, own, possess
2 *Will he have any pain after the operation?*
▷ experience, feel, sustain, undergo

MAKE IT MORE FORMAL
have fun play
have it in for have a grudge against
have it out argue until a dispute is settled
have on wear

haven
NOUN
The cat's haven was an old blanket.
▷ refuge, retreat, shelter

hazy
ADJECTIVE
The day was hazy, with no wind.
▷ foggy, misty, smoggy
ANTONYM clear

head
NOUN
His mother is the head of the company.
▷ boss, chief, director, leader, manager, president

VERB
He will head the project.
▷ be in charge of, control, direct, lead, manage

MAKE IT MORE FORMAL
come to a head reach a climax
head off turn something back or aside
keep your head remain calm
lose your head lose control of yourself
put our heads together discuss among ourselves

heal
VERB
Lots of rest will help to heal the injury.
▷ cure, mend, treat

healthy
ADJECTIVE
1 *My whole family is very healthy.*
▷ active, fit, robust, strong, well
ANTONYM ill
2 *Here is a list of healthy foods.*
▷ beneficial, nourishing, nutritious, wholesome
ANTONYM unwholesome

heap
NOUN
She dumped a heap of pennies on the table.
▷ mass, mound, pile, stack

hear
VERB
1 *I could not hear what they were whispering about.*
▷ catch, overhear
2 *How did you hear about the accident?*
▷ find out, learn

heartless
ADJECTIVE
That was a heartless thing to say!
▷ callous, cruel, merciless

heat
NOUN
1 *This heat makes me feel good.*
▷ temperature, warmth
ANTONYM cold
2 *We were upset by the heat of the discussion.*
▷ excitement, intensity, passion, vehemence

heave
VERB
Heave the anchor overboard.
▷ cast, fling, hurl, throw, toss

heavy
ADJECTIVE
We pushed the heavy box along the corridor.
▷ bulky, hefty, massive
ANTONYM light

H

hectic

ADJECTIVE

*Our **hectic** schedule left us with no spare time.*

▷ busy, excited, frantic, frenzied

ANTONYM leisurely

help

VERB

*If we **help** each other, the job will get done quickly.*

▷ aid, assist, support

helpful

ADJECTIVE

1 *Our **helpful** neighbour looked after the dog.*

▷ co-operative, kind, supportive

2 *The thesaurus was **helpful** when I wrote my essay.*

▷ advantageous, beneficial, useful

helpless

ADJECTIVE

*The bear defended her **helpless** cub.*

▷ dependent, powerless, vulnerable, weak

ANTONYM powerful

herb

NOUN

See picture below.

heroic

ADJECTIVE

*The firefighter's **heroic** and unselfish action saved the child.*

▷ bold, brave, fearless

ANTONYM cowardly

H

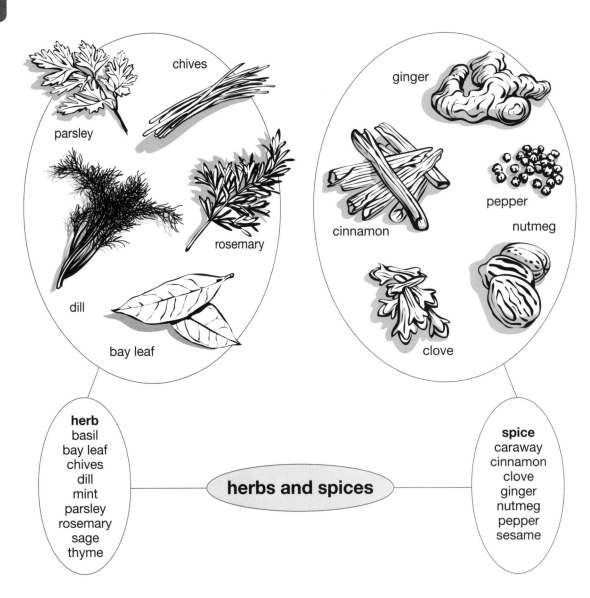

herb
basil
bay leaf
chives
dill
mint
parsley
rosemary
sage
thyme

herbs and spices

spice
caraway
cinnamon
clove
ginger
nutmeg
pepper
sesame

chives

parsley

rosemary

dill

bay leaf

ginger

cinnamon

pepper

nutmeg

clove

hesitate

VERB

*Do not **hesitate** to help someone in trouble.*

▷ be reluctant, delay

hidden

ADJECTIVE

*The bank uses **hidden** cameras.*

▷ concealed, covered, invisible, unseen

ANTONYM visible

high

ADJECTIVE

See box at foot of this page.

hijack

VERB

*The thieves tried to **hijack** a car.*

▷ seize, snatch, steal

hilarious

ADJECTIVE

*The movie was **hilarious**.*

▷ amusing, funny, hysterical, sidesplitting

hill

NOUN

*Which **hill** will we explore first?*

▷ butte, dune, foothill, knoll, moraine, mound

hinder

VERB

*Her injury will **hinder** her return to the team.*

▷ delay, frustrate, hamper, impede

ANTONYM help

hindrance

NOUN

*The snowstorm was a **hindrance** in getting to school.*

▷ barrier, obstacle

H

REPLACE AN OVERUSED WORD: HIGH

The adjective **high** has a number of meanings. Depending on what you are describing, you have a whole range of substitutes that can give your writing some added expressiveness.

- **a high object**

  ***Lofty** skyscrapers block out the sunshine.*

  *The **soaring** Confederation Bridge connects Prince Edward Island and New Brunswick.*

  *In the rainforest, **tall** trees form a canopy.*

  *The valley lies between two **towering** mountain ranges.*

- **a high amount or degree**

  *The score was tied, keeping the fans in a state of **acute** anxiety.*

  *A broken ankle produces an **extreme** level of pain.*

  *Her latest movie is stirring up a **great** amount of interest.*

  *The country is suffering from a **severe** shortage of water.*

- **a high cost or price**

  *The princess always wore **costly** jewellery.*

  *The price of admission is too **dear** for me.*

  *Dad is upset at the **expensive** charges for repairing his car.*

  *Why was there such a **steep** increase in the price?*

- **a high wind**

  *The leaves were blown in all directions by **blustery** winds.*

  ***Squally** gusts forced the cancellation of the sailboat race.*

  *A **strong** breeze blew from the west.*

  *The **violent** gale toppled many trees in this area.*

- **high in importance**

  *The **chief** reason for her success is hard work.*

  *He has an **influential** position on the Student Council.*

  *Many of the world's **leading** scientists will be at the conference.*

  *The magazine article gave short biographies of five **prominent** Canadians.*

- **a high voice or sound**

  *He let out a **high-pitched** yell to warn us that the bus was in sight.*

  *The train gave a **piercing** whistle as it approached the tunnel.*

  *The silence was broken by the **shrill** cry of a seagull.*

  *My sister has an attractive **soprano** voice.*

- **high spirits**

  *She woke up in a **buoyant** mood.*

  *He was grinning, obviously **elated** at the success of his presentation.*

  *The whole team felt **exhilarated** by the win.*

  *The dogs, in **exuberant** spirits, raced around the yard.*

---

hint

NOUN

1 *Her hint helped us to find the answer.*
▷ clue, indication, sign

2 *His cooking hint was helpful.*
▷ advice, pointer, suggestion, tip

VERB

Did you hint to her that you might visit?
▷ imply, indicate, insinuate, suggest

hire

VERB

The city plans to hire more bus drivers later in the year.
▷ appoint, employ, engage

ANTONYM fire

hit

VERB

See box at foot of this page.

hitch

NOUN

There is one hitch in the plan.
▷ drawback, problem, snag

hoard

VERB

A miser likes to hoard money.
▷ accumulate, save, stockpile, store

hoarse

ADJECTIVE

A sore throat made her voice hoarse.
▷ croaky, harsh, husky, rasping

REPLACE AN OVERUSED WORD: HIT

The verb **hit** is often overused. There are a number of more descriptive words that you can use to give additional information about the way in which something is hit, or how hard it is hit.

- If you **bang** on something, you hit it hard, making a loud noise.
  You will have to bang on the door till someone answers.

- If you **bang** a part of your body, you accidentally knock it against something and hurt it.
  If you bang your elbow, just bang the other one and neither elbow will hurt.

- If you **batter** something, you hit it hard, usually with your fists or a heavy object.
  If we can't open the door we'll have to batter it down.

- If you **beat** something, you hit it hard, usually several times or for a period of time.
  He offered to beat the drum as we marched.

- If you **hammer** on something, you hit it hard several times to make a noise.
  Some of the class applauded, and some began to hammer on the desks.

- If you **knock** something, you hit it roughly, especially so that it falls or moves.
  Be careful or you will knock the whole lot over.

- If you **knock** on something such as a door or window, you hit it several times, to attract someone's attention.
  Please knock on the back door, and I will let you in.

- If you **pat** something, you tap it lightly, usually with your hand held flat.
  The woman began to pat the baby's back.

- If you **pound** something, you hit it with great force, usually loudly and repeatedly.
  If you're going to pound all those nails in, I'm leaving.

- If you **punch** something, you hit it hard with your fist.
  Did you see him punch that hole in the wall?

- If you **rap** something, or rap on it, you hit it with a series of quick blows.
  I don't want to rap too hard on the window—it might break.

- If you **slap** something, you hit it with the palm of your hand.
  People crowded round to cheer the winner and slap him on the back.

- If you **swat** something such as an insect, you hit it with a quick, swinging movement using your hand or a flat object.
  Please get a newspaper to swat that fly.

- If you **tap** something, you hit it with a quick light blow or series of blows.
  Do not tap on the glass, because it frightens the goldfish.

- If you **thump** something, you hit it hard, usually with your fist.
  The gorilla began to thump its chest.

- If you **whack** something, you hit it hard.
  I want you to swing the bat and whack the ball as hard as you can.

hobby
NOUN
Do you have an unusual hobby?
▷ diversion, interest, pastime, recreation

hoist
VERB
We hoist the flag every morning.
▷ elevate, lift, raise

hold
VERB
1 *Hold one end of the box, please.*
▷ carry, clasp, clutch, grasp, grip
2 *I am not sure the jar will hold all the sauce.*
▷ contain, store

MAKE IT MORE FORMAL
get hold of contact
hold against resent
hold back restrain
on hold inactive

hole
NOUN
There is a hole in the wall, and the snow is blowing in from outside.
▷ cavity, gap, hollow, opening

MAKE IT MORE FORMAL
burn a hole in your pocket be easily spent
hole in the wall a small and unimportant place
hole up go into hiding
in the hole in debt
make a hole in use up a large amount of
pick holes in find fault with

holiday
NOUN
Is next Monday a holiday?
▷ celebration, festival

H

OFFICIAL HOLIDAYS IN CANADA
January 1: New Year's Day
March/April: Good Friday
March/April: Easter Sunday
March/April: Easter Monday
May: Victoria Day
July 1: Canada Day

September: Labour Day
October: Thanksgiving
November 11: Remembrance Day
December 25: Christmas Day
December 26: Boxing Day

HOLIDAYS IN PROVINCES AND TERRITORIES

Alberta
February: Family Day
August: Heritage Day

British Columbia
August: B.C. Day

Manitoba
August: Civic Holiday

New Brunswick
August: New Brunswick Day

Newfoundland & Labrador
March: St. Patrick's Day
April: St. George's Day
June 24: Discovery Day
July 1: Memorial Day
July 12: Orangemen's Day

Nova Scotia
August: Natal Day

Northwest Territories
August: Civic Holiday

Nunavut
July 9: Nunavut Day
August: Civic Holiday

Ontario
August: Civic Holiday

Prince Edward Island
August: Civic Holiday

Québec
June 24: Fête nationale

Saskatchewan
February: Family Day
August: Saskatchewan Day

Yukon
August: Discovery Day

home

NOUN
Their home is made of wooden logs.
▷ abode, dwelling, residence
See picture below.

> ### MAKE IT MORE FORMAL
>
> **a home away from home** a place where you feel at home
> **at home** relaxed, as if in your own home
> **bring** (*or* **drive**) **home** make clear
> **hit home** make an impression
> **home free** sure of success
> **home in on** narrow the attention to

honest

ADJECTIVE
She is honest and obeys the rules.
▷ law-abiding, reputable, trustworthy, truthful, virtuous
ANTONYM dishonest

honour

NOUN
1 *We expect honour from our elected officials.*
▷ decency, goodness, honesty, integrity
2 *Why did he receive that honour?*
▷ commendation, recognition, tribute

honourable

ADJECTIVE
We were honourable and returned the money.
▷ noble, respectable, virtuous

hoop

NOUN
The chain was attached to a metal hoop.
▷ circle, loop, ring

hope

VERB
I hope to hear from you soon.
▷ desire, wish
NOUN
The team has no hope of winning.
▷ chance, expectation, possibility, prospect

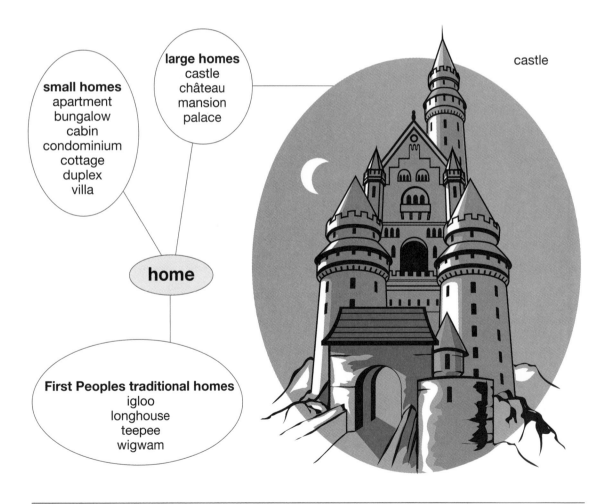

small homes
apartment
bungalow
cabin
condominium
cottage
duplex
villa

large homes
castle
château
mansion
palace

home

First Peoples traditional homes
igloo
longhouse
teepee
wigwam

castle

hopeful
ADJECTIVE
They are hopeful that they will win.
▷ confident, optimistic
ANTONYM pessimistic

hopeless
ADJECTIVE
This discussion is hopeless!
▷ futile, impossible, pointless, useless, vain

horde
NOUN
A horde of people got on the bus.
▷ crowd, throng

horrible
ADJECTIVE
1 *My sister was in a horrible mood this morning.*
▷ disagreeable, horrid, mean, nasty, unpleasant
2 *There was a horrible accident on the highway.*
▷ dreadful, grim, gruesome, terrible

horrid
ADJECTIVE
The medicine had a horrid taste.
▷ disagreeable, nasty, unpleasant
ANTONYM pleasant

horror
NOUN
They gazed in horror at the burning house.
▷ dread, fear, fright, panic, terror

horse
NOUN
The black horse is magnificent.
▷ mount, steed

hospitable
ADJECTIVE
The people we stayed with in Yukon Territory were very hospitable.
▷ sociable, welcoming
ANTONYM hostile

host
NOUN
A host of fans, screaming for autographs, rushed at the musicians.
▷ crowd, horde

hostile
ADJECTIVE
The other team had a hostile attitude.
▷ antagonistic, belligerent, malevolent, unfriendly
ANTONYM friendly

hot
ADJECTIVE
1 *The apple cider was hot.*
▷ boiling, fiery, heated, scalding, scorching
ANTONYM cold

2 *I like my chili hot!*
▷ peppery, spicy
ANTONYM bland

MAKE IT MORE FORMAL
hot and bothered angry and upset
hot under the collar angry
in hot water in trouble

house
NOUN
The house has three storeys.
▷ abode, building, dwelling, home, residence

MAKE IT MORE FORMAL
like a house on fire very well
on the house free

hover
VERB
The butterfly seemed to hover in the air.
▷ float, hang

howl
VERB
The baby began to howl.
▷ bawl, cry, scream, wail

hub
NOUN
The community centre is the hub of our town.
▷ centre, focus, heart

huff
NOUN
She left the room in a huff.
▷ mood, temper, snit

hug
VERB
I like to hug my puppy.
▷ clasp, cuddle, embrace

huge
ADJECTIVE
There are huge trees in the rainforest.
▷ colossal, enormous, giant, immense, massive
ANTONYM tiny

humane
ADJECTIVE
Our city provides for the homeless in a humane way.
▷ benevolent, caring, charitable, compassionate, kind, merciful, thoughtful

humble
ADJECTIVE
The popular actor found it hard to be humble.
▷ meek, modest, unassuming
ANTONYM haughty

H

H

humdrum

ADJECTIVE

I thought the story was humdrum.

▷ boring, dreary, dull, monotonous

ANTONYM exciting

humid

ADJECTIVE

Humid weather makes people uncomfortable.

▷ damp, clammy, moist, muggy, steamy, sticky

humiliate

VERB

Do not humiliate your sister like that.

▷ disgrace, embarrass, shame

humorous

ADJECTIVE

We laughed at the humorous cartoon.

▷ amusing, comical, funny, witty

humour

NOUN

1 *Did you find any humour in the story?*

▷ comedy, wit

2 *What kind of humour was she in?*

▷ mood, spirits, temper

hunch

NOUN

She had a hunch that the trip would be cancelled.

▷ feeling, guess, idea, impression, suspicion

hunger

NOUN

I have a hunger to sail on the ocean.

▷ appetite, craving, desire, longing

hungry

ADJECTIVE

He was hungry and ate everything on the plate.

▷ famished, ravenous

hunt

VERB

My dog likes to hunt rabbits.

▷ search for, seek, track

hurdle

NOUN

What was the most challenging hurdle to overcome?

▷ barrier, difficulty, obstacle

hurl

VERB

The children like to hurl stones into the lake.

▷ cast, fling, heave, pitch, throw, toss

hurry

VERB

1 *Hurry to the store before it closes.*

▷ dash, race, rush, speed

2 *The president of the Student Council tried to hurry the meeting.*

▷ accelerate, hasten, quicken

hurt

VERB

1 *Did the cat hurt the bird?*

▷ harm, injure, wound

2 *Gossip can hurt a lot of people.*

▷ distress, sadden, upset

hurtful

ADJECTIVE

A careless remark can be hurtful.

▷ cruel, distressing

husky

ADJECTIVE

1 *Her voice sounds husky.*

▷ gruff, harsh, hoarse

2 *Husky children are big for their age.*

▷ chunky, sturdy

hustle

VERB

You'll have to hustle to catch the bus.

▷ dash, rush, speed

hysterical

ADJECTIVE

1 *The children were hysterical at the disappearance of their dog.*

▷ frantic, frenzied, overwrought, raving

2 *She tells hysterical stories at parties.*

▷ comical, hilarious

I i

icy
ADJECTIVE
The icy wind made us shiver.
▷ cold, freezing, frigid, frosty

idea
NOUN
1 *Your idea is very creative.*
▷ plan, scheme, suggestion
2 *I have an idea that you are upset.*
▷ belief, notion, opinion, view
3 *We have no idea when he will arrive.*
▷ clue, guess, hint, inkling

> ### MAKE IT MORE FORMAL
> **don't get ideas** don't plan for things you shouldn't
> **have no idea** not know at all
> **The (very) idea!** That's outrageous!

ideal
NOUN
1 *Her main ideal is honesty.*
▷ principle, standard, value
2 *He is my ideal and I admire him very much.*
▷ epitome, model, paragon, standard
ADJECTIVE
Red is the ideal colour for you.
▷ best, model, perfect

identical
ADJECTIVE
They bought identical jackets.
▷ duplicate, matching, twin
ANTONYM different

identify
VERB
Can you identify this lost dog?
▷ name, recognize

idiotic
ADJECTIVE
The idiotic practical joke was not funny.
▷ foolish, senseless, stupid

idle
ADJECTIVE
He was too idle to complete any task.
▷ lazy, sluggish, slothful
ANTONYM industrious

idol
NOUN
The fans were excited to see their idol.
▷ celebrity, hero, star

ignorant
ADJECTIVE
He's not stupid, he's just ignorant.
▷ oblivious, unaware, uninformed

ignore
VERB
Our group did not ignore anyone's suggestions.
▷ discount, disregard, exclude, neglect, overlook, pass over

ill
ADJECTIVE
I became ill after I ate that hot dog.
▷ queasy, sick, unwell
ANTONYM well

> ### MAKE IT MORE FORMAL
> **ill at ease** uncomfortable
> **ill-tempered** irritable
> **ill-treat** abuse

illegal
ADJECTIVE
Smoking in public places is illegal.
▷ banned, illicit, outlawed, prohibited, unlawful
ANTONYM legal

illness
NOUN
The doctor identified the cause of my illness.
▷ ailment, disease, disorder, sickness

illusion
NOUN
1 *I think what you saw was an illusion.*
▷ apparition, dream, hallucination, mirage, vision
2 *The colour white gives the illusion of light.*
▷ appearance, effect, feeling, impression, sense

illustration
NOUN
1 *Please include an illustration with your story.*
▷ design, drawing, picture, sketch
2 *Our teacher gave an illustration of how magnets work.*
▷ demonstration, explanation, example

image
NOUN
She painted a realistic image of her father.
▷ likeness, portrait, representation

imagination
NOUN
Use your imagination to decorate the classroom.
▷ creativity, ingenuity, inventiveness

I

imagine

VERB

1 *Imagine what it would be like to be famous.*
▷ conceive, envisage, fantasize, picture, visualize
2 *Did you imagine that we would leave without you?*
▷ assume, believe, gather, guess, suppose, think

imitate

VERB

I can imitate my friend's way of speaking.
▷ ape, copy, impersonate, mimic

immaculate

ADJECTIVE

The white tablecloth was immaculate.
▷ clean, spotless, stainless
ANTONYM dirty

immature

ADJECTIVE

Their immature behaviour was unattractive.
▷ childish, juvenile
ANTONYM mature

immediately

ADVERB

She answered the phone immediately.
▷ at once, directly, instantly, promptly,
straightaway

immense

ADJECTIVE

During the storm, immense waves crashed onto the beach.
▷ colossal, enormous, gigantic, huge, massive
ANTONYM tiny

immerse

VERB

Immerse your wrists in cold water to cool yourself down.
▷ dip, dunk, plunge, submerge

imminent

ADJECTIVE

The clouds are getting dark, so the thunderstorm is imminent.
▷ approaching, coming, impending, looming

immune to

ADJECTIVE

Vaccination has made me immune to measles.
▷ protected from, resistant to, safe from,
unaffected by
ANTONYM vulnerable

impact

NOUN

We heard the impact from inside the house.
▷ blow, collision, crash, shock

impartial

ADJECTIVE

Her decision was impartial.
▷ fair, neutral, objective, unbiased
ANTONYM biased

impatient

ADJECTIVE

1 *Our teacher is never impatient.*
▷ brusque, curt, irritable
ANTONYM patient
2 *The children grew impatient while waiting for the movie to start.*
▷ anxious, eager, restless

impede

VERB

The snow will impede traffic.
▷ block, delay, disrupt, hamper, hinder, obstruct
ANTONYM aid

impending

ADJECTIVE

We must soon begin to study for the impending exam.
▷ approaching, coming, future, imminent,
looming

imperfect

ADJECTIVE

Imperfect jeans are sold for bargain prices.
▷ defective, faulty, flawed

impersonal

ADJECTIVE

He responded in an impersonal way.
▷ aloof, cold, detached, formal
ANTONYM warm

implement

NOUN

His workshop has an implement for every task.
▷ device, instrument, tool

implore

VERB

We implore you to tell us the news.
▷ beg, beseech, plead with, urge

imply

VERB

Did you just imply that I am lazy?
▷ hint, insinuate, suggest

impolite

ADJECTIVE

The employees in that store are never impolite.
▷ discourteous, ill-mannered, rude
ANTONYM polite

important

ADJECTIVE

1 *The premier will make an important announcement later today.*
▷ momentous, serious, significant, weighty
2 *She is an important member of the Cabinet.*
▷ eminent, influential, notable, powerful

impossible

ADJECTIVE

This plan seems impossible.
▷ hopeless, inconceivable, out of the question, unattainable
ANTONYM possible

impostor

NOUN

The impostor fooled all of us.
▷ fake, fraud, phony

impractical

ADJECTIVE

The idea was impractical.
▷ unrealistic, unworkable
ANTONYM practical

impress

VERB

Did the Canadian Rockies impress you too?
▷ affect, amaze, astound

impression

NOUN

1 *What impression did you have of the whole movie?*
▷ feeling, notion, sense, thoughts
2 *Her thumb left an impression in the soft clay.*
▷ dent, imprint, mark

improbable

ADJECTIVE

No one believed his improbable story.
▷ far-fetched, implausible, unbelievable, unlikely
ANTONYM probable

improper

ADJECTIVE

1 *They behaved in an improper way.*
▷ inappropriate, unsuitable, wrong
ANTONYM proper
2 *Her improper language upset everyone.*
▷ indecent, offensive, rude, shocking

improve

VERB

He wants to improve his woodworking skills.
▷ better, enhance, refine, sharpen

impulse

NOUN

I had a sudden impulse to look behind me.
▷ desire, inclination, urge, wish

impulsive

ADJECTIVE

My impulsive behaviour gets me into trouble.
▷ rash, reckless, spontaneous
ANTONYM cautious

MAKE IT MORE FORMAL

in fact really
in sight visible
in the end finally
in the long run finally

inaccessible

ADJECTIVE

The cabin is inaccessible in winter.
▷ unattainable, unreachable

inaccurate

ADJECTIVE

We received inaccurate information.
▷ false, imprecise, incorrect, wrong
ANTONYM correct

inadequate

ADJECTIVE

1 *Many countries have an inadequate supply of clean water.*
▷ insufficient, poor
ANTONYM plentiful
2 *He felt inadequate during the emergency.*
▷ incapable, incompetent, useless
ANTONYM competent

inane

ADJECTIVE

We are tired of listening to her inane stories.
▷ absurd, foolish, ridiculous, senseless, silly
ANTONYM sensible

inappropriate

ADJECTIVE

The writer has used inappropriate language.
▷ improper, unacceptable, unsuitable
ANTONYM acceptable

incentive

NOUN

What is your incentive to study?
▷ enticement, motivation, stimulus

incident

NOUN

I told my family about the amusing incident.
▷ episode, event, happening, occurrence

incite

VERB

The others tried to incite us to fight.
▷ encourage, provoke

I

incline

NOUN
The road had a very steep incline.
▷ grade, slant, slope

VERB
1 *The pile of books has started to incline.*
▷ lean, list, slant, slope, tilt
2 *Her ideas incline toward the creative.*
▷ lean, sway, tend

include

VERB
Your daily routine should include some exercise.
▷ contain, incorporate, involve
ANTONYM exclude

income

NOUN
I have no income.
▷ earnings, pay, salary, wages

incomparable

ADJECTIVE
Yukon Territory has incomparable natural beauty.
▷ unequalled, unparalleled, unrivalled

incompetent

ADJECTIVE
Incompetent drivers are a danger to us all.
▷ incapable, inept
ANTONYM expert

incomplete

ADJECTIVE
He gave an incomplete answer.
▷ insufficient, partial

inconceivable

ADJECTIVE
The number of stars in the universe is almost inconceivable.
▷ unbelievable, unimaginable, unthinkable

inconsiderate

ADJECTIVE
It was inconsiderate of you not to return my phone call.
▷ rude, selfish, thoughtless

inconvenience

NOUN
I lost my key, which was an inconvenience.
▷ bother, hassle, nuisance

inconvenient

ADJECTIVE
I find it inconvenient to jog in the morning.
▷ awkward, difficult, problematic, troublesome

incorrect

ADJECTIVE
There are incorrect quotes in this magazine article.
▷ false, inaccurate, untrue

increase

VERB
My mom wants to increase the size of the vegetable garden.
▷ enlarge, expand, extend
ANTONYM decrease

NOUN
Our town has had a huge increase in population.
▷ hike, rise, upsurge
ANTONYM decrease

incredible

ADJECTIVE
1 *We watched an incredible soccer game on TV.*
▷ amazing, astonishing, astounding, extraordinary, marvellous, sensational
2 *Those incredible results were faked.*
▷ absurd, far-fetched, improbable, unbelievable

incriminate

VERB
The thief did not incriminate anyone else.
▷ accuse, blame, implicate

indeed

ADVERB
Indeed I will go without you.
▷ actually, in reality, in truth, undeniably

indefinite

ADJECTIVE
The number of flights to be cancelled is indefinite.
▷ uncertain, unclear, undetermined

independent

ADJECTIVE
I like to be independent.
▷ self-reliant, self-sufficient

indication

NOUN
She gave no indication that she might change her mind.
▷ clue, hint, sign

indifference

NOUN
The indifference of the audience was upsetting to the cast of the play.
▷ apathy, disinterest
ANTONYM interest

indirect

ADJECTIVE
The creek takes an indirect route to the lake.
▷ meandering, roundabout, wandering

indispensable

ADJECTIVE
Smoke alarms are indispensable.
▷ essential, necessary, vital

individual

ADJECTIVE

1 *Divide the pie into individual portions.*
▷ separate, single

2 *She has an individual way of writing capital letters.*
▷ characteristic, distinctive, original, personal, unique

NOUN

Every individual is to be included in the census.
▷ human being, person

indulge

VERB

I like to indulge myself sometimes.
▷ gratify, pamper, spoil, treat

industrious

ADJECTIVE

Be industrious and the work will soon be done.
▷ busy, diligent, hard-working, tireless

ANTONYM lazy

inefficient

ADJECTIVE

The inefficient assistant gave us the wrong forms.
▷ disorganized, incompetent, unproductive

inevitable

ADJECTIVE

Is the result inevitable?
▷ certain, sure, unavoidable

inexpensive

ADJECTIVE

Choose an inexpensive watch for the child.
▷ cheap, low-priced

infallible

ADJECTIVE

Nobody is infallible.
▷ faultless, perfect

infant

NOUN

The infant began to cry.
▷ baby, child, newborn

infer

VERB

I infer from your frown that you are angry.
▷ conclude, deduce, guess, reason

inferior

ADJECTIVE

Don't put up with inferior service.
▷ lesser, lower, poor, second-rate, shoddy

ANTONYM superior

inflame

VERB

It is easy to inflame an angry mob.
▷ arouse, excite

ANTONYM calm

inflate

VERB

He tried to inflate his own importance.
▷ exaggerate, overstate

inflict

VERB

She is going to inflict stricter rules.
▷ deliver, enforce, impose

influence

NOUN

1 *I have no influence over my sister.*
▷ authority, control, power, sway

2 *What influence does television have?*
▷ effect, hold, power

VERB

What will influence the way you reply?
▷ affect, control, sway

inform

VERB

They will inform us when to leave.
▷ advise, notify, tell

informal

ADJECTIVE

Our meeting was informal and short.
▷ casual, natural, relaxed

information

NOUN

What information about the Annapolis Valley can you give me?
▷ data, facts, material, news

infrequent

ADJECTIVE

We make infrequent visits to see our cousins.
▷ few, irregular, rare, sporadic

infuriate

VERB

Do not infuriate the coach.
▷ anger, enrage, madden, vex

ingenious

ADJECTIVE

He has an ingenious way with language.
▷ bright, clever, creative, inventive, resourceful

ingredient

NOUN

The last ingredient to be added is flour.
▷ component, element, part

inhabit

VERB

Many Inuit inhabit the northern part of Canada.
▷ dwell in, live in, occupy, populate, reside in

I

inhuman
ADJECTIVE
His inhuman treatment of animals horrified us.
▷ barbaric, heartless, savage

initial
ADJECTIVE
My initial reaction was surprise.
▷ first, original, primary
ANTONYM final

initiate
VERB
The boys want to initiate a skateboarding club at school.
▷ begin, establish, found, start

initiative
NOUN
Use your initiative.
▷ drive, enterprise, resourcefulness

injure
VERB
I saw him injure his knee when he fell.
▷ harm, hurt, maim, wound

inkling
NOUN
Did you have any inkling about the surprise party?
▷ clue, hint, idea, notion, suspicion

inlet
NOUN
The boat was anchored in the inlet.
▷ bay, basin, gulf, harbour, fjord

innocent
ADJECTIVE
He was proved innocent of the crime.
▷ blameless, clear, not guilty
ANTONYM guilty

insecure
ADJECTIVE
1 *The rungs of the ladder are insecure.*
▷ loose, shaky, unstable, wobbly
2 *He feels insecure about speaking in public.*
▷ shy, timid, unconfident
ANTONYM confident

insensitive
ADJECTIVE
That was an insensitive comment to make!
▷ callous, thoughtless, uncaring, unfeeling

insert
VERB
Insert a space between the paragraphs in your report.
▷ introduce, place, put
ANTONYM remove

insight
NOUN
The new information gave us more insight.
▷ awareness, knowledge, understanding

insignificant
ADJECTIVE
Remove the insignificant details from your speech.
▷ little, minor, petty, trivial, unimportant

insincere
ADJECTIVE
I can tell when someone is being insincere.
▷ deceitful, dishonest, false

insinuate
VERB
How dare you insinuate that I lied!
▷ hint, imply, suggest

insist
VERB
I insist that my answer is correct.
▷ assert, claim, maintain, swear

inspect
VERB
Please inspect all the doors to make sure they are locked.
▷ check, examine, scrutinize

inspire
VERB
This video should inspire you to visit the beautiful beaches of Prince Edward Island.
▷ motivate, prompt, stimulate
ANTONYM deter

instance
NOUN
Can you name one instance where I was unhelpful?
▷ case, example, illustration

instant
NOUN
I will be ready in an instant.
▷ flash, minute, moment, second
ADJECTIVE
His instant reaction prevented an accident.
▷ immediate, instantaneous

instantly
ADVERB
The fire bell rang, so we left the classroom instantly.
▷ at once, immediately, right away

instinct
NOUN
1 *My instinct on the matter was correct.*
▷ feeling, intuition
2 *She has an instinct for saying the right thing.*
▷ ability, flair, gift, knack, talent

institution
NOUN
A charitable institution needs volunteers.
▷ association, establishment, organization

instruct
VERB
1 *Did you instruct them to be home on time?*
▷ command, direct, order, tell
2 *He will instruct us in gymnastics.*
▷ coach, educate, school, teach, train, tutor

instrument
NOUN
Mom has an instrument for measuring how many steps she takes in a day.
▷ contraption, device, gadget, implement, tool

insufficient
ADJECTIVE
Our plan had insufficient support.
▷ deficient, inadequate, incomplete

insult
VERB
Did you mean to insult her?
▷ affront, offend, snub
ANTONYM compliment

intact
ADJECTIVE
Some rooms were intact after the fire.
▷ complete, sound, whole

intelligent
ADJECTIVE
The intelligent child answered every question correctly.
▷ acute, bright, clever, quick, sharp, smart
ANTONYM stupid

intend
VERB
I intend to buy my friend a birthday present.
▷ aim, mean, plan, propose

intense
ADJECTIVE
His fear was so intense that it made him shake.
▷ acute, deep, extreme, fierce, powerful, severe

intention
NOUN
My intention is to work harder next year.
▷ aim, goal, objective, purpose

interest
NOUN
My main interest is swimming.
▷ activity, hobby, pastime, pursuit
VERB
This information will interest you.
▷ captivate, fascinate, intrigue, stimulate
ANTONYM bore

interfere
VERB
I get upset when you interfere.
▷ intervene, intrude, meddle

interfere with
VERB
Nothing will be allowed to interfere with my plans for the weekend.
▷ disrupt, hinder

interpret
VERB
We tried to interpret the look on his face.
▷ analyze, decipher, decode, explain, understand

interrogate
VERB
The lawyers will interrogate the witness.
▷ examine, grill, question, quiz

interrupt
VERB
1 *It is considered rude to interrupt when someone is speaking.*
▷ break in, butt in
2 *We had to interrupt our conversation.*
▷ break, discontinue, suspend

interval
NOUN
There is a short interval between classes.
▷ break, gap, interlude, pause, recess

interview
NOUN
I had an interview with the counsellor.
▷ consultation, meeting, talk

intimate
ADJECTIVE
We had an intimate chat about our problems.
▷ cozy, friendly, private

intimidate
VERB
Who tried to intimidate you?
▷ bully, frighten, threaten, scare

intricate
ADJECTIVE
I liked the intricate design on the cover.
▷ complex, complicated, elaborate, fancy
ANTONYM simple

intrigue
VERB
I think this blog will intrigue you.
▷ fascinate, interest

introduce
VERB
Please introduce the next topic.
▷ begin, initiate, start

invade
VERB
The terrorists' plan was to invade the town hall.
▷ assault, attack, enter, occupy, raid

invaluable
ADJECTIVE
These photographs are an invaluable part of our family history.
▷ precious, priceless

invent
VERB
I am going to invent a recipe for chocolate bread.
▷ concoct, create, devise

investigate
VERB
Our assignment is to investigate the water supply for our area.
▷ examine, explore, probe, research, study

invisible
ADJECTIVE
The bird was invisible among the bushes.
▷ concealed, hidden, unseen

invite
VERB
I invite you to explain your actions.
▷ ask, request, urge

involve
VERB
Our plan will involve several people.
▷ concern, include, require

involved
ADJECTIVE
He told a long and involved story.
▷ complex, complicated, elaborate

irate
ADJECTIVE
The irate fans jumped to their feet.
▷ angry, annoyed, furious, infuriated

irresponsible
ADJECTIVE
We do not want irresponsible team members.
▷ careless, reckless, thoughtless, undependable

irritable
ADJECTIVE
She gets irritable when she is hungry.
▷ bad-tempered, crabby, grumpy, grouchy

irritate
VERB
You irritate me when you keep interrupting.
▷ annoy, bother, exasperate

issue
NOUN
1 *We hope the health issue will be discussed.*
▷ concern, matter, problem, question, subject, topic
2 *The library has the May issue of that magazine.*
▷ copy, edition, instalment
VERB
Will the company issue an apology?
▷ deliver, pronounce, publish

item
NOUN
1 *Your complaint is the third item on the agenda.*
▷ article, matter, point
2 *The news item about food banks inspired me to volunteer.*
▷ article, feature, piece, report

I

J j

jab
VERB
*You will **jab** yourself in the eye if you keep waving that fork around.*
▷ dig, poke, stick

jabber
VERB
*He will **jabber** when he is nervous.*
▷ babble, chatter, mumble

jacket
NOUN
*Do you think my new **jacket** looks good with these pants?*
▷ blazer, coat, jerkin, mackinaw, parka, windbreaker

jagged
ADJECTIVE
*Take care when walking over this piece of **jagged** ground.*
▷ irregular, rough
ANTONYM smooth

jail
NOUN
*How many prisoners does that **jail** hold?*
▷ lockup, penitentiary, prison
VERB
*I wonder if they will **jail** her for committing that crime?*
▷ detain, imprison, incarcerate

jam
NOUN
1 *Losing my running shoes before the race put me in a real **jam**.*
▷ fix, predicament
2 *He likes to eat toast with **jam** for breakfast.*
▷ conserve, jelly, preserves
VERB
*If you **jam** your clothes into the drawer, it might not close properly.*
▷ cram, force, ram, stuff

jar
NOUN
*That **jar** will not hold any more water.*
▷ container, flask, vessel
VERB
*Try not to **jar** my desk when you walk by.*
▷ jog, jolt, shake

jealous
ADJECTIVE
*He is **jealous** of my relationship with his brother.*
▷ envious, resentful

jeer at
VERB
*It is unkind to **jeer at** someone under any circumstance.*
▷ insult, laugh at, mock, ridicule

jeopardize
VERB
*Do not **jeopardize** your life by crossing the street against the lights.*
▷ endanger, risk, threaten
ANTONYM protect

jerk
VERB
*I will try not to **jerk** my arm away when I get my flu shot.*
▷ pull, tug, wrench, yank

jest
NOUN
*Sometimes a **jest** can go wrong and people get hurt.*
▷ hoax, joke, prank

jester
NOUN
*The **jester** amused the crowd with his antics.*
▷ buffoon, clown, comedian, joker, prankster

jet
NOUN
*The geyser sprays a **jet** of water and steam every hour.*
▷ flow, gush, stream, spurt, squirt

jiffy
NOUN
*She said that she would return in a **jiffy**.*
▷ flash, instant, moment, twinkling

jilt
VERB
*I would never **jilt** a friend in need.*
▷ abandon, desert, drop, forsake, leave

jingle
VERB
*Whenever you **jingle** your keys, the dog opens its eyes.*
▷ clink, jangle, rattle

job
NOUN
1 *It is my **job** to ensure that everything runs smoothly.*
▷ concern, duty, function, responsibility, role, task
2 *You will have to get a **job** if you are to pay for your expensive hobbies.*
▷ career, occupation, position, post, profession, trade

jog
VERB
***Jog** his arm to get his attention.*
▷ bump, nudge, shake

J

join

VERB

1 *Let's **join** the gymnastics club.*
▷ enlist in, enrol in, sign up for
ANTONYM resign

2 *If we **join** both pieces of paper together we should have enough to wrap the gift.*
▷ attach, connect, fasten, link
ANTONYM separate

joint

NOUN

*The loose **joint** should hold until we can repair it properly.*
▷ bond, connection, fastening, link, union

joke

NOUN

*The **joke** didn't go over well and her feelings were hurt.*
▷ gag, jest, prank, trick

VERB

*Please don't **joke** about such serious matters.*
▷ jest, kid, tease

jolt

NOUN

*Her bicycle stopped with a **jolt** when she slammed on the brakes.*
▷ bump, jar, jerk

journal

NOUN

1 *He keeps track of daily events in his **journal**.*
▷ diary, ledger, log

2 *The story will appear in every major **journal**.*
▷ magazine, newspaper

journey

NOUN

*His **journey** took him across Canada.*
▷ excursion, expedition, tour, trek, trip, voyage

jovial

ADJECTIVE

*His bright smile revealed his **jovial** spirit.*
▷ cheerful, festive, good-humoured, jolly, light-hearted
ANTONYM sad

joy

NOUN

***Joy** showed on her face.*
▷ bliss, delight, happiness, pleasure
ANTONYM sorrow

joyful

ADJECTIVE

*We e-mailed the **joyful** news to the whole family.*
▷ glad, happy, joyous, merry
ANTONYM sorrowful

judge

NOUN

*We need a **judge** to decide who wins the award.*
▷ arbitrator, referee, umpire

VERB

*Could you **judge** the weight of this pumpkin, please?*
▷ assess, estimate, evaluate, rate

judgment

NOUN

1 *The court will announce a **judgment** this afternoon.*
▷ decision, decree, finding, ruling, sentence, verdict

2 *He has great **judgment** when it comes to people's feelings.*
▷ discretion, good sense, intelligence, understanding

jug

NOUN

*Fill the **jug** with water and set it next to the glasses.*
▷ pitcher, urn

juice

NOUN

*The **juice** dripped down her chin when she bit into the peach.*
▷ fluid, liquid

jump

VERB

*I'm going to **jump** over the puddle of water.*
▷ bound, hop, leap, skip, spring, vault

NOUN

*There was a **jump** in the cost of produce because of the drought.*
▷ increase, rise, surge

junction

NOUN

*Let's meet at the **junction** of King Street and Main.*
▷ crossing, crossroads, intersection

jungle

NOUN

*The dense **jungle** was alive with the sound of birds and insects.*
▷ bush, forest, thicket, wilderness

junior

ADJECTIVE

*The **junior** team members learned from the more experienced players.*
▷ lower, minor, secondary, subordinate, younger
ANTONYM senior

junk

NOUN

*Clear the **junk** from the garage and place it in the trash can.*
▷ garbage, litter, refuse, rubbish, scrap, trash, waste

just

ADJECTIVE

She received a just punishment for her crime.

▷ appropriate, fair, impartial, lawful, reasonable

ADVERB

1 *I have just enough flour for one batch of cookies.*

▷ exactly, precisely

2 *Actors are just ordinary people, the same as us.*

▷ merely, only, simply

justify

VERB

Being angry does not justify bad behaviour.

▷ excuse, explain, validate, vindicate, warrant

juvenile

ADJECTIVE

She was scolded for her juvenile behaviour.

▷ adolescent, childish, immature, young, youthful

ANTONYM mature

NOUN

A juvenile doesn't pay as much for admission as an adult.

▷ child, youngster, youth

J

K k

keen
ADJECTIVE
1 *He's a keen reader.*
▷ ardent, avid, eager, enthusiastic
ANTONYM uninterested
2 *Her keen mind understood the situation immediately.*
▷ brilliant, clever, perceptive, quick, sharp, shrewd
ANTONYM dull

keenness
NOUN
Actors play better when they feel the keenness of the audience.
▷ eagerness, enthusiasm, excitement, interest
ANTONYM boredom

keep
VERB
1 *Mountain bikes cost a lot to keep.*
▷ care for, maintain, preserve
ANTONYM neglect
2 *Keep the cash in a safe place.*
▷ deposit, hold, store
ANTONYM lose
3 *She will keep her promises.*
▷ carry out, fulfil, honour
ANTONYM break

MAKE IT MORE FORMAL
for keeps permanently
keep an eye on supervise
keep in with keep friendship with
keep on continue
keep out exclude
keep safe protect
keep to yourself not mix with others
keep up with do as well as
keep your eyes open watch

keepsake
NOUN
Please take this bracelet as a keepsake.
▷ memento, reminder, souvenir

key
ADJECTIVE
Eating sensibly is a key factor in good health.
▷ basic, chief, essential
ANTONYM unnecessary

kick
NOUN
I get a kick out of writing stories.
▷ delight, pleasure, thrill

kid
NOUN
The kid in the next apartment makes a lot of noise.
▷ child, infant, toddler, youngster
VERB
It can be fun to kid as long as it doesn't go too far.
▷ joke, pretend, tease

kidnap
VERB
She joked that aliens would kidnap me.
▷ abduct, capture, seize

kill
VERB
Should we kill whales to make dog food?
▷ butcher, destroy, execute, exterminate, massacre, murder, slaughter, slay

kin
NOUN
My friends are just like kin to me.
▷ family, people, relations, relatives

kind
NOUN
What kind of tree is that?
▷ breed, category, sort, type, variety
ADJECTIVE
He never smiles, but he has a kind nature.
▷ benevolent, benign, charitable, compassionate, considerate, good, humane, kind-hearted, kindly, thoughtful, unselfish
ANTONYM cruel

MAKE IT MORE FORMAL
all kinds of plenty of
kind of somewhat; rather
of a kind of the same kind

kindle
VERB
Is it time to kindle the bonfire?
▷ ignite, light
ANTONYM douse

kindness
NOUN
My foster family treats me with great kindness.
▷ benevolence, charity, compassion, generosity, gentleness, humanity
ANTONYM cruelty

king
NOUN
The king rules by permission of Parliament.
▷ monarch, sovereign

K

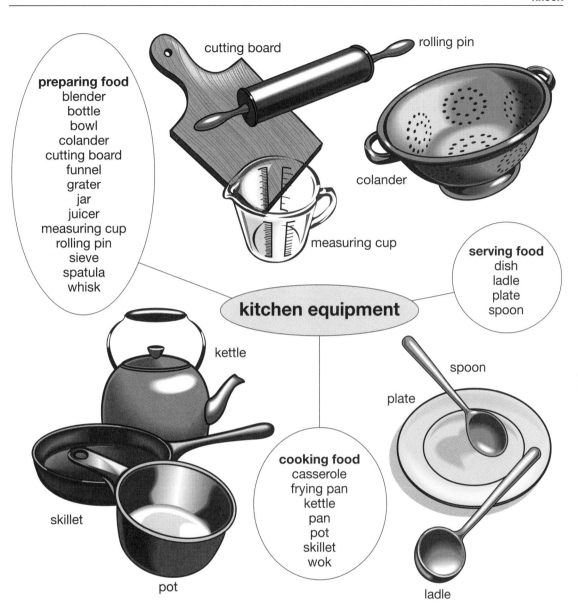

preparing food
blender
bottle
bowl
colander
cutting board
funnel
grater
jar
juicer
measuring cup
rolling pin
sieve
spatula
whisk

cutting board

rolling pin

colander

measuring cup

serving food
dish
ladle
plate
spoon

kitchen equipment

kettle

spoon

plate

skillet

cooking food
casserole
frying pan
kettle
pan
pot
skillet
wok

ladle

pot

K

kingdom

NOUN

*After years of war, the **kingdom** had no resources left.*

▷ country, state

kitchen equipment

NOUN

See picture above.

knack

NOUN

*She had the **knack** of getting people to tell their secrets.*

▷ ability, skill, talent

knob

NOUN

*Paint the door blue, and the **knob** red.*

▷ button, handle, opener

knock

VERB

1 *It hurts to **knock** your elbow on a hard surface like a desk.*

▷ bang, beat, bump, hit, strike, tap

2 *Don't **knock** it till you've tried it.*

▷ condemn, criticize

ANTONYM praise

MAKE IT MORE FORMAL

knock down overturn
knock it off Stop what you are doing!
knock out eliminate
knock over upset

---

knot

VERB

1 *Knot the string tightly, please.*
▷ fasten, secure, tie
ANTONYM untie

2 *It's annoying when kite strings begin to knot.*
▷ jumble, muddle, tangle, twist

know

VERB

1 *I know the answer.*
▷ comprehend, see, understand

2 *I know your brother.*
▷ be acquainted with, be familiar with, recognize

know-how

NOUN

He has the know-how to do the work properly.
▷ ability, expertise, knowledge, skill

knowledge

NOUN

She had a lot of knowledge of Canadian history.
▷ experience, understanding
ANTONYM ignorance

knowledgeable

ADJECTIVE

He's quite knowledgeable in many subjects.
▷ aware, experienced, expert
ANTONYM ignorant

K

label
NOUN
This label says the jacket is half price.
▷ sticker, tag, ticket

laborious
ADJECTIVE
Harvesting apples is laborious work.
▷ difficult, strenuous, tiring
ANTONYM easy

labour
NOUN
We put a lot of labour into our project.
▷ effort, toil, work

lack
NOUN
There was a lack of volunteers for the food drive.
▷ scarcity, shortage
ANTONYM abundance

lake
NOUN
The blue heron landed on the lake.
▷ lagoon, pond, pool, reservoir, slough

lame
ADJECTIVE
You have a very lame reason for being late.
▷ feeble, flimsy, pathetic, poor, unconvincing, weak

landscape
NOUN
The landscape looked magnificent at sunset.
▷ scene, scenery, view

lane
NOUN
Leave your bicycle in the lane beside our house.
▷ alley, passage, path

language
NOUN
We found an interpreter who knew our language.
▷ dialect, tongue

lanky
ADJECTIVE
The little boy has turned into a lanky teen.
▷ gangly, rangy
ANTONYM stout

large
ADJECTIVE
The sculpture was too large to fit into the gallery.
▷ colossal, enormous, gigantic, great, huge, immense, massive
ANTONYM small

lash
VERB
A good trainer never needs to lash a horse.
▷ beat, flog, whip

last
ADJECTIVE
We heard the last part of her speech.
▷ closing, concluding, final
ANTONYM first
VERB
The pain will not last very long.
▷ continue, persist, remain

MAKE IT MORE FORMAL

at last after a (seemingly) long time
last name surname or family name
last word most up-to-date style; something that cannot be improved
see the last of not see ever again

latch
NOUN
The latch on the door is broken.
▷ bolt, catch, fastener, lock

late
ADJECTIVE
The flight was late.
▷ delayed, overdue
ANTONYM early

laugh
VERB
See box at foot of next page.

launch
VERB
The hospital will launch its fundraiser today.
▷ begin, commence, initiate, start

lavish
ADJECTIVE
The winners were given lavish gifts.
▷ extravagant, generous, luxurious

law
NOUN
The city has passed an anti-littering law.
▷ act, bylaw, code, decree, regulation, rule, statute

lawyer
NOUN
He hired a lawyer to advise him.
▷ advocate, attorney, barrister, counsel, solicitor

L

lay
VERB
Lay the pizza box on the counter.
▷ place, put, set, set down

layer
NOUN
There is a dangerous layer of ice on the road.
▷ coat, coating, covering, film, sheet

lazy
ADJECTIVE
We do not want lazy people on our team.
▷ idle, slack
ANTONYM industrious

lead
VERB
1 *A teacher will lead you into the auditorium.*
▷ conduct, escort, guide, steer, usher
2 *Who will lead the team?*
▷ command, direct, govern, head

NOUN
The woman gave us a lead on where our dog went.
▷ clue, indication, tip

leader
NOUN
The group will elect a new leader.
▷ chief, commander, director, head

leak
VERB
Maple syrup began to leak from the can.
▷ escape, ooze, seep, spill

lean
ADJECTIVE
One of the twins is chubby, and the other is lean.
▷ slender, slim, thin
VERB
Straighten the picture so that it doesn't lean at all.
▷ slant, slope, tilt

leap
VERB
A dog couldn't leap over that fence.
▷ bounce, bound, jump, spring, vault

REPLACE AN OVERUSED WORD: LAUGH

There are a number of more interesting words that you can use in place of the basic verb **laugh**, if you want to say something about the way in which a person laughs.

- If you **cackle**, you laugh in a loud and unpleasant way, often at something bad which happens to someone else.
  When you slip and fall, some people will rush to help, but others will just cackle.

- If you **chuckle**, you laugh quietly.
  I didn't enjoy the whole movie, but some parts made me chuckle.

- If you **chortle**, you laugh in a pleased or amused way.
  While she was telling her story, the listeners began to chortle at her adventures.

- If you **giggle**, you laugh in a high-pitched way.
  Don't start to giggle, or I'll forget my lines.

- If you **guffaw**, you laugh very loudly because you think something is very funny.
  The audience would guffaw each time the clown tripped over his own feet.

- If you **snigger**, you laugh in a quiet, sly way, perhaps at something rude or unkind.
  The joke was so bad, I didn't even snigger.

- If you **titter**, you give a short, nervous laugh, often because you are embarrassed.
  The actor forgot his lines so often that the audience began to titter.

learn
VERB
What did you learn about earthquakes?
▷ discover, gather, understand

least
ADJECTIVE
Our class has the least number of students.
▷ fewest, lowest, minimum, smallest
ANTONYM most

leave
VERB
It's time to leave.
▷ depart, exit

lecture
NOUN
The whole school listened to the lecture.
▷ address, presentation, speech, talk

legal
ADJECTIVE
She had a legal claim to the money.
▷ authorized, lawful, legitimate, rightful, valid
ANTONYM illegal

legend
NOUN
The movie is based on an Inuit legend.
▷ fable, myth, tale

legitimate
ADJECTIVE
In the story, the girl discovers that she is the legitimate heir to the throne.
▷ lawful, legal, proper, rightful

leisure
NOUN
Always find time for some leisure.
▷ recreation, relaxation
ANTONYM work

leisurely
ADJECTIVE
They strolled along at a leisurely pace.
▷ comfortable, easy, gentle, relaxed, slow, unhurried

lend
VERB
Did you lend money to your brother?
▷ advance, loan, supply
ANTONYM borrow

lengthen
VERB
She proposes to lengthen her stay in Manitoba.
▷ extend, prolong, stretch
ANTONYM shorten

lenient
ADJECTIVE
My parents were lenient and did not ground me.
▷ merciful, tolerant
ANTONYM severe

lessen
VERB
This medicine will lessen the pain.
▷ decrease, diminish, ease, lower, reduce
ANTONYM increase

lesson
NOUN
The lesson on diving techniques was very useful.
▷ class, coaching, instruction

let
VERB
Will you let me help you?
▷ allow (to), permit (to)
ANTONYM forbid

MAKE IT MORE FORMAL

let down disappoint
let go *or* **let off** allow to go free
let in admit
let off steam give way to feelings
let someone in for involve someone in something unpleasant
let up stop

letter
NOUN
1 *I had to change one letter in my password.*
▷ character, sign, symbol
2 *I wrote a thank-you letter to my grandparents.*
▷ message, note

level
ADJECTIVE
It's easier to run on level ground.
▷ flat, horizontal
VERB
They will have to level the ground before they can build on it.
▷ flatten, smooth
NOUN
Which level have you reached in karate?
▷ grade, rank, stage

liable
ADJECTIVE
1 *We all have to be liable for our own actions.*
▷ accountable, answerable, responsible
2 *She is liable to fall without her cane.*
▷ inclined, likely, prone

L

liar

NOUN

*I will not associate with that **liar**.*

▷ deceiver, fibber, perjurer

liberal

ADJECTIVE

*The sponsor gave us a **liberal** cash donation.*

▷ generous, lavish

liberty

NOUN

*They have the **liberty** to leave when they want to.*

▷ freedom, independence

licence

NOUN

*He acts as if he has a **licence** to misbehave.*

▷ freedom, permission, permit

license

VERB

*The town will **license** her to catch stray animals.*

▷ allow, entitle, permit

lie

VERB

*I like to **lie** in the hammock.*

▷ lounge, recline, sprawl

NOUN

*Why did you make up such a **lie**?*

▷ deceit, fabrication, falsehood, fib, untruth

ANTONYM truth

life

NOUN

*He had many adventures during his **life**.*

▷ lifespan, lifetime

MAKE IT MORE FORMAL

as large as life in person
get a life find something worthwhile to do
not on your life under no circumstances

lifelike

ADJECTIVE

*My mom painted a **lifelike** picture of our cat.*

▷ exact, faithful, realistic

lift

VERB

1 ***Lift** both arms over your head.*

▷ elevate, hoist, raise

ANTONYM lower

2 *Dad will **lift** the punishment if I behave myself.*

▷ cancel, end, relax, remove

light

NOUN

*We saw a **light** in the distance.*

▷ brightness, brilliance, glare, glow, illumination, radiance

ADJECTIVE

1 *She painted the room in a **light** colour.*

▷ pale, pastel

ANTONYM dark

2 *The parcel was **light**, but awkward to carry.*

▷ lightweight, slight

ANTONYM heavy

VERB

1 *The moon helped to **light** the path.*

▷ brighten, illuminate

ANTONYM darken

2 *Don't **light** the campfire until the temperature goes down.*

▷ ignite, kindle

ANTONYM extinguish

lighting

NOUN

See picture on next page.

like

VERB

*I **like** the way you talk.*

▷ admire, appreciate, enjoy

ANTONYM dislike

MAKE IT MORE FORMAL

and the like and similar things
as like as not probably
like crazy (mad, etc.) with great speed, effort, etc.
nothing like not nearly
something like almost like
the likes of someone or something like

likeness

NOUN

*I noticed the **likeness** between the brothers.*

▷ resemblance, similarity

likewise

ADVERB

*You did well on the test and I hope to do **likewise**.*

▷ also, equally, similarly, too

limit

NOUN

*We walked as far as the town **limit**.*

▷ border, boundary, edge, end

VERB

***Limit** the amount of salt you use.*

▷ curb, ration, restrict

limp

ADJECTIVE

*Put the **limp** celery in some water.*

▷ drooping, floppy, soft

ANTONYM stiff

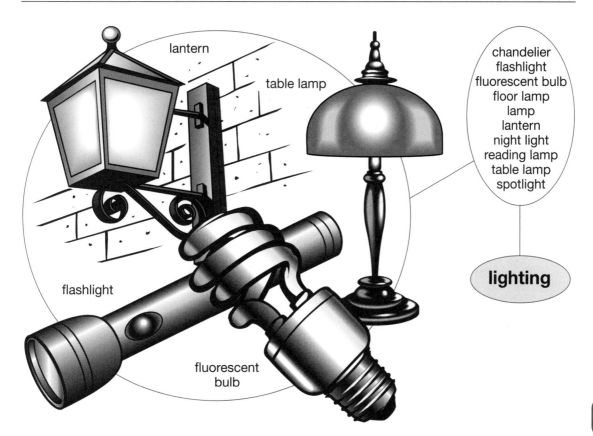

lantern

table lamp

chandelier
flashlight
fluorescent bulb
floor lamp
lamp
lantern
night light
reading lamp
table lamp
spotlight

flashlight

fluorescent
bulb

lighting

L

line

NOUN

1 *The artist painted a thick red line on the white canvas.*
▷ rule, streak, stripe

2 *Please stand over here and form a straight line.*
▷ column, file, queue, row

> ### *MAKE IT MORE FORMAL*
>
> **cross the line** do something unacceptable
> **hold the line** stand firm against an attack or challenge
> **in line with** in agreement with
> **lay it on the line** state firmly and clearly
> **on the line** at risk
> **out of line** unacceptable

linger

VERB

Come straight home and don't linger.
▷ dawdle, loiter, wait

link

NOUN

There is a close link between the twins.
▷ association, attachment, bond, connection, relationship, tie

liquid

NOUN

You can buy soap as a liquid or a solid.
▷ fluid, solution

list

NOUN

The list of home games is on the notice board.
▷ inventory, record, register, roster

listen

VERB

Please listen to what I am saying.
▷ hear, heed, pay attention

literate

ADJECTIVE

Students become literate in school.
▷ educated, learned

ANTONYM illiterate

litter

NOUN

She offered to help pick up litter in the park.
▷ garbage, refuse, trash

little

ADJECTIVE

See box on next page.

REPLACE AN OVERUSED WORD: LITTLE

Depending on what you are describing, you can choose from any of the following alternatives instead of the overused adjective **little**.

- **a little object**

  *On her ankle, she had a tattoo of a **miniature** heart.*

  *I think there's a **minute** bit of dust in my eye.*

  *These boots are too **small** for me.*

  ***Tiny** flakes of snow started to fall.*

- **a little time**

  *Let's take a **brief** break.*

  *He shot me a **fleeting** glance as he walked by.*

  *After a **momentary** pause, she continued reading aloud.*

  *I have a **quick** question for you.*

- **a little amount**

  *I've done **hardly** any studying this week.*

  *She complained about the **meagre** amount of tuna in the sandwich.*

  *The server handed me a **measly** plate of fries.*

  *He had a **paltry** fifty cents in his pocket.*

- **little in age**

  *My **baby** sister is only three months old.*

  *The father took his **infant** son to every ball game.*

  *The older children go to school, but the two **small** ones are in daycare.*

  *I was only a **young** child, but I remember what happened that day.*

- **little in importance**

  *The pain is **insignificant**, so I'll ignore it.*

  *A **minor** squabble can turn into a major feud.*

  *We spent too much time dealing with **petty** problems.*

  *There is no time to waste on **trivial** details.*

- **a little piece of something**

  *I'd like a **bit** of chocolate.*

  *Add a **dash** of salt to the soup.*

  *There's a **fragment** of paper stuck to your shoe.*

  *The mechanic spotted a **trace** of oil under the car.*

L

live

VERB

They are going to live by the ocean.

▷ dwell, reside

MAKE IT MORE FORMAL

live it up enjoy life to the full
live up to act according to
live with tolerate

lively

ADJECTIVE

My sister is very lively.

▷ active, animated, energetic, perky, sparkling

ANTONYM dull

livid

ADJECTIVE

I am livid that you borrowed my new shirt.

▷ angry, enraged, furious

load

NOUN

The truck was carrying a load of grain from Alberta.

▷ cargo, consignment, shipment

VERB

Load the groceries into the car.

▷ pack, pile, stack

loathe

VERB

I loathe him because he is dishonest.

▷ despise, detest, dislike, hate

ANTONYM like

lobby

NOUN

Wait in the lobby for me.

▷ entrance, foyer, vestibule

local

ADJECTIVE

We like to skate at our local rink.

▷ community, district, neighbourhood

locate

VERB

Can you locate Labrador City on the map?

▷ detect, find, pinpoint

location

NOUN

The new school is in a central location.

▷ place, point, position, site, situation, spot

lock

VERB

Do not forget to lock the door.

▷ bolt, fasten, secure

lodge

NOUN
*There is a new **lodge** near Whistler.*
▷ hotel, inn

logical

ADJECTIVE
*He gave a **logical** reply to the question.*
▷ rational, reasonable, sound, valid
ANTONYM illogical

lone

ADJECTIVE
*The hurricane left a **lone** tree standing.*
▷ single, sole, solitary

lonely

ADJECTIVE
1 *The girl was **lonely** without her friend.*
▷ alone, forlorn, lonesome
2 *An empty house stands on the **lonely** island.*
▷ deserted, desolate, isolated, remote, secluded, uninhabited

long

ADJECTIVE
*There may be a **long** delay before the next bus arrives.*
▷ extended, lengthy, prolonged
VERB
*The cold hikers began to **long** for a warm drink.*
▷ ache, crave, hunger, pine, yearn

longing

NOUN
*He had a **longing** to see his old home.*
▷ craving, desire, hankering, hunger, yearning

look

NOUN
*Take a **look** over there.*
▷ glance, glimpse, peek
VERB
1 See box at top of next page.
2 *Please **look** interested in what she has to say.*
▷ appear, seem

MAKE IT MORE FORMAL

look after take care of
look around consider many possibilities
look bad appear improper
look down on despise
look for search for
look into investigate
look like resemble
look out beware
look out for protect
look over inspect
look up to respect

loop

NOUN
*Twist the wire into a **loop**.*
▷ coil, ring

loose

ADJECTIVE
1 *The door handle is **loose**.*
▷ unsecured, wobbly
ANTONYM secure
2 ***Loose** clothes are comfortable in hot weather.*
▷ baggy, slack
ANTONYM tight

loosen

VERB
*Dad likes to **loosen** his tie when he gets home.*
▷ slacken, undo, unfasten, untie
ANTONYM tighten

loot

VERB
*People began to **loot** the stores during the riot.*
▷ pillage, plunder, raid, ransack
NOUN
*The pirates buried their **loot** on a deserted island.*
▷ booty, haul, plunder, spoils

lose

VERB
1 *Did you **lose** your pen?*
▷ mislay, misplace
ANTONYM find
2 *I'm afraid we're going to **lose**.*
▷ be beaten, be defeated
ANTONYM win

MAKE IT MORE FORMAL

lose hope despair
lose it lose control of emotions
lose out fail
lose your nerve panic
lose your temper rage

loser

NOUN
*Never consider yourself a **loser**.*
▷ dud, failure, flop

lost

ADJECTIVE
1 *The boat was **lost** in the fog.*
▷ adrift, astray, off course
2 *My **lost** running shoes turned up in my locker.*
▷ mislaid, misplaced, missing

lots or a lot

NOUN
*There was **lots** of potato salad at the picnic.*
▷ a great deal, plenty, quantities

L

REPLACE AN OVERUSED WORD: LOOK

All of the following words are more expressive substitutes for the verb **look**.

- If you **eye** something, you look at it carefully.
  Our cat would always eye its food with suspicion, then slowly begin eating.

- If you **examine** something, you look at it very carefully, to find out information from it.
  The jury must examine all the evidence.

- If you **gape** at something, you look at it in surprise, usually with your mouth open.
  She was obviously shocked at what I said, and could only gape at me.

- If you **gaze** at something, you look at it steadily for a long time, perhaps because you find it interesting, or because you are thinking about something else.
  She can sit and gaze out of the window for hours at a time.

- If you **glance** at something, you look at it quickly.
  He would glance at me sometimes, then quickly turn his head.

- If you **glare** at someone, you stare angrily.
  I didn't do it on purpose, so there's no need to glare at me.

- If you **goggle** at something, you look at it with your eyes wide open, usually because you are surprised.
  The special effects in the movie were spectacular enough to make us goggle in amazement.

- If you **observe** something, you look at it to see what is happening.
  We will observe the traffic on this street, and tally the number of vehicles travelling east.

- If you **peek** at something, you look at it quickly and secretly.
  Peek around the blind to see if anyone is out there.

- If you **peer** at something, you try to see it more clearly by narrowing your eyes.
  He went to peer through the window, but the glass was too dirty.

- If you **scan** something written, you look at it quickly without reading every word.
  I will have to scan several websites before I find one that I can use.

- If you **scowl** at someone, you stare at them sulkily.
  You look very ugly when you scowl.

- If you **squint** at something, you try to see it more clearly by screwing up your eyes.
  She couldn't find her glasses, and had to squint at the computer screen.

- If you **stare** at something, you look at it steadily for a long time. Staring is often thought to be rude.
  Don't stare at me like that.

- If you **study** something, you look at it very carefully, to learn as much as possible from it.
  Study the instructions before you begin.

- If you **survey** something, you look at it carefully, often to find out some information from it.
  The police officer will have to survey the scene before deciding what caused the accident.

loud
ADJECTIVE
1 *Turn the radio down—it's really loud!*
▷ blaring, deafening, noisy, thunderous
ANTONYM quiet
2 *The pants look fine, but the shirt is too loud.*
▷ flashy, garish, gaudy, lurid
ANTONYM dull

lovable
ADJECTIVE
What a lovable little kitten!
▷ adorable, charming, endearing, sweet

love
VERB
1 *I love my grandparents.*
▷ adore, cherish, treasure
ANTONYM hate
2 *I love your attitude and dedication.*
▷ appreciate, enjoy, like, relish
ANTONYM dislike
NOUN
They always show their love for one another.
▷ adoration, affection, devotion, passion
ANTONYM hatred

love of
NOUN
She has a love of the outdoors.
▷ fondness for, liking for
ANTONYM dislike of

lovely
ADJECTIVE
She has lovely eyes.
▷ attractive, beautiful, delightful, pretty

low
ADJECTIVE
There are two low steps just before the gate.
▷ little, short, small
ANTONYM high

lower
VERB
The government promised to lower the sales tax.
▷ cut, decrease, diminish, lessen, minimize, reduce, slash
ANTONYM increase

loyal
ADJECTIVE
A real friend is always loyal.
▷ faithful, staunch, true, trusty
ANTONYM disloyal

luck
NOUN
We found the place just by luck.
▷ accident, chance

ludicrous
ADJECTIVE
Going out in the snowstorm is a ludicrous idea.
▷ absurd, ridiculous

lug
VERB
We had to lug the box of newspapers to the curb.
▷ carry, drag, haul

luminous
ADJECTIVE
Her eyes were luminous with tears.
▷ bright, radiant, shining

lump
NOUN
1 *He dropped a lump of ice into the water.*
▷ bit, chunk, hunk, piece
2 *Where did you get that lump on your head?*
▷ bulge, bump, swelling

lure
VERB
The sale prices are sure to lure customers into the store.
▷ attract, draw, entice, tempt
NOUN
A free cellphone was the lure for entering the contest.
▷ attraction, bait, magnet

luscious
ADJECTIVE
Ripe strawberries are luscious.
▷ delicious, juicy, tasty

lush
ADJECTIVE
The grass is lush after all that rain.
▷ abundant, rich, thick

luxurious
ADJECTIVE
He said he did not want a luxurious lifestyle.
▷ deluxe, lavish, opulent, sumptuous
ANTONYM plain

luxury
NOUN
1 *He enjoys luxury.*
▷ affluence, opulence, wealth
2 *I think sleeping late on the weekend is a luxury.*
▷ extravagance, treat

lying
NOUN
Lying is the same as cheating.
▷ deceit, dishonesty, fibbing
ADJECTIVE
Her lying comments created a lot of trouble.
▷ deceitful, dishonest, false, untruthful
ANTONYM honest

L

M m

macabre
ADJECTIVE
Macabre campfire tales might scare the children.
▷ creepy, grisly, gruesome

machine
NOUN
This machine will help you do the job faster.
▷ apparatus, contraption, device, gadget, mechanism

mad
ADJECTIVE
He was mad because I read his private journal.
▷ angry, enraged, furious, irate, livid

magnet
NOUN
The rides at the fair are a magnet for young children.
▷ attraction, draw, lure, pull

magnetic
ADJECTIVE
She has a magnetic personality—everyone likes her!
▷ attractive, captivating, fascinating
ANTONYM repulsive

magnificent
ADJECTIVE
You did a magnificent job painting the fence.
▷ marvellous, superb, wonderful

main
ADJECTIVE
The main idea of the story is "Be kind to everyone."
▷ central, key, predominant

mainly
ADVERB
I am interested mainly in reading, but I also like sports.
▷ largely, mostly, primarily

maintain
VERB
Do you maintain that you didn't enter my room?
▷ assert, claim, insist, swear
ANTONYM deny

majestic
ADJECTIVE
The snow-capped mountains are majestic, especially at dawn.
▷ grand, magnificent, splendid

major
ADJECTIVE
The major reason for the delay was bad weather.
▷ chief, key, main

make
VERB
1 *Let's make a model of the school for our class project.*
▷ assemble, build, construct

2 *It can be difficult to make children eat food they dislike.*
▷ compel, force, oblige
3 *How much did we make from the bake sale?*
▷ bring in, earn, receive
4 *We plan to make her leader of our club.*
▷ appoint, elect, nominate
NOUN
Do you know the make of that MP3 player?
▷ brand, model

MAKE IT MORE FORMAL

make a difference matter
make a mistake err
make an attempt try
make an effort try
make certain ensure
make fun of tease
make it succeed
make known announce
make like imitate
make something of it start an argument about it
make up form; invent
make up for compensate
make up your mind decide
make use of employ

male
NOUN
A very polite male answered the phone.
▷ boy, gentleman, man

malevolent
ADJECTIVE
Most fairy tales have malevolent villains.
▷ evil, hateful, nasty, vicious, wicked

malicious
ADJECTIVE
That is a malicious and hurtful rumour.
▷ cruel, mean, spiteful, vicious

mammoth
ADJECTIVE
Mom says that cleaning my room will be a mammoth job.
▷ colossal, enormous, giant, massive
ANTONYM tiny

man
NOUN
That man has a very trim beard.
▷ fellow, gentleman, guy, lad, male

manage
VERB
I offered to manage the lemonade stand.
▷ control, direct, oversee, run, supervise

manager
NOUN
His manager asked him to mop the floors.
▷ boss, director, supervisor

mangle
VERB
Take care not to mangle the map.
▷ crush, deform, twist

manipulate
VERB
Some people are able to manipulate the actions of others.
▷ control, exploit, influence

manner
NOUN
Her manner of dress is modest but stylish.
▷ fashion, mode, style, way

manoeuvre
VERB
It is easy to manoeuvre a boat through calm water.
▷ guide, navigate, steer
NOUN
Convincing me that you were sick was a clever manoeuvre.
▷ ploy, ruse, strategy, tactic

manual
NOUN
The manual shows how to program the cellphone.
▷ guide, handbook

many
ADJECTIVE
I have many hobbies, so I'm never bored.
▷ numerous, umpteen
ANTONYM few

map
NOUN
If you follow the map, you will not get lost.
▷ diagram, drawing, plan

mar
VERB
Some people think that tall buildings mar the landscape.
▷ damage, ruin, spoil
ANTONYM enhance

margin
NOUN
The margin of his notebook is filled with doodles.
▷ border, edge

mark
NOUN
See box at foot of this page.

M

REPLACE AN OVERUSED WORD: MARK

The noun **mark** is not very specific. There are a number of more interesting synonyms that you can use in its place.

- **a stain**
  There's a smudge of ketchup on your chin.
  I'm trying to remove this greasy spot from my jacket.
  Does orange juice leave a stain?
  He didn't realize there was a streak of paint in his hair.

- **a damaged area**
  The blemish on your nose isn't noticeable.
  I have a red blotch on my neck.
  Harry Potter has a jagged scar on his forehead.
  Who made this scratch on the desk?

- **a written or printed symbol**
  The purple saxifrage is the floral emblem of Nunavut.
  The city wants a new logo.

I can't read the date stamp on the envelope.
In the centre of the Canadian flag there is a maple leaf symbol.

- **a characteristic of something**
  A generous nature is one attribute of a good person.
  White fur is a characteristic of Arctic animals.
  Multiculturalism is a basic feature of Canadian society.
  Look for one trait of good writing in this story.

- **an indication of something**
  Nodding the head is usually a gesture of agreement.
  There was no indication of any injury to his arm.
  Wave a white flag as a sign of surrender.
  We exchanged gifts as a token of our friendship.

---

marked
ADJECTIVE
*There was a **marked** change in the weather overnight.*
▷ noticeable, obvious, striking

market
NOUN
*Please go to the **market** for some bread and milk.*
▷ grocery store, shop, store, supermarket

marsh
NOUN
*Many insects live in the **marsh**.*
▷ bayou, bog, fen, marshland, mire, morass, mud flat, muskeg, quagmire, quicksand, swamp, swampland, wetland

marvel
NOUN
*It was a **marvel** that you weren't hurt.*
▷ miracle, wonder

marvellous
ADJECTIVE
*She is a **marvellous** athlete.*
▷ excellent, magnificent, remarkable, splendid, superb, wonderful

mash
VERB
***Mash** the ingredients together.*
▷ crush, grind, pound, squash

M

mask
VERB
*He tried to **mask** his disappointment with a smile.*
▷ conceal, cover, disguise, hide

mass
NOUN
*I raked the leaves into a single **mass**.*
▷ heap, load, pile
ADJECTIVE
*This is a movie with **mass** appeal.*
▷ general, popular, universal, widespread

massive
ADJECTIVE
*The Great Lakes cover a **massive** area.*
▷ colossal, enormous, gigantic, huge, immense
ANTONYM small

match
NOUN
*Our team won the **match** and will play in the finals.*
▷ competition, contest, game
VERB
*Those shoes don't **match** that outfit.*
▷ complement, suit
ANTONYM clash

material
NOUN
*This **material** irritates my skin.*
▷ cloth, fabric

matter
NOUN
*Discuss the **matter** before making up your mind.*
▷ issue, situation, subject, topic

maximum
ADJECTIVE
*The **maximum** capacity of this elevator is 20 people.*
▷ greatest, highest
ANTONYM minimum

maybe
ADVERB
***Maybe** we could go to a movie later.*
▷ perhaps, possibly

meadow
NOUN
*I can see a few cows standing in the **meadow**.*
▷ field, grassland, pasture

meagre
ADJECTIVE
*She was still hungry after the **meagre** lunch.*
▷ inadequate, measly, paltry
ANTONYM substantial

mean
VERB
1 *Do you know what these symbols **mean**?*
▷ denote, indicate, signify
2 *I **mean** to finish this book before I go to bed.*
▷ aim, intend, plan
ADJECTIVE
1 *Her **mean** comments nearly made me cry.*
▷ cruel, hurtful, malicious, nasty, unkind
2 *Don't be **mean** with your money!*
▷ miserly, stingy
ANTONYM generous

meaning
NOUN
*The **meaning** of the story is not clear to me.*
▷ importance, message, significance
ANTONYM insignificance

meaningless
ADJECTIVE
*If you don't feel sorry, your apology is **meaningless**.*
▷ pointless, useless, worthless

means
NOUN
*Not everyone has the **means** to own a car.*
▷ money, resources, wealth

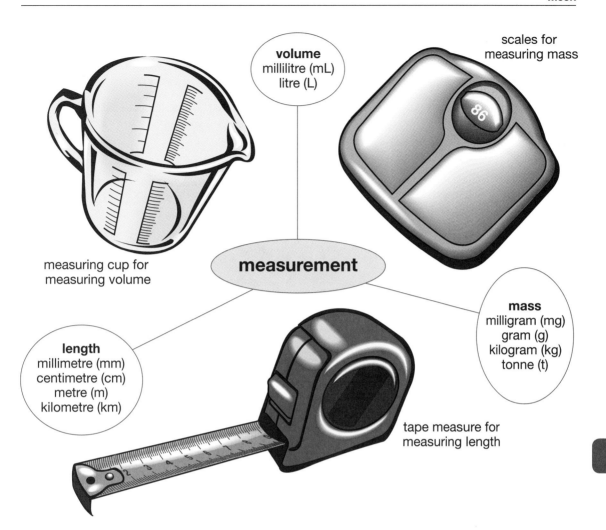

volume
millilitre (mL)
litre (L)

scales for
measuring mass

*measuring cup for
measuring volume*

measurement

mass
milligram (mg)
gram (g)
kilogram (kg)
tonne (t)

length
millimetre (mm)
centimetre (cm)
metre (m)
kilometre (km)

*tape measure for
measuring length*

M

measure
VERB
Measure the distance between these two points.
▷ calculate, determine

NOUN
We take every safety measure to ensure the security of the rides.
▷ action, procedure, step

measurement
NOUN
See picture at top of this page.

mechanical
ADJECTIVE
Breathing is a mechanical action.
▷ automatic, unthinking

meddle
VERB
Don't meddle in other people's lives.
▷ interfere, intervene

medicine
NOUN
The medicine tasted bitter.
▷ drug, medication, pill, remedy

meditate on
VERB
Meditate on all of the benefits of reducing air pollution.
▷ consider, contemplate, ponder, reflect on

medley
NOUN
I chose a banana and an apple from the medley of fruit at the buffet.
▷ assortment, collection, mixture

meek
ADJECTIVE
He was too meek to defend himself.
▷ docile, submissive, timid, unassuming
ANTONYM bold

meet
VERB
1 *Use a dot to mark the point where the two lines meet.*
▷ join, link, touch, unite
ANTONYM separate
2 *You must meet the minimum height requirement in order to go on that ride.*
▷ fulfill, satisfy

melancholy
ADJECTIVE
His melancholy mood affected the rest of us.
▷ depressed, gloomy, glum, sad
ANTONYM cheerful

melody
NOUN
The melody was easy to sing.
▷ air, song, tune

memorable
ADJECTIVE
What is the most memorable event of your life?
▷ historic, notable, unforgettable

menace
NOUN
My clumsy brother is a menace in the kitchen.
▷ danger, hazard, threat

mend
VERB
Will you mend the tear in my jeans?
▷ fix, patch, repair

merchandise
NOUN
Most hockey leagues sell merchandise with the team logo.
▷ goods, products

merchant
NOUN
The flower merchant opens her store at 7 a.m.
▷ dealer, retailer, trader, vendor

merciful
ADJECTIVE
The convicted man begged the judge to be merciful.
▷ compassionate, humane, kind
ANTONYM merciless

merciless
ADJECTIVE
The merciless villain threw the princess into the dungeon.
▷ callous, cruel, heartless
ANTONYM merciful

merit
NOUN
No one saw any merit in his plan.
▷ asset, strength, virtue
VERB
Your ideas merit careful consideration.
▷ deserve, earn, justify

merry
ADJECTIVE
His laugh was so merry, we all laughed too.
▷ cheerful, gleeful, jolly
ANTONYM gloomy

mess
NOUN
Please tidy up the mess in here.
▷ clutter, disorder, jumble

mess up
VERB
If you mess up the cake, we will have no dessert.
▷ botch, damage, ruin, spoil

> ### MAKE IT MORE FORMAL
> **mess about** (*or* **around**) be busy without seeming to accomplish anything
> **mess with** provoke

message
NOUN
1 *Send me a message by e-mail.*
▷ letter, memo, note
2 *Does every story have to have a message?*
▷ moral, point, significance

method
NOUN
Show us your method for drawing perfect circles.
▷ procedure, system, technique

middle
NOUN
Cars are not permitted in the middle of the town.
▷ centre, core, heart

midget
ADJECTIVE
My little brother has a set of midget cars.
▷ little, miniature, small, tiny
ANTONYM giant

might
NOUN
They pushed with all their might, but the boulder wouldn't budge.
▷ force, power, strength

M

mild

ADJECTIVE

1 *Add pepper if the soup is too mild.*
▷ bland, tasteless, weak
ANTONYM strong
2 *His manner was mild but firm.*
▷ easygoing, gentle, kind, placid
3 *Do you think it is mild enough to go out without my jacket?*
▷ balmy, temperate, warm

mimic

VERB

I can mimic the way she sings.
▷ ape, copy, imitate

MAKE IT MORE FORMAL

give someone a piece of your mind speak angrily to someone
have a mind to intend to
keep in mind remember
make up your mind decide
never mind pay no attention to
on your mind much in your thoughts
speak your mind give your opinion
take someone's mind off something distract someone from something unpleasant

mingle

VERB

I know you're shy, but try to mingle at the party.
▷ circulate, socialize

miniature

ADJECTIVE

The miniature book fits in the palm of my hand.
▷ tiny, toy
NOUN
A miniature of the famous schooner sat on the display shelf.
▷ model, replica

minimum

ADJECTIVE

What is the minimum amount of time you need to finish your report?
▷ least, lowest
ANTONYM maximum

minor

ADJECTIVE

That is a minor detail.
▷ insignificant, slight, small, trivial
ANTONYM major
NOUN
In Canada, you are a minor until you turn eighteen.
▷ child, juvenile, youth
ANTONYM adult

minute

NOUN

She said she'd be back in a minute, but I'm still waiting.
▷ flash, instant, moment
ADJECTIVE
A minute speck of dust will seem large under a microscope.
▷ microscopic, small, tiny
ANTONYM huge

miracle

NOUN

It was a miracle that nobody was seriously hurt.
▷ marvel, wonder

miraculous

ADJECTIVE

The injured skydiver made a miraculous recovery.
▷ extraordinary, phenomenal, unbelievable, wondrous

miscellaneous

ADJECTIVE

The cupboard is full of miscellaneous items.
▷ assorted, mixed, varied, various

mischievous

ADJECTIVE

He's a mischievous child.
▷ impish, naughty, playful

miserable

ADJECTIVE

1 *She was miserable when her best friend moved away.*
▷ sad, unhappy, wretched
ANTONYM cheerful
2 *Tidying my room is a miserable task.*
▷ cheerless, depressing, dismal, wretched

misery

NOUN

She groaned in misery.
▷ anguish, despair, grief, sadness, sorrow, unhappiness, woe
ANTONYM joy

mislay

VERB

If you mislay your permission form, you can't come on the field trip.
▷ lose, misplace

mislead

VERB

She tried to mislead us into believing she was sick.
▷ deceive, delude, fool

miss

VERB

When you are on holiday, do you miss your home?
▷ long for, pine for, yearn for

M

missing
ADJECTIVE
*One of my gloves is **missing**.*
▷ lost, mislaid, misplaced

mission
NOUN
*It was our **mission** to find fresh water.*
▷ assignment, job, task

mist
NOUN
*The **mist** made it difficult to see across the lake.*
▷ fog, haze, smog

mistake
NOUN
*If you see a **mistake**, fix it.*
▷ blunder, error, fault, oversight
VERB
*Don't **mistake** my yawn for boredom—I'm just tired.*
▷ confuse, misinterpret

mistaken
ADJECTIVE
*You were **mistaken** if you thought I didn't want dessert.*
▷ incorrect, misguided, wrong

mistreat
VERB
*What kind of person would **mistreat** an animal?*
▷ abuse, ill-treat

mistrust
VERB
*I **mistrust** some of the things that I read online.*
▷ disbelieve, distrust, doubt, suspect

misunderstanding
NOUN
*We had a **misunderstanding**, but now we're friends again.*
▷ argument, disagreement, quarrel

mix
VERB
1 *Mix the ingredients with a wooden spoon.*
▷ blend, combine
2 *You have to **mix** if you want to meet new people.*
▷ mingle, socialize

mixture
NOUN
*The **mixture** of flour and water was very sticky.*
▷ blend, combination

mix-up
NOUN
*The server apologized for the **mix-up** with our order.*
▷ error, mistake, misunderstanding

moan
VERB
*You always **moan** about how many chores you have.*
▷ complain, grumble, whine

mob
NOUN
*There was a **mob** of people at the mall.*
▷ crowd, horde, mass, throng

mock
VERB
*Don't **mock** him just because he doesn't play the game as well as you.*
▷ deride, ridicule, scoff at, tease
ADJECTIVE
*These boots are made of **mock** leather.*
▷ fake, false, imitation, phony, sham

model
NOUN
*This is a **model** of the solar system.*
▷ mock-up, replica, representation
VERB
*I'm going to **model** a dinosaur out of clay.*
▷ fashion, form, mould, sculpt, shape

moderate
ADJECTIVE
*A **moderate** amount of exercise is part of a well-balanced lifestyle.*
▷ average, fair, reasonable

modern
ADJECTIVE
1 *Sorting garbage for recycling is a part of **modern** society.*
▷ contemporary, current, present-day
2 *Does the lab have **modern** equipment?*
▷ the latest, new, up-to-date, up-to-the-minute
ANTONYM old-fashioned

modest
ADJECTIVE
1 *There's a **modest** improvement in her work.*
▷ limited, moderate, small
2 *She is **modest** about her achievements.*
▷ humble, unassuming, unpretentious
ANTONYM conceited

modify
VERB
Modify the recipe by adding peaches or pears.
▷ adapt, adjust, alter, change

moist
ADJECTIVE
*I don't like this **moist** weather.*
▷ clammy, damp, humid
ANTONYM dry

M

moisture
NOUN
*A dehumidifier takes the **moisture** out of the air.*
▷ damp, dampness, humidity, wetness

moment
NOUN
1 *He stopped for a **moment** to catch his breath.*
▷ minute, second, split second
2 *At the same **moment**, we both looked up.*
▷ instant, point, time

monarch
NOUN
*The **monarch** owned many castles throughout the kingdom.*
▷ king, queen, ruler, sovereign

money
NOUN
*I have no **money**.*
▷ cash, currency, funds

MAKE IT MORE FORMAL
for my money in my opinion
on the money exact

monotonous
ADJECTIVE
*The speaker had a **monotonous** voice.*
▷ boring, dull, repetitive, tedious

monster
NOUN
*The **monster** in the cartoon had red eyes.*
▷ beast, fiend, savage

mood
NOUN
*Not even the rain will spoil my cheerful **mood**.*
▷ humour, spirits, state of mind, temper

moody
ADJECTIVE
*You get very **moody** when things don't go your way.*
▷ grumpy, irritable, sulky, sullen

mope
VERB
*My little brother will **mope** if we don't let him play with us.*
▷ brood, sulk

moral
ADJECTIVE
*Helping others is a **moral** thing to do.*
▷ ethical, honourable, virtuous
ANTONYM immoral

more
ADJECTIVE
*May I have **more** time to finish my work?*
▷ additional, extra, supplementary

morning
NOUN
*Is it **morning** already?*
▷ dawn, daybreak, sunrise
ANTONYM evening

morose
ADJECTIVE
*She was feeling **morose** and would not speak.*
▷ broody, glum, sullen
ANTONYM cheerful

morsel
NOUN
*I couldn't eat another **morsel**.*
▷ bit, bite, crumb, scrap

mortal
ADJECTIVE
*This spider's bite is **mortal**.*
▷ deadly, fatal, lethal

most
ADJECTIVE
*She received the **most** number of votes.*
▷ greatest, highest

mostly
ADVERB
***Mostly**, I eat lunch at school.*
▷ as a rule, mainly, normally, usually

motion
NOUN
1 *The **motion** of the boat made me ill.*
▷ action, movement
2 *What does that **motion** mean?*
▷ gesture, signal

motionless
ADJECTIVE
*He stood **motionless** with fear.*
▷ immobile, stationary, still, unmoving
ANTONYM moving

motivate
VERB
*How do you **motivate** yourself to keep exercising?*
▷ drive, inspire, move, prompt

motive
NOUN
*I think that she is hiding her true **motive**.*
▷ aim, intention, purpose, reason

motto
NOUN
*He said his **motto** is "Enjoy life."*
▷ catchphrase, saying, slogan

mould
VERB
***Mould** the clay into any shape you like.*
▷ form, shape

M

mouldy
ADJECTIVE
The bread is mouldy.
▷ musty, rotten, stale

mound
NOUN
1 *Place the garbage in a mound by the curb.*
▷ heap, pile, stack
2 *We climbed a mound to get a better view.*
▷ bank, hill, rise

mount
VERB
1 *Mount the stairs and wait at the top.*
▷ ascend, climb, scale
ANTONYM descend
2 *In most mystery stories, tension will mount just before the villain is caught.*
▷ build up, escalate, increase, intensify, rise

mourn
VERB
He will mourn the loss of his friend.
▷ grieve, lament
ANTONYM rejoice

mournful
ADJECTIVE
The mournful sound turned out to be the wind.
▷ doleful, sorrowful
ANTONYM cheerful

mouth
NOUN
We set up camp at the mouth of the cave.
▷ entrance, opening

mouthful
NOUN
Try a mouthful of this pasta.
▷ bite, morsel, taste, tidbit

move
VERB
1 See box on next page.
2 *Our family might move to the Maritimes.*
▷ migrate, relocate, transfer
3 *This story will move you deeply.*
▷ affect, touch

MAKE IT MORE FORMAL

get a move on hurry
make your move take action
on the move moving about

movement
NOUN
This equipment tracks the movement of the hurricane.
▷ flow, motion, progress

moving
ADJECTIVE
The speech was deeply moving.
▷ affecting, emotional, stirring, touching

much
ADJECTIVE
I don't have much time.
▷ abundant, ample, considerable
ADVERB
I feel much better now.
▷ considerably, greatly, noticeably, significantly

mud
NOUN
The dog tracked mud all over the house.
▷ dirt, filth, mud, ooze, scum, slime

muddle
NOUN
My notes are in a hopeless muddle.
▷ jumble, mess, tangle

muddy
ADJECTIVE
1 *Put your muddy soccer uniform in the washing machine.*
▷ dirty, filthy, grimy, grubby
ANTONYM clean
2 *The stream was too muddy to see any fish.*
▷ cloudy, murky, unclear
ANTONYM clear

muffle
VERB
These earplugs should muffle some of the noise.
▷ dampen, deaden, stifle

mug
VERB
The thief was caught before he could mug another victim.
▷ ambush, assault, attack, rob

muggy
ADJECTIVE
A swim is refreshing when the weather is muggy.
▷ clammy, humid, sticky

mumble
VERB
I can't understand what you say when you mumble.
▷ murmur, mutter

munch
VERB
It's impossible to munch quietly on an apple.
▷ chew, chomp

murder
VERB
Is it acceptable to murder animals for food?
▷ assassinate, execute, kill, slaughter, slay

REPLACE AN OVERUSED WORD: MOVE

Move is not a very expressive verb. You can use a more vivid substitute to say something about the way in which a person or thing moves.

- If you **bolt**, you suddenly start to run very fast, often because something has frightened you.
  If I hear any strange noises, I'll just bolt for the door.

- If you **crawl**, you move slowly.
  I was so tired, I could hardly crawl out of bed.

- If you **creep** somewhere, you move slowly and quietly.
  He came home late, and tried to creep to his room without waking his brother.

- If you **dash** (or **dart**), you move quickly and suddenly.
  She jumped up, ready to dash away.

- If you **fly**, you move with a lot of speed.
  I must fly, or I'll be late for school.

- If you **hurry** (or **race**, or **rush**), you move as quickly as you can.
  If we hurry, we might be able to catch the last train.

- If you **jog**, you run slowly.
  Do you prefer to jog in the morning, or after school?

- If you **run**, you move quickly because you are in a hurry to get somewhere.
  I can't get there in time, even if I run all the way.

- If you **scamper**, you move quickly with small, light steps.
  The little girl will scamper off as soon as you say "Go."

- When you **scurry**, you move hurriedly, usually to avoid something.
  As soon as he saw me, he turned around and started to scurry back inside.

- If you **slither** somewhere, you move by sliding along the ground in an uneven way.
  First she slipped, then she began to slither along the icy path.

- If you **tear** (or **tear off**) somewhere, you move there very quickly, often in an uncontrolled or dangerous way.
  Look at him tear off down the street! He'll knock someone over!

- If you **wriggle**, you move there by twisting and turning your body.
  Sit still and don't wriggle.

M

muscular
ADJECTIVE
The gymnast was muscular yet very graceful.
▷ athletic, brawny, powerful
ANTONYM puny

mushy
ADJECTIVE
Carrots become mushy when overcooked.
▷ soft, soggy, squashy, squishy

musical instrument
NOUN
See picture on next page.

must
NOUN
Being on time is an absolute must.
▷ duty, necessity, obligation, requirement

mutiny
NOUN
The crew held a mutiny and took control of the ship.
▷ protest, rebellion, revolt, uprising

mysterious
ADJECTIVE
1 *Some mysterious symbols had been scratched on the rock.*
▷ baffling, mystifying, puzzling, strange, unexplained
2 *I wonder why my sister is being so mysterious.*
▷ furtive, secretive
ANTONYM open

mystery
NOUN
The mystery may never be solved.
▷ enigma, puzzle, riddle

mystify
VERB
This riddle is sure to mystify you.
▷ baffle, bewilder, confuse, puzzle

myth
NOUN
The storyteller told us a myth about dragons.
▷ fable, fantasy, legend, tale

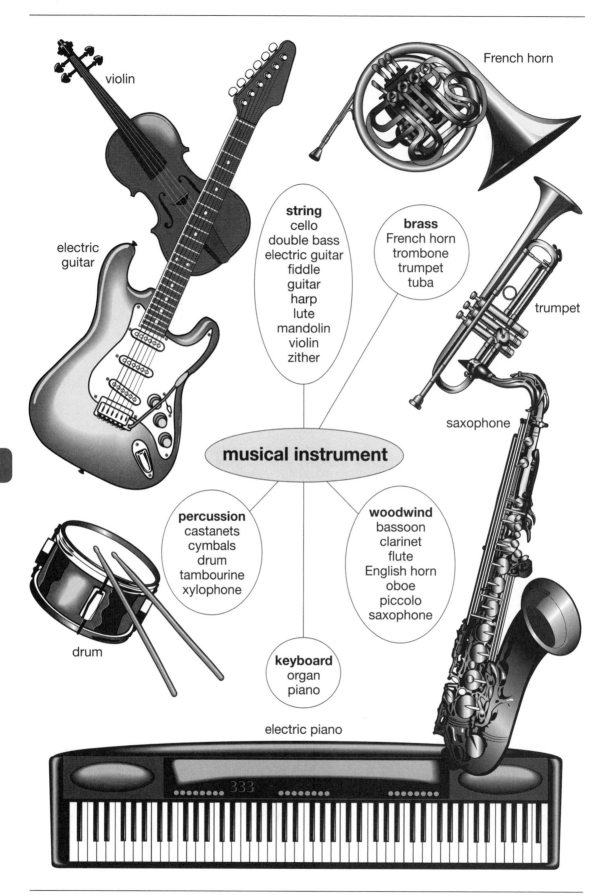

violin

French horn

electric
guitar

string
cello
double bass
electric guitar
fiddle
guitar
harp
lute
mandolin
violin
zither

brass
French horn
trombone
trumpet
tuba

trumpet

saxophone

musical instrument

M

percussion
castanets
cymbals
drum
tambourine
xylophone

woodwind
bassoon
clarinet
flute
English horn
oboe
piccolo
saxophone

drum

keyboard
organ
piano

electric piano

N n

nab
VERB
Nab the thief before he gets away!
▷ apprehend, arrest, capture, catch

nag
VERB
If you nag, I won't do what you ask.
▷ badger, harass, hassle, pester

naive
ADJECTIVE
He's naive enough to believe that story.
▷ gullible, innocent, trusting
ANTONYM cunning

naked
ADJECTIVE
The sun will burn your naked shoulders.
▷ bare, nude, unclothed
ANTONYM clothed

name
NOUN
1 *Do you know the name for that gadget?*
▷ designation, label, term
2 *Your name will be ruined if you cheat.*
▷ character, reputation
VERB
We will name the committee at our next meeting.
▷ appoint, assign, choose, nominate

MAKE IT MORE FORMAL

call names insult by swearing at
you name it whatever you like
name after give someone the same name as
the name of the game the main objective
give something a bad name cause disrepute
    to something

nap
VERB
I'm going to nap for an hour.
▷ doze, rest, sleep, slumber, snooze

narrate
VERB
She will narrate her poem now.
▷ recite, recount, relate, tell

narrow
ADJECTIVE
I do not think the piano will go through that narrow space.
▷ constricted, cramped, slender, tight
ANTONYM wide

nasty
ADJECTIVE
The rotting food had a nasty odour.
▷ disagreeable, disgusting, foul, unpleasant, vile
ANTONYM pleasant

nation
NOUN
1 *Our nation is Canada.*
▷ country, homeland, land
2 *The nation can vote for a new government.*
▷ citizens, people, population

native
NOUN
Are you a native of Toronto?
▷ citizen, inhabitant, local, resident

natural
ADJECTIVE
1 *Tears are a natural reaction to sad news.*
▷ normal, typical, usual
2 *She was so natural with the children.*
▷ genuine, real, unaffected
ANTONYM false
3 *He's a natural comedian.*
▷ effortless, instinctive, intuitive

nature
NOUN
It's not in my nature to sit still.
▷ character, disposition, makeup, personality, temperament

naughty
ADJECTIVE
She was a naughty child.
▷ bad, disobedient, mischievous
ANTONYM well-behaved

navigate
VERB
Navigate the boat toward the shore.
▷ guide, manoeuvre, pilot, steer

near
ADJECTIVE
1 *Is there a library near here?*
▷ close by, nearby
ANTONYM far
2 *The start of the school year is near.*
▷ approaching, imminent, looming, upcoming
PREPOSITION
Sit with me near the fire.
▷ alongside, by, close to, next to

nearly
ADVERB
The theatre was nearly empty.
▷ almost, practically, virtually

N

neat
ADJECTIVE
My bedroom is always neat.
▷ orderly, tidy
ANTONYM untidy

necessary
ADJECTIVE
Warm clothing is necessary if you plan to ski.
▷ essential, indispensable, required, vital

negative
ADJECTIVE
Don't be so negative.
▷ critical, discouraging, pessimistic
ANTONYM positive

neglect
VERB
1 *Don't neglect your health.*
▷ disregard, forget, ignore, overlook
2 *Did you neglect to look both ways?*
▷ fail, forget

negotiate
VERB
Try to negotiate a better deal.
▷ bargain for, discuss, haggle for

neighbourhood
NOUN
My neighbourhood has many apartment buildings.
▷ environs, surroundings, vicinity

N

nerve
NOUN
It took nerve to dive into the cold water.
▷ bravery, courage, daring, pluck

nervous
ADJECTIVE
I'm always a bit nervous before a test.
▷ anxious, apprehensive, edgy, jittery, jumpy, worried
ANTONYM calm

neutral
ADJECTIVE
Some countries remain neutral during a war.
▷ disinterested, impartial, nonaligned

never
ADVERB
I would never tell a secret.
▷ at no time, not ever, under no circumstances

new
ADJECTIVE
See box at foot of this page.

news
NOUN
What news is there?
▷ information, intelligence

next
ADVERB
What should I do next?
▷ afterwards, subsequently
ADJECTIVE
He's in the next room.
▷ adjacent, adjoining

nibble
VERB
Nibble on some carrots if you're hungry.
▷ gnaw, munch, snack

nice
ADJECTIVE
See box on next page.

nick
NOUN
I noticed a nick on the fender of mom's car.
▷ cut, dent, score, scratch

night
NOUN
Bats fly at night.
▷ dark, dusk, evening
ANTONYM day

REPLACE AN OVERUSED WORD: NEW

Depending on the sense of **new** that you mean, there are other adjectives that you can use to add more interest to your writing.

- **recently discovered or created**
  I've seen all the current movies.
  What's the title of her latest book?
  The local TV stations compete to have up-to-the-minute information.

- **unfamiliar**
  You are too young to travel alone in a strange country.

I'm unaccustomed to living downtown.
This topic is completely unknown to me.

- **untried**
  Let's take a different route to school for a change.
  Can you think of a novel way to keep fit?
  I believe he has come up with an original idea.

REPLACE AN OVERUSED WORD: NICE

When you are about to use the adjective **nice**, try to think of a more descriptive and interesting word instead. Here are some ideas for words that you might use.

- **a nice appearance**
  *He's an **attractive** man.*
  *She looked **beautiful**.*
  *Her brother is **good-looking**.*
  *You look very **pretty** in that outfit.*

- **a nice place**
  *There is a **beautiful** beach nearby.*
  *She made a **comfortable** home for her children.*
  *This would be a **delightful** spot for a picnic.*
  *There is a **relaxing** atmosphere at her apartment.*

- **nice clothes**
  *Those are **fashionable** jeans.*
  *Mom gave me a pair of very **elegant** boots.*
  *I bought a pair of **smart** black pants.*
  *My brother has really **stylish** clothes.*

- **a nice time**
  *Going skating is an **agreeable** way to spend a Saturday afternoon.*

*Thank you; I had a **delightful** evening.*
*The trip was **enjoyable**, apart from the weather.*
*What a **pleasant** surprise!*

- **a nice personality**
  *She's **considerate** to everyone.*
  *He is always **good-natured**.*
  *Be **kind** to your brother.*
  *Thank you for the **thoughtful** card.*

- **nice food**
  *The soup had an **appetizing** smell.*
  *Dad bakes **delicious** pies.*
  *These peaches are **mouthwatering**.*
  *There were several **tasty** dishes at the buffet.*

- **nice weather**
  *It was a **beautiful** evening.*
  *The morning was **bright**.*
  *Cut the grass in **fine** weather.*
  *What a **glorious** day!*

nimble
ADJECTIVE
The nimble gymnast did four backflips in a row.
▷ agile, lively
ANTONYM awkward

noble
ADJECTIVE
It is noble to volunteer in your community.
▷ decent, generous, gracious, honourable
ANTONYM ignoble

nod
VERB
Just nod when you want me to come over there.
▷ beckon, signal

nod off
VERB
I'm so tired, I could nod off.
▷ doze, nap, sleep, snooze

noise
NOUN
There's too much noise in here.
▷ clamour, commotion, din, racket
ANTONYM silence

noisy
ADJECTIVE
Fire alarms have to be noisy.
▷ deafening, earsplitting, loud, piercing
ANTONYM quiet

nominate
VERB
I would like to nominate her for president.
▷ name, recommend, submit, suggest

nonsense
NOUN
His speech sounded like complete nonsense.
▷ drivel, garbage, gibberish, rubbish

non-stop
ADJECTIVE
Non-stop rain caused severe flooding in several areas.
▷ constant, continuous, relentless, steady

norm
NOUN
Sharing household chores is the norm in our family.
▷ custom, rule, standard

normal

ADJECTIVE

Drinking lots of water is part of my normal routine.

▷ average, ordinary, regular, standard, typical, usual

ANTONYM unusual

nosey

ADJECTIVE

My nosey brother listens to my phone conversations.

▷ curious, inquisitive, prying

MAKE IT MORE FORMAL

not at all no
not far from near
not guilty innocent
not many few
not quite almost

---

notable

ADJECTIVE

She is a notable scientist.

▷ celebrated, important, noteworthy, prominent

ANTONYM insignificant

note

NOUN

1 *Put a note on the calendar.*

▷ memo, message, reminder

2 *I detect a note of anger in your voice.*

▷ hint, shade, tone, touch, trace

VERB

Note how gracefully the actor moves.

▷ notice, observe, perceive

notice

VERB

If you notice anything unusual, tell me.

▷ detect, discern, note, observe, perceive

NOUN

The notice gave the date of the performance.

▷ ad, advertisement, announcement, bill, poster, sign

noticeable

ADJECTIVE

There was a noticeable mark on the wall.

▷ clear, evident, obvious, prominent, visible

notify

VERB

Notify us of any change to the rules.

▷ advise, alert, inform, tell, warn

notion

NOUN

I don't know where he got that notion.

▷ belief, idea, impression

nourishing

ADJECTIVE

Fruit is a nourishing snack.

▷ beneficial, healthful, nutritious, wholesome

novel

ADJECTIVE

Try to come up with a novel idea.

▷ fresh, original, unique, unusual

ANTONYM well-worn

now

ADVERB

I feel ill and would like to see the doctor now.

▷ at once, immediately, right now, straightaway, without delay

ANTONYM later

MAKE IT MORE FORMAL

now and again sometimes
now and then occasionally

---

nude

ADJECTIVE

People can swim nude at that beach.

▷ naked, unclothed, undressed

ANTONYM covered

nudge

VERB

Nudge him with your elbow.

▷ poke, prod

nuisance

NOUN

Missing the bus is a nuisance.

▷ annoyance, bother, hassle, inconvenience

numb

ADJECTIVE

We were numb with fear during the storm.

▷ deadened, frozen, paralyzed

number

NOUN

1 *He chose a number between one and twenty.*

▷ digit, figure, numeral

See picture on next page.

2 *A number of people were waiting to enter the arena.*

▷ crowd, group, horde, multitude

MAKE IT MORE FORMAL

do a number on someone treat someone badly
have someone's number know someone's character

---

nutritious

ADJECTIVE

Eating a nutritious breakfast is a good way to start the day.

▷ healthful, nourishing, wholesome

cardinal number

one	eleven	fifty
two	twelve	hundred
three	thirteen	thousand
four	fourteen	million
five	fifteen	
six	sixteen	
seven	seventeen	
eight	eighteen	
nine	nineteen	
ten	twenty	

ordinal number

first	eleventh	fiftieth
second	twelfth	hundredth
third	thirteenth	thousandth
fourth	fourteenth	millionth
fifth	fifteenth	
sixth	sixteenth	
seventh	seventeenth	
eighth	eighteenth	
ninth	nineteenth	
tenth	twentieth	

number

Roman numeral

1	I	11	XI
2	II	12	XII
3	III	13	XIII
4	IV	14	XIV
5	V	15	XV
6	VI	16	XVI
7	VII	17	XVII
8	VIII	18	XVIII
9	IX	19	XIX
10	X	20	XX

50	L
100	C
1000	M
1 000 000	$\overline{M}$

N

Oo

oath
NOUN
The witness gave an oath to tell the truth.
▷ pledge, promise, vow

obey
VERB
She promised to obey the rules.
▷ abide by, comply with, follow
ANTONYM disobey

object
NOUN
1 *What is that object you are holding?*
▷ article, item
2 *The object of the game is to score points.*
▷ aim, goal, intention, point, purpose

object to
VERB
I object to your unfair comment.
▷ oppose, protest
ANTONYM approve

obligation
NOUN
He has an obligation to finish his project.
▷ commitment, duty, responsibility

obnoxious
ADJECTIVE
The obnoxious fans were asked to leave the arena.
▷ loathsome, offensive, repulsive
ANTONYM pleasant

observant
ADJECTIVE
An observant person will be a good witness.
▷ attentive, perceptive, watchful

observation
NOUN
1 *The police have the store under observation.*
▷ scrutiny, study, surveillance
2 *She made the observation that they should hurry.*
▷ comment, remark, statement

observe
VERB
1 *She used a telescope to observe the moon.*
▷ monitor, study, survey, watch
2 *I could observe that you are late, but I suppose you know that already.*
▷ comment, mention, remark, state
3 *We should all observe the laws of Canada.*
▷ abide by, follow, respect

obsession
NOUN
My obsession is to reduce, reuse, and recycle.
▷ fixation, preoccupation

obsolete
ADJECTIVE
This computer is obsolete.
▷ archaic, old-fashioned, outdated, outmoded
ANTONYM current

obstacle
NOUN
I can't sing in tune, which is an obstacle to my joining the choir!
▷ barrier, hindrance, obstruction

obtain
VERB
He has to obtain permission.
▷ acquire, procure, secure

obvious
ADJECTIVE
She told an obvious lie.
▷ apparent, clear, evident, plain, self-evident

occasion
NOUN
1 *Our school graduation was an important occasion.*
▷ affair, event
2 *Saturday was a good occasion to read my book.*
▷ chance, opportunity, time

occupant
NOUN
The new occupant has moved in next door.
▷ inhabitant, resident

occupation
NOUN
You do not have to choose your occupation yet.
▷ calling, job, profession, trade

occupied
ADJECTIVE
He was occupied when I called.
▷ busy, engaged, unavailable
ANTONYM free

occur
VERB
Will trouble occur if they do not show up?
▷ appear, arise, happen

occurrence
NOUN
She lost the race, which was a rare occurrence.
▷ circumstance, event, happening, incident

O

REPLACE AN OVERUSED WORD: OLD

Depending on the meaning of **old** that you want, there are a number of adjectives that you can use instead.

- **having lived for a long time**

  He has an *aging* aunt who lives next door.

  The whole family has deep respect for my *ancient* grandparents.

  Is your uncle an *elderly* man?

  My grandmother is a *senior* member of the curling club.

- **in the past**

  Museums hold treasures from *bygone* civilizations.

  Don't keep talking about my *past* mistakes.

  The *previous* owner kept this bike in good condition.

  There are no written records from those *remote* times.

- **out of date**

  Slang quickly becomes *dated*.

  Does a new computer become *obsolete* as soon as you unpack it?

  Try to imitate an *old-fashioned* style of writing.

  The city wants to replace all its *outmoded* streetcars.

odd
ADJECTIVE
He is behaving in a very odd way.
▷ bizarre, peculiar, strange, unusual

odour
NOUN
1 *What is that delicious odour coming from the kitchen?*
▷ aroma, scent, smell
2 *We smelled the odour of skunk in our yard.*
▷ reek, stench, stink

offence
NOUN
He was convicted of the offence and put in jail.
▷ crime, violation

offend
VERB
Her outspoken comments always offend someone.
▷ affront, insult, outrage

offensive
ADJECTIVE
Their behaviour was offensive, and they should apologize.
▷ disgusting, distasteful, insulting, objectionable, rude

offer
VERB
Will you offer the guests something to eat when they arrive?
▷ give, present
NOUN
He accepted my offer to trade skateboards.
▷ bid, proposal

official
ADJECTIVE
I have an official NHL hockey sweater.
▷ authorized, certified
NOUN
She is the official in charge of complaints.
▷ executive, officer, representative

offspring
NOUN
My grandparents had just one offspring.
▷ child, descendant, heir
ANTONYM ancestor

often
ADVERB
We often go to the park to walk the dog.
▷ frequently, regularly, repeatedly
ANTONYM seldom

OK
ADJECTIVE
Is it OK to turn the music up a bit?
▷ acceptable, satisfactory, tolerable

old
ADJECTIVE
See box at top of this page.

old-fashioned
ADJECTIVE
Our old-fashioned black-and-white TV still works.
▷ dated, obsolete, outdated, outmoded
ANTONYM fashionable

omen
NOUN
It was a bad omen that we missed the bus.
▷ sign, warning

O

ominous

ADJECTIVE

He looked up and saw ominous grey clouds.

▷ sinister, threatening

on

PREPOSITION

We enjoyed the debate on global warming.

▷ about, concerning, related to

MAKE IT MORE FORMAL

on account of because of
on and off at some times and not other times
on and on without stopping
on edge restless
on guard alert
on hand handy
on the dot exactly
on the whole as a rule
on time punctual

---

once

ADVERB

She played soccer once, but now she plays hockey.

▷ earlier, formerly, previously

MAKE IT MORE FORMAL

once in a while sometimes
once more again

---

onlooker

NOUN

I was an onlooker and not involved in the fight.

▷ bystander, observer, spectator, witness

only

ADJECTIVE

He is my only brother.

▷ one, single, sole

onset

NOUN

I usually get a very sore throat at the onset of a cold.

▷ beginning, commencement, start

ANTONYM conclusion

onslaught

NOUN

The onslaught caused the enemy to surrender.

▷ assault, attack

ooze

VERB

The honey started to ooze from the cracked jar.

▷ flow, leak, seep

NOUN

My shoes got covered in ooze.

▷ mire, muck, slime

open

ADJECTIVE

He was open with me when I asked for advice.

▷ candid, frank, honest

MAKE IT MORE FORMAL

be open with speak candidly
into the open not concealed
open up fully reveal

---

opening

ADJECTIVE

She went to the art show on the opening day.

▷ first, initial

ANTONYM closing

NOUN

1 *At the opening of the play, the actors are in a cave.*

▷ beginning, commencement, start

ANTONYM conclusion

2 *He looked through the opening in the fence.*

▷ crack, gap, hole, slot, space

operate

VERB

Does the old computer still operate?

▷ function, run, work

opinion

NOUN

In my opinion, we should leave now.

▷ belief, estimation, judgment, point of view, view

opponent

NOUN

Who was your toughest opponent?

▷ adversary, competitor, enemy, foe, rival

ANTONYM ally

opportune

ADJECTIVE

Morning is an opportune time for me to walk.

▷ favourable, fitting, suitable

ANTONYM inopportune

opportunity

NOUN

Did you have an opportunity to visit the RCMP Centennial Museum in Regina?

▷ chance, occasion

opposite

ADJECTIVE

The two local newspapers had opposite viewpoints.

▷ conflicting, contrary, opposed

opposition

NOUN

There was opposition when the pool shut down.

▷ disapproval, hostility, resistance

ANTONYM support

opt for
VERB
Which flavour of ice cream did you opt for?
▷ choose, decide on, pick, select

optimistic
ADJECTIVE
He is optimistic that he will do well in the spelling bee.
▷ confident, hopeful, positive
ANTONYM pessimistic

option
NOUN
We have the option of going today or tomorrow.
▷ alternative, choice

opulent
ADJECTIVE
We visited the opulent historic house.
▷ lavish, luxurious, sumptuous

oral
ADJECTIVE
They had an oral agreement on the price.
▷ spoken, verbal

orange
ADJECTIVE
The orange carpet made the room look cheerful.
▷ amber, apricot, peach, tangerine

ordeal
NOUN
Getting lost was a terrible ordeal.
▷ agony, nightmare, torture, trial

order
NOUN
1 *The army officer gave the order to march.*
▷ command, instruction
2 *He quickly restored order to the group.*
▷ harmony, organization, regularity
ANTONYM disorder

> ### MAKE IT MORE FORMAL
> **in short order** quickly
> **order about** (*or* **around**) constantly command
> **out of order** not arranged properly; not working properly

orderly
ADJECTIVE
Our orderly desks pleased the teacher.
▷ neat, organized, tidy
ANTONYM disorderly

ordinary
ADJECTIVE
We do our ordinary chores after school.
▷ normal, regular, routine, standard, usual
ANTONYM special

organization
NOUN
1 *The charitable organization supports the food bank.*
▷ association, body, group, institution
2 *The organization of the bake sale was well done.*
▷ planning, structuring

organize
VERB
I will organize the trip.
▷ arrange, plan, set up

origin
NOUN
Try to find the origin of that word.
▷ derivation, root, source

original
ADJECTIVE
1 *The sale price is fifty percent of the original price.*
▷ earliest, first, initial
2 *We need an original topic for the debate.*
▷ fresh, new, novel

originate
VERB
Where did that idea originate?
▷ begin, start

ornament
NOUN
See picture on next page.

ornate
ADJECTIVE
That old picture frame is too ornate for me.
▷ elaborate, fancy, showy
ANTONYM plain

out
ADVERB
He will be out for the afternoon.
▷ absent, away, elsewhere
ANTONYM in
ADJECTIVE
Bell-bottoms are definitely out this year.
▷ dated, old-fashioned, outdated, unfashionable
ANTONYM trendy

> ### MAKE IT MORE FORMAL
> **out loud** aloud
> **out of danger** safe
> **out of shape** unfit
> **out of the ordinary** exceptional
> **out of the question** impossible

outcome
NOUN
What was the outcome of the argument?
▷ consequence, effect, result

O

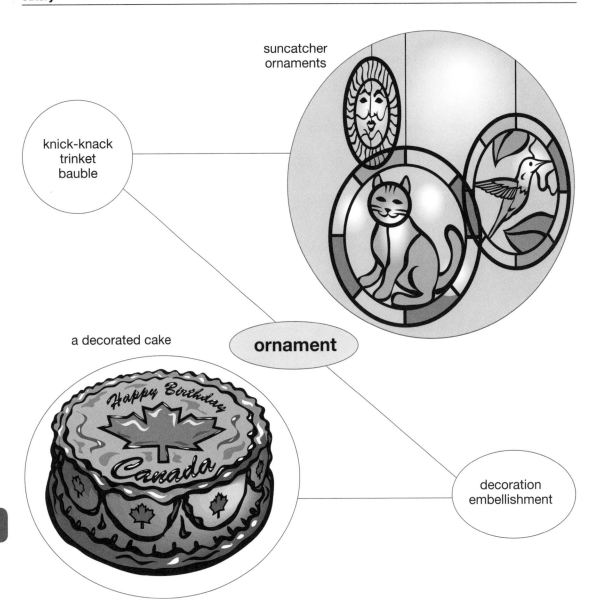

suncatcher
ornaments

knick-knack
trinket
bauble

a decorated cake

ornament

decoration
embellishment

outcry
NOUN
There was a great outcry about the abused dog.
▷ commotion, uproar

outdated
ADJECTIVE
We replaced our outdated computer equipment.
▷ dated, obsolete, old-fashioned
ANTONYM modern

outdo
VERB
They always try to outdo each other in class.
▷ beat, outshine, surpass, top

outfit
NOUN
Our camping outfit is ready for the trip.
▷ equipment, gear, kit

outing
NOUN
Where did you go on your outing?
▷ excursion, expedition, trip

outlandish
ADJECTIVE
I have never heard such an outlandish remark!
▷ bizarre, eccentric, odd, strange
ANTONYM ordinary

outlaw
VERB
Will the city outlaw skateboarding on roads?
▷ ban, forbid, prohibit

outline
VERB
Please outline your plan.
▷ describe, draft, sketch, summarize
NOUN
1 *He was asked for an outline of his project.*
▷ rundown, summary
2 *Draw an outline in black crayon.*
▷ profile, shape, silhouette

outlook
NOUN
1 *She has a practical outlook for the future.*
▷ attitude, perspective, viewpoint
2 *The weather outlook is not good.*
▷ forecast, future, prospect

outrage
NOUN
The theft of the pension money was an outrage.
▷ atrocity, crime, disgrace, scandal
VERB
If the town closes the library, it will certainly outrage the citizens.
▷ anger, horrify, offend, scandalize, shock

outrageous
ADJECTIVE
The price of the basketball was outrageous.
▷ excessive, exorbitant, extreme
ANTONYM moderate

outright
ADJECTIVE
He told an outright lie.
▷ absolute, complete, pure, total, utter

outset
NOUN
She was against the plan from the outset.
▷ beginning, start
ANTONYM end

outside
ADJECTIVE
Please leave the outside light on for me.
▷ exterior, external, outdoor
ANTONYM inside

MAKE IT MORE FORMAL

an outside chance a small chance
at the outside at the most
outside of with the exception of

---

outskirts
NOUN
The new mall is on the outskirts of town.
▷ bounds, edge, limits, perimeter

outspoken
ADJECTIVE
He is outspoken, but fair.
▷ blunt, candid, frank

outstanding
ADJECTIVE
1 *She gave an outstanding piano performance.*
▷ excellent, exceptional, first-rate, great, superb
2 *You must pay the outstanding amount now.*
▷ due, overdue, owing, payable

outward
ADJECTIVE
His outward reaction did not show how he really felt.
▷ exterior, external, surface

over
PREPOSITION
We spent over an hour playing in the park.
▷ above, beyond, in excess of
ADJECTIVE
When school was over, they went home.
▷ at an end, complete, done, finished

MAKE IT MORE FORMAL

over again once more
over and over again and again
over (and done) with finished

---

overall
ADJECTIVE
The overall attendance for the school play was 725.
▷ complete, general, total

overbearing
ADJECTIVE
No one likes an overbearing person.
▷ arrogant, bossy, domineering

overcast
ADJECTIVE
Plant the seeds on an overcast day.
▷ cloudy, dark, dull
ANTONYM bright

overcome
VERB
I have been able to overcome my fear of snakes.
▷ conquer, surmount, vanquish

overjoyed
ADJECTIVE
We were overjoyed to see our friends from Whitehorse.
▷ delighted, ecstatic, elated, jubilant
ANTONYM disappointed

O

overlook

VERB

1 *I will try to overlook your rudeness.*
▷ excuse, forgive, pardon
2 *He always seems to overlook my requests.*
▷ disregard, ignore, neglect

overpower

VERB

Their basketball team managed to overpower us.
▷ conquer, crush, overwhelm, subdue

oversee

VERB

She was asked to oversee the department.
▷ direct, manage, supervise

oversight

NOUN

The oversight created a problem for everyone.
▷ blunder, error, fault, mistake

overturn

VERB

1 *The waves caused the boat to overturn.*
▷ capsize, topple, upset
2 *Can a judge overturn the verdict of a jury?*
▷ overrule, reverse

own

ADJECTIVE

How can he help others if he can't solve his own problems?
▷ individual, personal, private

MAKE IT MORE FORMAL

come into your own get the success you deserve
get your own back take revenge
hold your own keep your position of strength

O

P p

pack
NOUN
A pack of children raced around the beach.
▷ crowd, gang, group
VERB
Pack the cooler with lots of food.
▷ cram, fill, load, stuff

package
NOUN
We sent a package of books to my brother.
▷ bundle, carton, parcel

pact
NOUN
The two countries have a peace pact.
▷ agreement, contract, deal

pain
NOUN
The pain in my ankle is worse.
▷ ache, cramp, discomfort, soreness, twinge

painful
ADJECTIVE
1 *This is a painful topic for him.*
▷ distressing, unpleasant, upsetting
2 *My broken thumb was painful.*
▷ aching, agonizing, excruciating

paint
VERB
Will you paint a picture for me?
▷ colour, draw, illustrate

painting
NOUN
My painting is hanging in the hall.
▷ canvas, mural, picture

pair
NOUN
The dancers make an attractive pair.
▷ couple, duo, twosome

pal
NOUN
She has been my pal since grade one.
▷ buddy, chum, friend, mate

pale
ADJECTIVE
The child has a pale face and looks tired.
▷ ashen, colourless, pallid

pamper
VERB
We like to pamper our new kitten.
▷ baby, coddle, indulge, spoil

panic
NOUN
They seemed to be in a state of panic.
▷ alarm, fear, hysteria

paper
NOUN
We need to stock up on paper this week.
▷ cardboard, crepe paper, letterhead, newsprint, stationery, tissue paper, toilet paper, tracing paper, writing paper

parcel
NOUN
The courier delivered a parcel for you.
▷ bundle, carton, package

part
NOUN
1 *A small part of the page is torn.*
▷ bit, fraction, fragment, piece, portion, section
2 *He plays the part of the rock star.*
▷ character, role

MAKE IT MORE FORMAL

for my part as far as I am concerned
for the most part mostly
in part to some extent
part and parcel a necessary part
part company separate
part from go away from
part with give up
play a part be a contributing factor
take in good part not be offended by
take part in participate

particular
ADJECTIVE
1 *I'm looking for a particular shade of green.*
▷ distinct, exact, precise, specific, unique
2 *I am particular about my food.*
▷ fussy, picky, selective

partner
NOUN
Bring your partner with you.
▷ companion, mate, spouse

party
NOUN
There will be a party on the last day of school.
▷ celebration, function, gathering, get-together, reception

P

pass

VERB

1 *She is trying to pass her previous score.*
▷ exceed, go beyond, outdo, surpass

2 *I will pass if I study hard.*
▷ meet the requirements, qualify, succeed
ANTONYM fail

3 *Please pass the cookies to the children.*
▷ distribute, hand out

NOUN

We have a pass to get into the building.
▷ permit, ticket

MAKE IT MORE FORMAL

pass around distribute
pass away die
pass down hand down
pass on communicate
pass out faint
pass over fail to notice
pass round distribute

passage

NOUN

He read a short passage from his book.
▷ excerpt, paragraph, section

passion

NOUN

We could hear the passion in her voice.
▷ emotion, excitement, intensity, zeal

passionate

ADJECTIVE

They made a passionate appeal for help.
▷ emotional, heartfelt, intense, strong
ANTONYM indifferent

past

ADJECTIVE

Do not judge me by my past behaviour.
▷ bygone, earlier, former, previous
ANTONYM future

pastime

NOUN

My favourite pastime is writing poetry.
▷ activity, diversion, hobby

pasture

NOUN

Sheep were standing in the pasture.
▷ field, grassland, meadow

patch

VERB

I will patch that rip in your sleeve.
▷ fix, mend, repair

path

NOUN

Which path should she take to become a teacher?
▷ course, direction, route

pathetic

ADJECTIVE

They had a pathetic excuse for being late.
▷ feeble, pitiful, poor, sorry

patient

ADJECTIVE

The patient customers waited in line.
▷ calm, tolerant, understanding

patrol

VERB

A company was hired to patrol the area.
▷ guard, protect, watch

pattern

NOUN

1 *I like the pattern on the wallpaper.*
▷ design, motif

2 *They used a pattern to make the toys.*
▷ blueprint, design, template

pause

VERB

I want to pause on this bench for a while to get my breath back.
▷ halt, rest, wait

NOUN

There was a short pause in the program.
▷ break, breather, intermission

pay

NOUN

Mom gets her pay on Fridays.
▷ earnings, income, salary, wages

MAKE IT MORE FORMAL

pay attention listen
pay attention to heed
pay back repay
pay for buy
pay off give all the money that is owed
pay out spend
pay someone back get revenge on someone
pay up pay in full
pay tribute to praise
pay your way contribute your share

peace

NOUN

I enjoy the peace in the library.
▷ quiet, serenity, silence, stillness, tranquility

peaceful

ADJECTIVE

1 *He had a peaceful look on his face.*
▷ calm, quiet, serene, tranquil
2 *Most people are peaceful.*
▷ nonviolent, passive
ANTONYM violent

peak

NOUN

The climbers will reach the peak tomorrow.
▷ crest, mountaintop, summit

peculiar

ADJECTIVE

She gave me a peculiar look.
▷ bizarre, curious, strange, unusual, weird

peek

NOUN

Did you get a peek at the new uniforms?
▷ glance, glimpse, preview

pen

NOUN

We put the ducks in their new pen.
▷ cage, coop, corral, enclosure, stall

penalty

NOUN

What is the penalty for throwing garbage on the street?
▷ fine, punishment

people

NOUN

1 *Many people are homeless because of the fire.*
▷ humans, individuals
2 *The people of Canada are proud of their Olympic athletes.*
▷ citizens, inhabitants, nation, population

peppery

ADJECTIVE

She made a peppery sauce for the pasta.
▷ fiery, hot, spicy

perfect

ADJECTIVE

1 *Their skating routine was perfect.*
▷ flawless, ideal, polished
ANTONYM imperfect
2 *I felt like a perfect fool.*
▷ absolute, complete, total

VERB

She wants to perfect her speaking skill.
▷ improve, polish, refine

perform

VERB

1 *Did you perform your tasks quickly?*
▷ accomplish, complete, execute, fulfill
2 *He will perform the part of the hero.*
▷ act, play

perfume

NOUN

The perfume of the lilacs filled the air.
▷ aroma, fragrance, scent

perhaps

ADVERB

Perhaps we can meet later.
▷ conceivably, maybe, possibly

perimeter

NOUN

We often run around the perimeter of the football field.
▷ border, boundary, edge

period

NOUN

1 *For a long period they lived in Trois-Rivières.*
▷ interval, stretch, term
2 *They studied the pre-Confederation period.*
▷ age, epoch, era, time

perky

ADJECTIVE

She is always perky and smiles a lot.
▷ animated, cheerful, energetic, lively, playful

permanent

ADJECTIVE

There should be no permanent damage to my knee.
▷ enduring, lasting, perpetual
ANTONYM temporary

permission

NOUN

Do you have permission to go?
▷ approval, authorization, consent

permit

VERB

Will she permit me to bring my dog?
▷ allow, authorize, grant
ANTONYM forbid

NOUN

The builder has a permit to build townhouses.
▷ authorization, licence

persecute

VERB

The dictator will persecute those who oppose him.
▷ hound, oppress, torment, torture

person

NOUN

The census counts each person in the country.
▷ human, human being, individual

personality

NOUN

1 *Each individual has a unique personality.*
▷ character, disposition, identity, nature
2 *She used to be a famous personality.*
▷ celebrity, public figure, star

P

persuade
VERB
*Can you **persuade** her to come to the game?*
▷ coax, convince, influence
ANTONYM dissuade

pessimistic
ADJECTIVE
*Do not spend time with **pessimistic** people.*
▷ cynical, defeatist, negative
ANTONYM optimistic

pest
NOUN
*My little sister is a **pest** sometimes.*
▷ annoyance, bother, nuisance

pester
VERB
*He will **pester** you until you answer him.*
▷ badger, bother, harass

petition
NOUN
*We need more signatures on the **petition**.*
▷ appeal, plea, request

petrified
ADJECTIVE
*I was so **petrified** that I couldn't move a muscle.*
▷ frightened, scared, terrified

petty
ADJECTIVE
*I am tired of their **petty** arguments.*
▷ insignificant, minor, trivial, unimportant
ANTONYM important

phase
NOUN
*That **phase** of my life is over.*
▷ chapter, period, point, stage

P

phenomenal
ADJECTIVE
*We saw a **phenomenal** movie on TV.*
▷ exceptional, extraordinary, outstanding, remarkable

phobia
NOUN
*He has a **phobia** of spiders.*
▷ dread, fear

phony
ADJECTIVE
*The actor wore a **phony** nose in her latest film.*
▷ fake, false, imitation
ANTONYM real

phrase
NOUN
*I do not understand that **phrase**.*
▷ expression, saying, slogan

pick
VERB
1 *Pick a number between one and ten.*
▷ choose, select, settle on
2 *We went to pick blueberries.*
▷ gather, harvest

MAKE IT MORE FORMAL

pick and choose be very fussy
pick apart find many flaws in
pick on bully
pick out distinguish
pick up learn
pick up on notice and understand

picture
NOUN
*That **picture** isn't straight.*
▷ drawing, illustration, painting, photograph, portrait, sketch
VERB
*Close your eyes and **picture** a calm lake.*
▷ imagine, visualize

MAKE IT MORE FORMAL

get the picture understand without further explanation
out of the picture not part of a certain situation

piece
NOUN
*We ate a **piece** of the cake.*
▷ chunk, fragment, part, portion, slice

MAKE IT MORE FORMAL

a piece of cake a very easy task
a piece of my mind a scolding
a piece of work a difficult person to deal with
go to pieces break down
piece together assemble
speak your piece express your opinion

pierce
VERB
*Did the nail **pierce** your bicycle tire?*
▷ perforate, prick, puncture

pile
NOUN
*I have a **pile** of clothes to wash.*
▷ heap, mound, mountain, stack
VERB
*He began to **pile** the DVDs on the shelf.*
▷ heap, load, stack

pilot

VERB

The driver was afraid to pilot the bus through the narrow alley.
▷ drive, guide, manoeuvre, steer

pinch

NOUN

1 *We are in a pinch and need your help.*
▷ crisis, difficulty, jam
2 *The soup needs a pinch of salt.*
▷ dash, smidgen, touch

pink

ADJECTIVE

I like your pink sweater.
▷ coral, fuchsia, rose, salmon

pioneer

NOUN

He was a pioneer in computer technology.
▷ explorer, innovator, trailblazer

pitch

VERB

Please pitch my sweater over to me.
▷ cast, fling, hurl, throw

pitcher

NOUN

Here is a pitcher of lemonade.
▷ carafe, decanter, jug

pitiful

ADJECTIVE

1 *Well, that was a pitiful excuse.*
▷ feeble, pathetic, wretched
2 *I'm still hungry after that pitiful lunch.*
▷ inadequate, insignificant, meagre

pity

NOUN

1 *She had pity for the homeless cat.*
▷ compassion, kindness, sympathy
2 *It is a pity that so few people voted.*
▷ misfortune, shame

place

NOUN

Is this the right place?
▷ area, location, site, spot

VERB

Place your boots on the mat.
▷ deposit, position, situate

MAKE IT MORE FORMAL

all over the place everywhere
go places achieve success
put someone in his or her place tell or show that someone is conceited
take place occur

plain

ADJECTIVE

1 *I like the plain shoes better.*
▷ simple, unadorned
ANTONYM fancy
2 *He made it plain that he dislikes peas.*
▷ clear, evident, obvious, unmistakable

NOUN

The plain has few trees.
▷ flat, flatland, grassland, lowland, mesa, plateau, prairie, savanna, steppe

plan

NOUN

1 *Our plan is to get to Bathurst by Friday.*
▷ proposal, scheme, strategy
2 *Our group drew a plan of the school.*
▷ blueprint, diagram, layout

VERB

Why didn't we plan our route before we left?
▷ design, devise, draft, prepare

plane

NOUN

The family went to Whitehorse by plane.
▷ aircraft, airplane

ADJECTIVE

That artist works on a plane surface.
▷ even, flat, horizontal, level, smooth

plant

VERB

He was told to plant himself at the door.
▷ establish, post, station

plaster

VERB

I like to plaster jam on my toast.
▷ slather, smear, spread

platform

NOUN

The speaker stood on the platform.
▷ dais, podium, stage

play

VERB

We will play you in the next game.
▷ compete with, contend with

NOUN

I liked the ending of the play.
▷ performance, presentation, production, show

MAKE IT MORE FORMAL

play a trick on fool
play for time delay (to get an advantage)
play the part of act
play up emphasize
play up to try to gain through flattery

P

playful
ADJECTIVE
The playful children ran around the park.
▷ active, frisky, lively

plea
NOUN
She made a plea for mercy.
▷ appeal, petition, request

plead
VERB
Maybe we should plead for more time to finish the project.
▷ appeal, beg, implore

pleasant
ADJECTIVE
1 *Yesterday was a pleasant day.*
▷ agreeable, delightful, enjoyable, lovely
2 *He is pleasant to everyone.*
▷ amiable, charming, friendly, likeable

please
VERB
1 *This gift will please my sister.*
▷ delight, gratify, satisfy
2 *May I do what I please with this money?*
▷ choose, desire, prefer, wish

pleasure
NOUN
Do you get a lot of pleasure from teasing me?
▷ delight, enjoyment, happiness, satisfaction

pledge
NOUN
They made a pledge to be best friends forever.
▷ guarantee, oath, promise, vow
VERB
New citizens pledge loyalty to their country.
▷ promise, swear, vow

plentiful
ADJECTIVE
The plentiful crop is due to good weather.
▷ abundant, ample, copious
ANTONYM scarce

plot
NOUN
1 *The thieves had a plot to steal the jewels.*
▷ conspiracy, plan, scheme
2 *In your book report, describe the plot.*
▷ action, scenario, storyline
VERB
1 *The traitors began to plot against the government.*
▷ conspire, intrigue, scheme
2 *They had to plot their escape route.*
▷ chart, draw, graph, map

pluck
VERB
I like to pluck weeds from the garden.
▷ pull, tug, yank
NOUN
We admire his pluck for opposing the bully.
▷ boldness, bravery, courage, nerve
ANTONYM cowardice

plug
NOUN
Remove the plug and pour the liquid out.
▷ cork, stopper
VERB
What will you use to plug the hole?
▷ block, fill, seal

plump
ADJECTIVE
See box at **fat**.

plunge
VERB
1 *She had to plunge the shovel into the snow.*
▷ force, sink, stab, thrust
2 *Let's plunge into the pool!*
▷ dive, drop, fall, plummet

point
NOUN
1 *The point of going is to see my uncle.*
▷ aim, goal, intention, object, purpose
2 *At what point should we break for lunch?*
▷ instant, moment, time

> ### MAKE IT MORE FORMAL
> **point of view** opinion
> **point out** comment

pointless
ADJECTIVE
It was pointless to argue with him.
▷ futile, meaningless, senseless

poison
NOUN
That is a dangerous poison.
▷ toxin, venom
VERB
Exhaust fumes poison the air.
▷ contaminate, infect, pollute, taint

poisonous
ADJECTIVE
Firefighters wear masks against poisonous gases.
▷ deadly, lethal, toxic

poke
VERB
Why did you poke me just now?
▷ elbow, jab, nudge, prod

pole

NOUN

She finally had to use a pole to prop up the tent.

▷ bar, post, rod, staff, stick

polish

VERB

1 *I have to polish my shoes, so I will do yours as well.*

▷ buff, shine, wax

2 *He didn't take time to polish his speech, but it was very interesting.*

▷ improve, perfect, refine

polite

ADJECTIVE

We were taught to be polite to everyone, whether we liked them or not.

▷ civil, courteous, gracious, respectful, well-mannered

ANTONYM rude

poll

NOUN

Are the results of the poll accurate?

▷ ballot, survey, vote

pollute

VERB

Burning coal will pollute the air.

▷ contaminate, poison, taint

polygon

NOUN

See picture below.

pompous

ADJECTIVE

The mayor acted in a pompous way.

▷ arrogant, self-important

ponder

VERB

I will ponder your request carefully.

▷ consider, contemplate, reflect, think

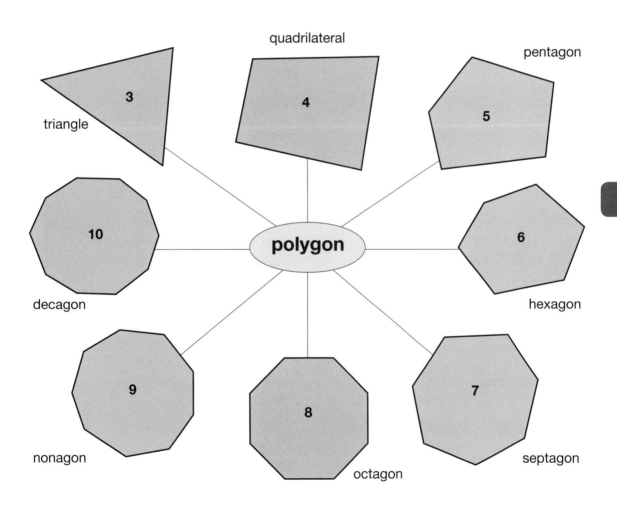

P

pool

NOUN
*There were a lot of insects near the **pool**.*
▷ lagoon, pond, reservoir

VERB
*If we **pool** our money, we can buy the DVD.*
▷ combine, merge, share

poor

ADJECTIVE
1 *Our neighbourhood helped the **poor** family.*
▷ impoverished, penniless, poverty-stricken
ANTONYM rich
2 *The employee did **poor** work and was fired.*
▷ inferior, second-rate, unsatisfactory
ANTONYM superior

pop

VERB
*The balloon will **pop** if you keep blowing air into it.*
▷ bang, burst, explode

popular

ADJECTIVE
1 *Which cellphone is the most **popular**?*
▷ in demand, in favour, sought-after, well-liked
2 *It's **popular** knowledge that the weather is getting warmer.*
▷ common, general, widespread

populate

VERB
*Settlers from France and Britain came to **populate** Canada.*
▷ colonize, inhabit, occupy, settle

portion

NOUN
*Give each person a **portion** of the pie.*
▷ helping, piece, serving, share, slice

portrait

NOUN
*This is a **portrait** of my parents.*
▷ painting, picture

portray

VERB
*Who will **portray** the doctor in the movie?*
▷ depict, represent

pose

VERB
*The students were asked to **pose** questions.*
▷ present, submit

positive

ADJECTIVE
1 *Are you **positive** you know where the library is?*
▷ certain, confident, convinced, sure
ANTONYM uncertain
2 *The witness made a **positive** identification.*
▷ clear-cut, conclusive, definite

3 *I like to be with **positive** people.*
▷ constructive, encouraging, helpful
ANTONYM negative

possess

VERB
*How many CDs does she **possess**?*
▷ have, own

possessions

NOUN
*All their **possessions** were destroyed in the fire.*
▷ belongings, property

possible

ADJECTIVE
1 *It will be **possible** to practise after school.*
▷ doable, feasible, workable
2 *Here is a **possible** solution to the problem.*
▷ conceivable, imaginable, likely, potential

poster

NOUN
*They put up copies of the **poster** all around town.*
▷ advertisement, notice, sign

postpone

VERB
*I must **postpone** my visit to the dentist.*
▷ defer, delay

potential

NOUN
*Always work to your full **potential**.*
▷ ability, capability, power, promise

pound

VERB
***Pound** the nail into the wood.*
▷ beat, hammer, strike

pour

VERB
*The dam cracked and water began to **pour** out.*
▷ flow, gush, spout, stream

power

NOUN
1 *Who has the **power** to make the decision?*
▷ authority, control, supremacy
2 *He played with **power** and speed.*
▷ strength, vigour

powerful

ADJECTIVE
1 *She has a **powerful** personality.*
▷ commanding, dominant, influential
2 *He has become a tall and **powerful** young man.*
▷ mighty, strapping, strong
ANTONYM weak
3 *The councillor gave a **powerful** speech.*
▷ compelling, convincing, effective, persuasive

P

practical
ADJECTIVE
1 *Mom always gives me practical advice.*
▷ down-to-earth, level-headed, realistic
2 *Waterproof jackets are practical.*
▷ functional, sensible, useful
ANTONYM impractical

practice
NOUN
1 *It is my practice to drink lots of water.*
▷ custom, habit, method, ritual, routine
2 *Practice for the school play starts at four o'clock.*
▷ rehearsal, training

practise
VERB
I have to practise my gymnastics routine.
▷ rehearse, learn

praise
VERB
Did he praise them for all their hard work?
▷ admire, applaud, congratulate, honour
NOUN
The praise she received was deserved.
▷ admiration, approval, honour, recognition
ANTONYM criticism

prank
NOUN
The prank was cruel and hurt his feelings.
▷ hoax, joke, trick

precious
ADJECTIVE
1 *The princess wears precious jewels.*
▷ costly, expensive, valuable
ANTONYM worthless
2 *My most precious possession is a book that my grandmother gave me.*
▷ beloved, cherished, dear, loved

precipitation
NOUN
More precipitation is expected.
▷ drizzle, freezing rain, hail, rain, sleet, snow

precise
ADJECTIVE
I know the precise size of the picture.
▷ actual, correct, exact
ANTONYM approximate

predict
VERB
Can you predict which team will win?
▷ forecast, foresee, foretell

prejudice
NOUN
Racial prejudice has no place in our society.
▷ bias, discrimination, intolerance

preoccupied
ADJECTIVE
She is preoccupied with her problems.
▷ absorbed, engrossed, immersed

prepare
VERB
I need time to prepare my speech.
▷ arrange, organize, plan

present
ADJECTIVE
The whole school was present at the pep rally.
▷ at hand, in attendance, there
ANTONYM absent

preserve
VERB
The city plans to preserve many of our historic buildings.
▷ conserve, protect, safeguard
ANTONYM neglect

press
VERB
1 *Press the pages flat with your hand.*
▷ compress, push, squeeze
2 *I will press her to help with the food drive.*
▷ beg, implore, plead, urge

pressure
NOUN
1 *Apply pressure to stop the bleeding.*
▷ force, weight
2 *He quit his job because of the pressure.*
▷ burden, demand, strain, stress
VERB
She tried to pressure me into buying more software.
▷ compel, force, push

presume
VERB
I presume you have an excuse.
▷ assume, guess, imagine, suppose

pretend
ADJECTIVE
My little sister has a pretend friend.
▷ false, imaginary, invented, make-believe
VERB
He likes to pretend he is a superhero.
▷ imagine, make believe

pretty
ADJECTIVE
The little girl wore a pretty dress.
▷ attractive, beautiful, cute, lovely
ADVERB
I am pretty sure that you are wrong.
▷ fairly, quite

P

prevent
VERB
A security guard was hired to prevent vandalism.
▷ avert, discourage, impede, obstruct
ANTONYM permit

previous
ADJECTIVE
She preferred the previous version of my essay.
▷ earlier, former, prior

price
NOUN
What is the price of tomatoes today?
▷ amount, charge, cost
VERB
The real estate agent will price their house.
▷ appraise, assess, estimate, value

priceless
ADJECTIVE
1 *Our priceless photographs have been stolen.*
▷ cherished, costly, invaluable, precious
2 *She always has a priceless story to tell.*
▷ amusing, funny, hilarious

prick
VERB
The doctor had to prick my finger to draw blood.
▷ jab, pierce, puncture

pride
NOUN
1 *With pride, I presented the trophy to the winners.*
▷ delight, pleasure, satisfaction
2 *He has too much pride to admit he was wrong.*
▷ arrogance, conceit
ANTONYM humility

primary
ADJECTIVE
What is your primary goal right now?
▷ chief, foremost, main, major, principal

primitive
ADJECTIVE
1 *Her drawings are primitive but colourful.*
▷ basic, crude, rough, simple
2 *They have discovered more primitive cave paintings.*
▷ ancient, archaic, prehistoric
ANTONYM modern

principal
ADJECTIVE
The principal reason that I swim is for exercise.
▷ foremost, main, major, primary

print
VERB
The newspaper had to print an apology.
▷ issue, produce, publish

NOUN
1 *I bought fabric with a flowered print.*
▷ design, motif, pattern
2 *He bought a print of a famous painting.*
▷ copy, duplication, replica, reproduction

prior
ADJECTIVE
She has no prior gardening experience.
▷ earlier, former, preceding, previous

prison
NOUN
That prison is for dangerous offenders.
▷ jail, penitentiary

private
ADJECTIVE
1 *The queen has her own private train.*
▷ exclusive, personal
2 *The two men had a private talk.*
▷ confidential, secret
ANTONYM public

prize
NOUN
A prize is given for perfect attendance.
▷ award, honour, trophy
VERB
I prize my books and reread them often.
▷ cherish, esteem, treasure, value

problem
NOUN
1 *Do you need help with your problem?*
▷ difficulty, dilemma, predicament, trouble
2 *The teacher gave us a problem to solve.*
▷ challenge, puzzle, riddle

proceed
VERB
1 *We will proceed with our project after recess.*
▷ carry on, continue
2 *The parade will proceed to the town centre.*
▷ advance, continue, progress, travel

process
NOUN
What process do you use to mix paint colours?
▷ method, practice, procedure, system

proclaim
VERB
It is too soon to proclaim a winner.
▷ announce, declare, pronounce, state

produce
VERB
It takes a lot of sap to produce a litre of maple syrup.
▷ create, make, manufacture

profession

NOUN

The counsellor will help her choose a profession.

▷ career, job, occupation

professional

ADJECTIVE

Congratulations on doing such a professional job.

▷ efficient, expert, skilled

NOUN

They should have hired a professional.

▷ authority, expert, specialist

profit

NOUN

1 *We donated our bake-sale profit to the food bank.*

▷ earnings, proceeds, return, revenue

ANTONYM loss

2 *The profit I get from reading is knowledge.*

▷ advantage, benefit, gain, use

program

NOUN

The track-and-field program has been finalized.

▷ agenda, outline, schedule

progress

NOUN

I'm making some progress in my work.

▷ advance, development, improvement

prolong

VERB

They decided to prolong their stay in Annapolis Royal.

▷ extend, lengthen, stretch

ANTONYM shorten

prominent

ADJECTIVE

1 *A prominent scientist visited our class.*

▷ famous, important, leading, notable, renowned, well-known

2 *He has a prominent bruise on his arm.*

▷ conspicuous, eye-catching, noticeable

promise

VERB

We had to promise to return the DVD player.

▷ pledge, swear, vow

NOUN

The government made a promise to lower taxes.

▷ commitment, guarantee, oath, pledge, vow

promote

VERB

1 *The tennis star intends to promote healthy living.*

▷ back, encourage, endorse, support

2 *The government will promote tourism in Canada.*

▷ advertise, market, publicize

3 *The company plans to promote her to manager.*

▷ advance, upgrade

prompt

VERB

High gas prices may prompt people to take public transit.

▷ inspire, motivate, spur

ADJECTIVE

Please give me a prompt reply.

▷ immediate, quick, rapid, speedy

pronounce

VERB

1 *I find it hard to pronounce some words.*

▷ speak, utter

2 *The TV station will pronounce the winner of the election.*

▷ affirm, declare, proclaim

proof

NOUN

A passport is proof of citizenship.

▷ confirmation, evidence, verification

prop

NOUN

We need a prop to support the fence.

▷ brace, reinforcement, strut

proper

ADJECTIVE

1 *Use the proper tools for the job.*

▷ appropriate, correct, fitting, suitable

2 *It is proper to stand for the national anthem.*

▷ accepted, conventional, orthodox

property

NOUN

Their property is stored in a rental unit.

▷ assets, belongings, possessions

propose

VERB

I propose we spend an hour planning our project.

▷ advise, recommend, suggest

prosper

VERB

The business will prosper if they work hard.

▷ flourish, succeed, thrive

protect

VERB

See picture on next page.

protest

VERB

They did not protest the judge's decision.

▷ dispute, object to, oppose

NOUN

1 *Our protest was sent to the mayor.*

▷ complaint, objection

2 *She joined the protest for affordable housing.*

▷ demonstration, march, rally

P

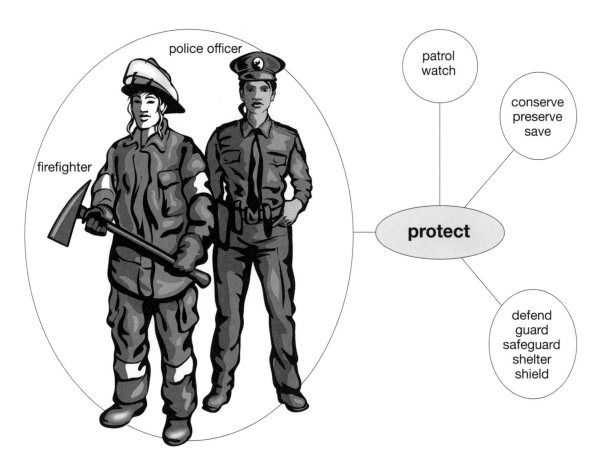

firefighter | police officer

patrol
watch

conserve
preserve
save

protect

defend
guard
safeguard
shelter
shield

proud

ADJECTIVE

*Why does he behave in such a **proud** way?*

▷ arrogant, conceited, smug

ANTONYM humble

prove

VERB

*She can **prove** where she was at seven o'clock.*

▷ confirm, demonstrate, establish

ANTONYM disprove

provoke

VERB

1 *Do not **provoke** the skunk.*

▷ anger, annoy, enrage, irritate

2 *The newspaper article is sure to **provoke** anger.*

▷ cause, produce, prompt, spark

prowl

VERB

*Why do you always **prowl** around like that?*

▷ roam, sneak, stalk

public

NOUN

*The **public** will be upset if there is another election so soon.*

▷ community, nation, people, populace

ADJECTIVE

*The polluted water in the lake caused a **public** outcry.*

▷ popular, universal

ANTONYM private

pull

VERB

*The child tried to **pull** the heavy wagon.*

▷ drag, haul, tow

ANTONYM push

NOUN

*I do not understand the **pull** of that movie.*

▷ appeal, attraction, lure

MAKE IT MORE FORMAL

pull back retreat

pull down receive as a salary

pull for give help to

pull off successfully complete

pull out withdraw

pull someone's leg playfully fool someone

pull through survive

pull together co-operate

pull up halt

pull yourself together recover your self-control

---

pump
VERB
They had to pump the water from the basement.
▷ drain, draw, extract

punish
VERB
The judge will punish the offenders.
▷ discipline, penalize, sentence

punishment
NOUN
Their punishment was not harsh.
▷ penalty, retribution, sentence

puny
ADJECTIVE
The puny dog needed food.
▷ feeble, frail, scrawny, sickly, skinny, weak
ANTONYM robust

pure
ADJECTIVE
1 *Her company sells pure spring water.*
▷ clean, germ-free, sterilized, uncontaminated, unpolluted
ANTONYM impure
2 *Our meeting like this is pure luck.*
▷ absolute, complete, outright, sheer, utter

purple
ADJECTIVE
You can mix blue and red paint to get purple.
▷ amethyst, aubergine, gentian, heather, heliotrope, indigo, lavender, lilac, magenta, mauve, mulberry, plum, puce, violet

purpose
NOUN
The purpose of my visit was to bring her some muffins.
▷ function, intention, object, point, reason (for)

pursue
VERB
I had to pursue the runaway dog.
▷ chase, follow, track, trail

push
VERB
1 *Push your backpack into the locker.*
▷ ram, shove, thrust
ANTONYM pull
2 *They had to push him because he was too lazy to try.*
▷ encourage, persuade, press, urge

MAKE IT MORE FORMAL
push around treat roughly
pushed for limited by some lack
push for promote strongly

pushy
ADJECTIVE
I do not like pushy people.
▷ aggressive, assertive, bossy, forceful

put
VERB
1 *Put your boots over there.*
▷ deposit, lay, place, position, rest
2 *Is there a better way to put your question?*
▷ express, phrase, word

MAKE IT MORE FORMAL
put across express
put back return
put down criticize
put off delay
put on wear
put together assemble
put up with tolerate

puzzle
VERB
Did the ending of the story puzzle you?
▷ baffle, bewilder, confuse, mystify, stump
NOUN
She likes any kind of word puzzle.
▷ brainteaser, problem, riddle

P

Q q

quack

NOUN

The TV program was about a doctor who was really a quack.

▷ fake, fraud, impostor

quake

VERB

I quake whenever I think of a tsunami.

▷ quiver, shake, shiver, shudder, tremble

qualification

NOUN

What qualification do I need for the job?

▷ accomplishment, capability, credential, skill

quality

NOUN

1 *His skill as a carpenter is of high quality.*

▷ calibre, grade, merit, value, worth

2 *A good quality to have is a sense of humour.*

▷ characteristic, feature, mark, trait

quantity

NOUN

We sold a huge quantity of books at the yard sale.

▷ amount, lot, number

quarrel

NOUN

Let's end this quarrel.

▷ argument, disagreement, dispute, feud, fight, row, squabble, tiff

VERB

She did not want to quarrel with her friend.

▷ argue, bicker, clash, fight, squabble

ANTONYM agree

quarter

NOUN

There are many restaurants in that quarter.

▷ area, district, neighbourhood, region, section

queasy

ADJECTIVE

The rocking of the boat made me queasy.

▷ ill, nauseous, sick, squeamish

question

NOUN

1 *Do you have a question?*

▷ inquiry, query

ANTONYM response

2 *They discussed the question of pollution.*

▷ issue, subject, topic

VERB

1 *She was afraid to question the guard's authority.*

▷ challenge, dispute

2 *The police want to question the witness.*

▷ examine, interrogate, interview

3 *I question his ability to do a good job.*

▷ distrust, doubt

questionable

ADJECTIVE

This video game is of questionable quality.

▷ doubtful, dubious, suspect, suspicious

queue

NOUN

The queue for tickets got longer and longer.

▷ line, lineup

quick

ADJECTIVE

1 *They went for a quick walk.*

▷ brisk, fast, hasty, rapid, speedy, swift

ANTONYM slow

2 *I made a quick telephone call.*

▷ brief, hurried

ANTONYM long

MAKE IT MORE FORMAL

be quick act quickly

cut someone to the quick deeply offend someone

quick and dirty hastily done

---

quickly

ADVERB

We took a shortcut to get to school quickly.

▷ fast, hastily, hurriedly, rapidly, speedily, swiftly

ANTONYM slowly

quiet

ADJECTIVE

1 *She speaks in a quiet voice.*

▷ hushed, low, soft

ANTONYM loud

2 *He looked for a quiet place to read.*

▷ peaceful, restful, serene, tranquil

NOUN

There was total quiet during the ceremony.

▷ silence, stillness

MAKE IT MORE FORMAL

keep quiet about something keep something secret

on the quiet secretly

---

quip

NOUN

Her quip was very funny.

▷ gag, jest, joke, wisecrack

quit

VERB

1 *Please quit interrupting.*

▷ cease, discontinue, stop

2 *Why did he quit the team?*

▷ leave, resign

quite

ADVERB

1 *Our food drive was quite successful.*

▷ fairly, moderately, somewhat

2 *I am quite busy, so please call me later.*

▷ absolutely, completely, entirely, fully, perfectly, totally

quiver

VERB

The actor began to quiver just as the play began.

▷ quake, shake, shiver, shudder, tremble

quiz

VERB

Did you quiz her about the broken window?

▷ ask, interrogate, question, test

NOUN

She completed the quiz quickly.

▷ contest, examination, puzzle, test

quota

NOUN

They are allowed a small quota of candy per day.

▷ allowance, ration, share

quotation

NOUN

The author read a quotation from his book.

▷ extract, passage, selection

quote

VERB

She likes to quote poetry.

▷ cite, recite, state

Q

R r

race
NOUN
The Beothuk race were the original inhabitants of Newfoundland.
▷ ethnic group, nation, people
VERB
We must race to the bus stop.
▷ dash, fly, hurry, run

racket
NOUN
1 *Who is making that annoying racket?*
▷ commotion, din, hubbub, noise, rumpus
2 *That free vacation offer is a racket.*
▷ fraud, scam, scheme

radiant
ADJECTIVE
The radiant bride walked slowly up the aisle.
▷ beaming, glowing, happy

rage
NOUN
1 *Rage is difficult to control.*
▷ anger, frenzy, fury, wrath
2 *Beaded jewellery is the rage right now.*
▷ fad, fashion
VERB
He began to rage at the server.
▷ fume, rave, storm

ragged
ADJECTIVE
1 *He wants to keep his ragged teddy bear.*
▷ scruffy, shabby, torn
2 *The ragged edge of the metal cut my finger.*
▷ jagged, rough

raid
VERB
They will raid the terrorists' hideout.
▷ assault, attack, invade

rain
NOUN
The rain went on for three days.
▷ deluge, downpour, drizzle, rainfall, showers
VERB
Will it rain tomorrow?
▷ drizzle, pour, shower

raise
VERB
1 *He was able to raise the bar over his head.*
▷ elevate, heave, hoist, lift
ANTONYM lower
2 *The aunt offered to raise the orphan.*
▷ nurture, rear

ram
VERB
1 *Can you ram one more item into the suitcase?*
▷ cram, force, stuff
2 *I watched him ram the bicycle into the wall.*
▷ push, shove, slam

ramble
VERB
We like to ramble along the beach.
▷ hike, walk, wander

ramp
NOUN
Cars slow down on the ramp.
▷ gradient, incline, slope

rancid
ADJECTIVE
A rancid smell came from the refrigerator.
▷ musty, putrid, sour

random
ADJECTIVE
I made a random guess.
▷ arbitrary, haphazard
ANTONYM deliberate

range
NOUN
1 *What is the range of the radar?*
▷ extent, limit, scope
2 *The shoe store sells a range of sizes.*
▷ assortment, selection, variety
VERB
Their ages range from nine to twelve.
▷ extend, stretch, vary

rank
NOUN
He works at the lowest rank right now.
▷ class, grade, level, position, status

ransack
VERB
The mob started to ransack the stores.
▷ loot, plunder, scour

rant
VERB
Do not rant about that unimportant event.
▷ rave, roar, shout

rap
VERB
Rap on the door loudly.
▷ bang, knock, pound
NOUN
He offered to take the rap for his friend.
▷ blame, responsibility

rapid
ADJECTIVE
She made a rapid choice.
▷ fast, quick, slow, speedy, swift

rapture
NOUN
The rapture showed on his face.
▷ bliss, delight, ecstasy, joy

rare
ADJECTIVE
Rain was rare last summer.
▷ exceptional, scarce, sparse, uncommon, unusual
ANTONYM common

rash
ADJECTIVE
Do not make a rash decision.
▷ foolhardy, hasty, headstrong, impetuous, impulsive, reckless
NOUN
I received a rash of unwelcome e-mails.
▷ flood, plague, wave

rate
NOUN
1 *My heart beats at a normal rate.*
▷ frequency, pace, speed, tempo
2 *What is the rate for washing windows?*
▷ charge, cost, fee, price
VERB
I rate his work as excellent.
▷ appraise, assess, consider, evaluate, judge, rank, regard

MAKE IT MORE FORMAL
at any rate under any circumstances
at this (*or* **that**) **rate** under such circumstances

ration
NOUN
We each received one ration of meat.
▷ helping, portion, share

rational
ADJECTIVE
Judges are expected to be rational.
▷ logical, reasonable, sensible, wise
ANTONYM unreasonable

rattle
VERB
1 *The baby likes to rattle the noisy toy.*
▷ clatter, jangle, shake
2 *He tried to rattle me with that question.*
▷ confuse, fluster, muddle

rave
VERB
1 *She began to rave about unfair treatment.*
▷ babble, rage, rant
2 *The critics always rave about that group's performance.*
▷ enthuse, gush

ravenous
ADJECTIVE
The ravenous children ate everything.
▷ famished, hungry, starving

ravine
NOUN
Is there a stream at the bottom of this ravine, or is it dry?
▷ canyon, coulee, gorge, gulch, gully

raw
ADJECTIVE
1 *The wound is still raw.*
▷ painful, sensitive, sore, tender
2 *A raw wind blew all day.*
▷ chilly, cold, harsh
3 *The raw soldiers learned quickly.*
▷ inexperienced, untrained

reach
VERB
1 *We expect to reach Fort McMurray by Friday.*
▷ arrive at, get as far as, get to, make it to
2 *Can you reach the top shelf?*
▷ extend to, touch

reaction
NOUN
The positive reaction was very encouraging.
▷ acknowledgment, feedback, response

read
VERB
Did you read that magazine article yet?
▷ look at, scan, study

MAKE IT MORE FORMAL
read between the lines find a meaning not actually expressed
read into interpret in a certain way
read out read aloud
read up on study

ready
ADJECTIVE
1 *I like to get ready for school early.*
▷ organized, prepared, primed
2 *Mom is ready to try skateboarding.*
▷ eager, keen, willing

R

real

ADJECTIVE
1 *The real story will be published soon.*
▷ actual, authentic, factual, genuine, true
ANTONYM imaginary
2 *The jeweller said my ring is real gold.*
▷ authentic, genuine
ANTONYM fake

> **MAKE IT MORE FORMAL**
>
> **for real** in fact
> **get real** be serious
> **in real life** in reality
> **the real McCoy** a genuine object or person
> **the real thing** a genuine object or feeling

realistic

ADJECTIVE
1 *Try to be realistic.*
▷ practical, sensible
2 *The sculpture of the horse is realistic.*
▷ authentic, lifelike

realize

VERB
I realize the importance of studying.
▷ appreciate, comprehend, grasp, recognize, understand

really

ADVERB
1 *He swims really well.*
▷ extremely, remarkably
2 *Will you really come to the school play?*
▷ actually, in fact, in reality, truly

rear

VERB
My aunt and uncle rear chickens.
▷ breed, raise
NOUN
They marched at the rear of the parade.
▷ back, end, tail

reason

NOUN
What's the reason for their actions?
▷ cause, grounds, incentive, motive

reasonable

ADJECTIVE
1 *She made a reasonable request.*
▷ fair, moderate, rational, sensible
2 *The new recycling rules are reasonable.*
▷ logical, sensible, sound, understandable
3 *They have reasonable prices at that store.*
▷ cheap, fair, inexpensive, low, modest
ANTONYM expensive

rebel

VERB
The sailors plan to rebel.
▷ mutiny, resist, revolt

rebellion

NOUN
The rebellion took place in 1869.
▷ mutiny, revolt, revolution, uprising

rebuke

VERB
The coach does not usually rebuke the team.
▷ reprimand, reproach, scold
ANTONYM praise

recall

VERB
1 *Can you recall his cellphone number?*
▷ recollect, remember
2 *The company may recall its software program.*
▷ cancel, retract, withdraw

recede

VERB
We watched the mist recede.
▷ ebb, retreat, shrink

recent

ADJECTIVE
Do you have a recent copy of the magazine?
▷ current, fresh, up-to-date

recess

NOUN
The committee members took a short recess.
▷ break, intermission, pause

recite

VERB
Can you recite the poem from memory?
▷ quote, recount, relate

reckless

ADJECTIVE
The reckless children fell off the toboggan.
▷ foolhardy, heedless, impetuous, irresponsible, rash
ANTONYM cautious

reckon

VERB
1 *I reckon that we will see them tomorrow.*
▷ assume, believe, suppose, think
2 *Can you reckon how many apples are on that tree?*
▷ calculate, estimate

recognize

VERB
1 *I could recognize him by his voice.*
▷ distinguish, identify
2 *The hospital plans to recognize its volunteers.*
▷ acknowledge, appreciate, honour

R

recollect
VERB
I don't recollect what you said.
▷ recall, remember
ANTONYM forget

recommend
VERB
Which restaurant do you recommend?
▷ advise, endorse, suggest

record
NOUN
1 *Did you keep a record of the group's suggestions?*
▷ account, file, journal, log
2 *She has no criminal record.*
▷ background, past
VERB
Record your ideas in a journal.
▷ document, enter, log, note, register

recover
VERB
1 *He has begun to recover from the accident.*
▷ convalesce, improve, recuperate
2 *Did the police recover the stolen goods?*
▷ reclaim, regain, repossess, retrieve

recovery
NOUN
The doctor predicted my recovery would be fast.
▷ healing, improvement, recuperation

recreation
NOUN
What do you do for recreation?
▷ entertainment, fun, leisure

recruit
VERB
The soccer club needs to recruit more players.
▷ draft, enlist, enrol
NOUN
The youngest recruit is doing an excellent job.
▷ apprentice, beginner, novice, trainee

rectify
VERB
I would like to rectify my mistake.
▷ correct, remedy

recuperate
VERB
He will recuperate faster if he rests.
▷ convalesce, improve, mend, recover

red
ADJECTIVE
Red is my favourite colour.
▷ burgundy, carmine, cerise, cherry, crimson, magenta, maroon, raspberry, ruby, scarlet, vermilion

reduce
VERB
We can all help to reduce the amount of garbage.
▷ decrease, diminish, lessen, lower
ANTONYM increase

reek
NOUN
There is a strong reek of rotten fish.
▷ smell, stench, stink

referee
NOUN
A referee must deal with all disagreements.
▷ arbitrator, judge, umpire

refined
ADJECTIVE
Her manner is very refined.
▷ civilized, genteel, polite

reflect on
VERB
Take time to reflect on the problem before you decide.
▷ consider, contemplate, deliberate, ponder

refrain from
VERB
Refrain from chewing gum in class.
▷ abstain from, avoid, resist

refresh
VERB
Exercise will refresh you.
▷ energize, enliven, invigorate, rejuvenate, revive, stimulate

refrigerate
VERB
Refrigerate the cake.
▷ chill, cool, freeze

refuge
NOUN
Injured animals seek a safe refuge.
▷ asylum, haven, sanctuary, shelter

refund
VERB
The store promised to refund my money.
▷ reimburse, repay, return

refuse
VERB
Why did you refuse my offer of help?
▷ decline, reject, spurn
ANTONYM accept
NOUN
Someone left refuse in the parking lot.
▷ garbage, litter, trash, waste

R

regain
VERB
The team is struggling to regain the championship.
▷ reclaim, recover, retrieve

regal
ADJECTIVE
She is very young to have such a regal manner.
▷ majestic, noble, royal

regard
VERB
1 *I regard her as my best friend.*
▷ consider, judge, view
2 *Please regard his every movement.*
▷ scrutinize, watch

region
NOUN
Which region has the highest population?
▷ area, district, sector, territory, zone

register
NOUN
The register has the names of the players.
▷ list, note, record

regret
NOUN
We expressed regret at our rude behaviour.
▷ remorse, repentance, sorrow

regular
ADJECTIVE
1 *His pulse is regular at the moment.*
▷ consistent, constant, even, rhythmic, steady, uniform
ANTONYM irregular
2 *We took our regular route to school.*
▷ customary, normal, ordinary, routine, usual

regulation
NOUN
The anti-noise regulation will be enforced.
▷ law, rule

rehearse
VERB
Rehearse your speech until you have it memorized.
▷ practise, repeat

reinforce
VERB
Can you reinforce the wobbly fence?
▷ strengthen, supplement, support

reject
VERB
He decided to reject the offer.
▷ decline, deny, rebuff, refuse, spurn
ANTONYM accept

rejoice in
VERB
Let us rejoice in our good fortune.
▷ celebrate, delight in, glory in

relate
VERB
Ask her to relate her experience.
▷ describe, recount, tell

related to
ADJECTIVE
Good health is closely related to good eating habits.
▷ associated with, connected to, linked to

relation
NOUN
He is a distant relation.
▷ family member, kin, relative

relationship
NOUN
There is no relationship between those two events.
▷ association, connection, correlation, link, parallel

relax
VERB
Just relax until lunch is ready.
▷ laze, rest, unwind

release
VERB
1 *Release the prisoner.*
▷ discharge, free, liberate
2 *The company will release the report soon.*
▷ issue, publish

relentless
ADJECTIVE
The relentless hammering went on for two hours.
▷ incessant, non-stop, persistent

relevant
ADJECTIVE
Give me all the relevant information.
▷ applicable, appropriate, necessary
ANTONYM irrelevant

reliable
ADJECTIVE
Is the witness reliable?
▷ dependable, trustworthy

religious
ADJECTIVE
See picture on next page.

relish
VERB
The friends relish every moment together.
▷ enjoy, savour
ANTONYM loathe

R

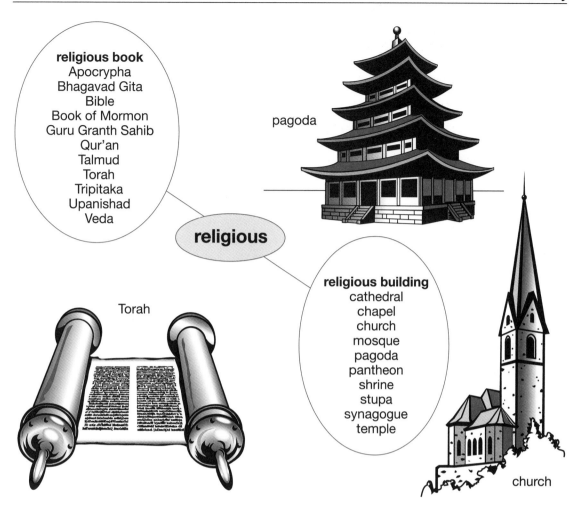

religious

religious book
Apocrypha
Bhagavad Gita
Bible
Book of Mormon
Guru Granth Sahib
Qur'an
Talmud
Torah
Tripitaka
Upanishad
Veda

pagoda

Torah

religious building
cathedral
chapel
church
mosque
pagoda
pantheon
shrine
stupa
synagogue
temple

church

reluctant
ADJECTIVE
He was reluctant to jump into the cold water.
▷ hesitant, unwilling
ANTONYM eager

rely on
VERB
I rely on your good judgment.
▷ count on, depend on, trust

remain
VERB
1 *Can you remain here for a while?*
▷ linger, stay, wait
2 *The pleasure of that day will remain in my mind.*
▷ continue, persist

remainder
NOUN
You may do the remainder of your homework later.
▷ balance, rest

remark
VERB
I heard him remark that he liked me.
▷ mention, say, state
NOUN
Which remark upset you so much?
▷ comment, observation, statement

remarkable
ADJECTIVE
He has a remarkable memory.
▷ exceptional, extraordinary, marvellous,
uncommon, wonderful

remedy
VERB
I can remedy my mistake.
▷ correct, rectify
NOUN
Her remedy for a cold is hot soup.
▷ cure, medicine, treatment

R

remember

VERB
I can remember names quite easily.
▷ recall, recollect, retain
ANTONYM forget

remnant

NOUN
The remnant of the cake was really just crumbs.
▷ remains, residue

remote

ADJECTIVE
1 *Nunavut has many remote communities.*
▷ isolated, secluded
2 *He is remote sometimes and difficult to talk to.*
▷ aloof, cold, detached, distant, reserved, withdrawn
3 *She has only a remote chance of making the team.*
▷ poor, slender, slight, slim, small

remove

VERB
Remove the unused folders from the computer.
▷ delete, eliminate, erase, withdraw

renew

VERB
I want to renew my library privileges.
▷ reopen, restore, resume

renovate

VERB
My dad wants to renovate the kitchen.
▷ recondition, refurbish

renowned

ADJECTIVE
The renowned singer is coming to our town.
▷ celebrated, famous, notable

rent

VERB
Our family will rent a boat for a month.
▷ charter, hire, lease

repair

VERB
Can you repair my bicycle?
▷ fix, mend

repay

VERB
You don't have to repay me the money yet.
▷ refund, reimburse

repel

VERB
1 *Did the scenes in the movie repel you?*
▷ disgust, offend, revolt, sicken
ANTONYM attract
2 *Use this spray to repel mosquitoes.*
▷ repulse, ward off

repellent

ADJECTIVE
I think his behaviour is repellent.
▷ disgusting, distasteful, offensive, repulsive
ANTONYM attractive

replace

VERB
What program will replace the cancelled show?
▷ succeed, supersede, substitute for

replacement

NOUN
Is there a replacement for the injured dancer?
▷ stand-in, substitute, successor

replica

NOUN
I bought a replica of the painting in the museum shop.
▷ copy, duplicate, facsimile

reply

VERB
Please reply as soon as possible.
▷ answer, respond
NOUN
He may not give you a reply immediately.
▷ answer, response

report

VERB
Report what you discovered.
▷ describe, relate, state, tell
NOUN
Can you give a report of the accident?
▷ account, description, statement

represent

VERB
1 *What does that logo represent?*
▷ mean, signify, symbolize
2 *Can you represent your idea in a drawing?*
▷ depict, describe, portray

representative

NOUN
The mayor sent her representative to the meeting.
▷ agent, delegate, deputy, spokesperson
ADJECTIVE
The maple leaf is a representative symbol of Canada.
▷ characteristic, illustrative, typical

repress

VERB
He tried to repress his sneeze.
▷ smother, stifle, suppress

reprimand

VERB
Did he reprimand you for being late?
▷ caution, lecture, rebuke, reproach
ANTONYM praise

R

reproach

VERB

I would like to reproach them for their bad manners.
▷ censure, rebuke, reprimand, scold
ANTONYM compliment

reproduce

VERB

1 *Some animals do not reproduce in captivity.*
▷ breed, multiply
2 *A digital piano can reproduce the sound of each piano note.*
▷ copy, duplicate, imitate

repulsive

ADJECTIVE

There's a bowl of something repulsive in the fridge.
▷ disgusting, offensive, unpleasant
ANTONYM attractive

reputation

NOUN

His reputation as a musician is unequalled.
▷ standing, stature

request

VERB

Request permission before you enter her room.
▷ ask, seek
NOUN
Her request for time off is being considered.
▷ appeal, application, plea

require

VERB

1 *What do you require from me?*
▷ crave, need, want
2 *The school may require us to wear uniforms next year.*
▷ compel, direct, instruct, order

required

ADJECTIVE

Is Geography a required subject in high school?
▷ compulsory, mandatory, necessary, obligatory

rescue

VERB

He managed to rescue some of his things from the flooded basement.
▷ salvage, save

research

NOUN

His research proved a link between lifestyle and illness.
▷ analysis, examination, exploration, investigation, study
VERB
Our group will research acid rain.
▷ examine, explore, investigate, study

resemblance

NOUN

I can see the resemblance between you and your younger brother.
▷ likeness, similarity

resent

VERB

I hope you did not resent my comment.
▷ begrudge, dislike, object to

resentful

ADJECTIVE

She becomes resentful at other people's success.
▷ bitter, embittered, jealous

reserve

VERB

Please reserve two tickets for us.
▷ hold, keep, save, set aside
NOUN
We have a reserve of emergency supplies.
▷ fund, hoard, stock, store, supply

reserved

ADJECTIVE

He is polite but reserved.
▷ distant, remote, secretive

reside

VERB

They reside in the south part of town.
▷ live, stay

residence

NOUN

Their permanent residence is in Fredericton, but they have a summer home on Cape Breton Island.
▷ dwelling, home

resign

VERB

He plans to resign from his job soon.
▷ leave, quit, retire

resist

VERB

The residents agreed to resist the zoning bylaw.
▷ defy, fight, oppose
ANTONYM accept

resistance

NOUN

There was resistance to the fare increase.
▷ defiance, opposition

resolve

VERB

How will you resolve who is correct?
▷ decide, determine, settle

R

respect
VERB
I deeply respect firefighters.
▷ admire, honour, value
ANTONYM disrespect
NOUN
I have a lot of respect for her opinions.
▷ admiration, esteem, regard
ANTONYM disrespect

respectable
ADJECTIVE
He has a respectable character.
▷ decent, good, honourable, reputable, upright
ANTONYM disreputable

respectful
ADJECTIVE
Be respectful to others.
▷ courteous, deferential, polite
ANTONYM rude

respond
VERB
Do not respond while you are angry.
▷ answer, reply, retort

responsible
ADJECTIVE
1 *Our group is responsible for collecting the data.*
▷ accountable, liable
2 *We need a responsible person for this job.*
▷ dependable, reliable, sensible, trustworthy
ANTONYM irresponsible

rest
NOUN
1 *Please clean up the rest of the mess.*
▷ balance, remainder
2 *Take a rest after you finish half the work.*
▷ break, pause

restful
ADJECTIVE
I am looking for a restful place to read.
▷ calm, peaceful, quiet, relaxing
ANTONYM hectic

restless
ADJECTIVE
He was restless because he was worried.
▷ edgy, fidgety, fretful, jumpy, uneasy, unsettled

restore
VERB
The experts will try to restore the ruined building.
▷ rebuild, reconstruct, renovate, repair

restrain
VERB
We could hardly restrain our excitement.
▷ control, curb, inhibit

restrict
VERB
The curfew will restrict your activities.
▷ hamper, limit, regulate

restriction
NOUN
There's a height restriction on some fairground rides.
▷ limit, regulation

result
NOUN
The result of our hard work was a perfect score.
▷ consequence, effect, outcome, product, upshot
VERB
An argument will result from your careless remark.
▷ arise, develop, follow, stem

resume
VERB
May we resume our conversation later?
▷ continue, renew
ANTONYM interrupt

retire
VERB
I plan to retire from the competition.
▷ resign, withdraw

retort
NOUN
He gave a rude retort.
▷ answer, reply

retreat
VERB
We received the order to retreat.
▷ flee, retire, withdraw
ANTONYM advance
NOUN
1 *The army's retreat began yesterday.*
▷ departure, evacuation, flight, withdrawal
ANTONYM advance
2 *The peaceful retreat is just outside the city.*
▷ haven, refuge, sanctuary

retrieve
VERB
Can you retrieve my deleted files?
▷ recover, regain, rescue, salvage
ANTONYM lose

return
VERB
Return the books to the correct shelf.
▷ replace, restore

reveal
VERB
Clean the silver bowl to reveal its beauty.
▷ expose, show, uncover, unveil
ANTONYM hide

R

revel in
VERB
I revel in my brother's success.
▷ celebrate, enjoy

revenge
NOUN
The players' revenge was to win the next game.
▷ reprisal, retaliation, retribution, vengeance

revere
VERB
I revere my grandparents.
▷ esteem, honour, respect

reverse
VERB
The judge will reverse the conviction.
▷ overrule, overturn

review
NOUN
1 *We read a review of the movie.*
▷ commentary, criticism
2 *We will spend some time on a review of this topic.*
▷ examination, inspection, study, survey

revise
VERB
Revise the paragraph and ask your partner to check it.
▷ amend, correct, edit, rewrite, update

revolt
VERB
The people will revolt against the cruel tyrant.
▷ mutiny, rebel

revolting
ADJECTIVE
The smell of the gas was revolting.
▷ disgusting, obnoxious, repugnant, repulsive

revolution
NOUN
In what year did the revolution take place?
▷ rebellion, uprising

revolve
VERB
I watched the merry-go-round revolve.
▷ spin, turn

reward
NOUN
There is a reward for finding the dog.
▷ award, bounty, payment, prize
ANTONYM penalty
VERB
You don't need to reward me for my help.
▷ pay, compensate
ANTONYM punish

rhythm
NOUN
I like the rhythm of that music.
▷ beat, pulse, tempo

rich
ADJECTIVE
1 *The rich family gave money for medical research.*
▷ affluent, prosperous, wealthy
ANTONYM poor
2 *Canada has rich natural resources.*
▷ abundant, plentiful

riddle
NOUN
We could not solve the riddle of the lost key.
▷ mystery, problem, puzzle

ridge
NOUN
Hiking on the ridge is popular with local residents.
▷ esker, hogback, moraine, range

ridicule
VERB
Do not ridicule others.
▷ mock, insult, sneer at, taunt, tease

ridiculous
ADJECTIVE
She was amused by the ridiculous behaviour of the clowns.
▷ absurd, laughable, ludicrous, preposterous, silly

rift
NOUN
The rift between the families has ended.
▷ breach, clash, disagreement, split

right
ADJECTIVE
See box on next page.

> **MAKE IT MORE FORMAL**
>
> **in the right** morally correct
> **right away** *or* **right now** immediately

rigid
ADJECTIVE
1 *The school has rigid rules to prevent bullying.*
▷ fixed, inflexible, set, strict
2 *Let the clay dry until it is rigid.*
▷ firm, hard, stiff
ANTONYM flexible

rim
NOUN
He drew a wavy line around the rim of his sketch.
▷ border, edge, margin

R

REPLACE AN OVERUSED WORD: RIGHT

Depending on the sense of **right** that you mean, there are a number of adjectives that you can use to vary your writing and make it more interesting.

- **the right thing**

  The use of slang words is not *appropriate* in a formal speech.

  You must bow in the *approved* manner when being presented to the monarch.

  Make sure your behaviour is *fitting* for such a solemn occasion.

  It was not *honourable* of you to cheat.

  Find out what kind of conduct is *proper* in that country.

  It is not *seemly* to stare at other people.

  I want to wear something *suitable* for such a grand party.

- **the right information**

  Is that clock *accurate*?

  Make sure you buy the *correct* size.

  You need the *exact* amount of money, because they will not give you any change.

  Please make sure all the information in your report is *factual*.

  The measurements have to be *precise*.

  Please tell us whether the story is *true* or not.

  Do you know if this password is *valid*?

ring
VERB
Ring the bell to assemble the villagers.
▷ chime, clang, toll

riot
NOUN
The police dealt quickly with the riot.
▷ brawl, clash, disturbance

ripe
ADJECTIVE
The peaches are ripe.
▷ developed, mature, ready

rise
VERB
1 *We watched the smoke rise from the bonfire.*
▷ ascend, climb, mount
ANTONYM fall
2 *The price of gas will rise due to a shortage.*
▷ grow, increase
ANTONYM decrease

risk
VERB
Do not risk your health by smoking.
▷ endanger, gamble, jeopardize

risky
ADJECTIVE
That was a risky thing to do.
▷ dangerous, perilous, unsafe

rite
NOUN
The team performs a special rite before games.
▷ ceremony, custom, ritual

ritual
NOUN
One common ritual is to blow out candles on a birthday cake.
▷ ceremony, custom, rite

rival
NOUN
Who will be your rival in the tournament?
▷ adversary, challenger, opponent
ADJECTIVE
The rival team is coming by bus.
▷ competing, opposing

road
NOUN
The road through our town has been widened.
▷ highway, route, street

roam
VERB
The hikers like to roam through the countryside.
▷ ramble, rove, wander

roar
VERB
You don't have to roar—I can hear you.
▷ bawl, bellow, blare, shout, yell

robust
ADJECTIVE
He looked robust and happy all summer.
▷ healthy, sound, strong, sturdy, tough, vigorous
ANTONYM fragile

rock
NOUN
Put the rock in the middle of the lawn.
▷ boulder, stone

R

role
NOUN
What role do you have in the group?
▷ function, job, position

roll
NOUN
Mark the absentees on the roll.
▷ list, record, register

romantic
ADJECTIVE
They played a romantic couple in the movie.
▷ amorous, loving, passionate, tender

room
NOUN
1 *The judge received them in a room in the courthouse.*
▷ chamber, hall, office
2 *Is there room in the trunk for my books?*
▷ capacity, space

root
NOUN
The root of the quarrel is jealousy.
▷ basis, cause, origin

rot
VERB
The vegetables began to rot in the heat.
▷ decay, decompose, fester, moulder, spoil

rotate
VERB
Rotate the doorknob to the right.
▷ spin, turn

rotten
ADJECTIVE
We threw the rotten apples into the compost.
▷ bad, decayed, decomposed, mouldy

rough
ADJECTIVE
1 *The rough path was hard to walk on.*
▷ bumpy, rocky, uneven
ANTONYM smooth
2 *They had a rough time driving in the snow.*
▷ difficult, hard, unpleasant
ANTONYM easy
3 *My rough guess is that he'll arrive about noon.*
▷ approximate, estimated, vague
4 *She needs to improve her rough manners.*
▷ crude, discourteous, impolite, rude

MAKE IT MORE FORMAL
rough in (*or* **out**) shape or sketch roughly
rough it do without conveniences

round
ADJECTIVE
He formed the clay into a round shape.
▷ circular, curved, spherical

route
NOUN
They took the easier route.
▷ path, road, way

routine
ADJECTIVE
Our routine time for breakfast is eight o'clock.
▷ everyday, normal, ordinary, regular, standard, typical, usual
NOUN
She dislikes anything that disturbs her daily routine.
▷ habit, pattern, practice, procedure, program, schedule, system

row
NOUN
1 *Stand in a row until your name is called.*
▷ column, line, queue
2 *They had a row over which TV program to watch.*
▷ argument, disagreement, dispute, fight, quarrel, squabble

rowdy
ADJECTIVE
The rowdy fans spoiled the game for everyone.
▷ boisterous, disorderly, noisy, unruly, wild

rub
VERB
Rub the dirt off your face.
▷ brush, polish, scrub, wipe

rubbish
NOUN
People should not drop rubbish on the ground.
▷ garbage, litter, refuse, trash, waste

rude
ADJECTIVE
I scolded the rude child.
▷ disrespectful, impertinent, impolite, impudent, insolent
ANTONYM polite

ruffle
VERB
Do not joke about her mistake because it will ruffle her.
▷ agitate, fluster, irritate, upset, worry

ruin
VERB
The flood will ruin the crops.
▷ demolish, destroy, devastate, wreck

R

rule

NOUN

The new rule is reasonable.
▷ decree, guideline, law, order, regulation

VERB

The dictator will rule till he dies.
▷ govern, lead, reign

ruler

NOUN

What would you do if you were the ruler of that country?
▷ commander, head of state, leader, monarch, premier, prime minister, sovereign

rumour

NOUN

The rumour is totally untrue.
▷ gossip, hearsay, scandal

run

VERB

1 *He started to run because he was late.*
▷ bolt, gallop, jog, race, sprint
2 *Can he run the business by himself?*
▷ administer, control, direct, manage

MAKE IT MORE FORMAL

run across (*or* **into**) meet by chance
run around with associate with
run away *or* **run off** flee
run out on someone desert someone
run through use up
run up against face a problem
run with go ahead creatively with a plan

---

rush

VERB

They had to rush to get to school on time.
▷ dash, hurry, hustle, race, run, scramble, scurry

ruthless

ADJECTIVE

The people feared the ruthless tyrant.
▷ harsh, merciless, pitiless

R

S s

sack
VERB
Her boss could sack her for being late.
▷ discharge, dismiss, fire

sacred
ADJECTIVE
Many religions have sacred books.
▷ holy, religious

sacrifice
VERB
He will sacrifice some free time to help us.
▷ forfeit, forgo, relinquish, surrender

sad
ADJECTIVE
1 *We were sad to hear about the accident.*
▷ dejected, depressed, downcast, glum, grief-stricken, mournful, unhappy
ANTONYM happy
2 *I do not like sad movies.*
▷ depressing, dismal, gloomy, mournful, tragic

sadden
VERB
This news may sadden you.
▷ depress, dishearten, dismay, distress, grieve

safe
ADJECTIVE
They kept the injured bird in a safe place.
▷ protected, secure, sheltered

salary
NOUN
He saved his salary to travel to Labrador.
▷ earnings, income, pay, wages

salvage
VERB
She could not salvage her electronic files.
▷ reclaim, recover, rescue, save

same
ADJECTIVE
I eat the same amount of food that you eat.
▷ equal, equivalent, identical
ANTONYM different

sample
NOUN
Please give me a sample of your handwriting.
▷ example, model

sanction
VERB
Only the principal can sanction a field trip.
▷ allow, approve, authorize, permit
ANTONYM veto

sanctuary
NOUN
He created a sanctuary for injured animals.
▷ haven, refuge, retreat, shelter

sane
ADJECTIVE
City council made a sane decision.
▷ lucid, rational, sensible
ANTONYM insane

sap
VERB
Lack of sleep will sap your energy.
▷ deplete, drain, exhaust, weaken

sarcastic
ADJECTIVE
We did not like her sarcastic comments, and we told her so.
▷ cutting, ironic, mocking, sardonic

satisfaction
NOUN
I get satisfaction from doing my best.
▷ contentment, delight, enjoyment, fulfillment

satisfactory
ADJECTIVE
His answer was satisfactory.
▷ acceptable, adequate, sufficient

satisfy
VERB
1 *Nothing will satisfy her.*
▷ gratify, please, suit
2 *Can you satisfy me that you will be careful?*
▷ convince, persuade, reassure

savage
ADJECTIVE
They had never seen such a savage attack.
▷ barbaric, brutal, ferocious, vicious, violent

save
VERB
1 *I had to save the magazines from being thrown out.*
▷ rescue, salvage
2 *I save quarters in a special jar.*
▷ hoard, keep, reserve

say
NOUN
See box on the next two pages.

saying
NOUN
I like the saying "Teachers open the door, but you enter by yourself."
▷ adage, maxim, proverb

S

There are a number of more interesting or creative words you can use in place of the basic verbs **say**, **speak**, and **talk**, if you want to describe the way in which a person says something, or the way in which something was said.

- If you **add** something when you are speaking, you say something more.

  I'd like to add my thanks to all of you.

- If you **announce** something, you speak about it publicly or officially.

  When will they announce the result of the soccer game?

- If you **answer** someone who has just spoken, you say something back to them.

  Are you going to answer the question?

- If you **ask** something, you say it in the form of a question because you want to know the answer.

  Wait until he has finished speaking before you ask any questions.

- If you **babble**, you talk in a confused or excited way.

  He tried to tell us what happened, but he was so upset that he could only babble.

- If you **breathe** something, you say it very quietly.

  Don't breathe a word to anyone about this.

- If you **chat** with someone, you talk in a friendly and informal way.

  We stopped to chat for a few minutes.

- If you **chatter**, you talk quickly and excitedly about things that are not important.

  Each group began to chatter, until it became impossible to follow what anyone was saying.

- If you **comment on** something, you say something about it.

  The prime minister refused to comment on the report.

- If you **converse** with someone, you talk to them. This is a formal word.

  They would sometimes converse in French.

- If you **croak** something, you say it in a low, rough voice.

  His mouth was so dry with fear, he could only croak for help.

- If you **declare** something, you say it firmly.

  Do you solemnly declare that you did not leave the room?

- If you **explain** something, you talk about it so that it can be understood.

  She managed to explain her idea with the help of a diagram.

- If you **gabble**, you say things so quickly that it is difficult for people to understand you.

  Slow down! I can't understand anything when you gabble.

- If you **gasp** something, you say it in a short, breathless way, especially because you are surprised, shocked, or in pain.

  First there was a loud noise, then I heard someone gasp, "What was that?"

- If you **gossip** with someone, you talk informally, especially about other people or events.

  If the two of you are going to gossip, I don't want to hear.

- If you **groan** something, you say it in a low voice, usually because you are in pain.

  We rushed over to help, and heard her groan, "I think my arm is broken."

- If you **growl** something, you say it in a low, rough, and angry voice.

  I tried and tried to help, but each time she would just growl, "Go away."

- If you **grunt** something, you say it in a low voice, often because you are annoyed or not interested.

  She was almost speechless with fury, and just managed to grunt a refusal.

- If you **hiss** something, you say it forcefully in a whisper.

  I heard him hiss something, but I was too scared to make out the words.

- If you **inquire about** something, you ask for information about it. This is a formal word.

  I would like to inquire about renewing my library card.

- If you **interrupt**, you say something while someone else is speaking.

  Please do not interrupt while she is telling her story.

- If you **mention** something, you say something about it, usually briefly.

  Did he mention that he knew my brother?

S

REPLACE AN OVERUSED WORD: SAY

Here are some more words that you can use in place of the basic verbs **say**, **speak**, and **talk**, if you want to describe the way in which a person says something, or the way in which something was said.

- If you **moan** something, you say it in a low voice, usually because you are unhappy.

  The lights went out, all the computers in the room crashed, then we heard someone ***moan***, *"I'll have to do the whole thing over again."*

- If you **mumble**, you speak very quietly and not clearly, so that your words are hard to make out.

  She started to ***mumble*** *something, then burst into tears.*

- If you **murmur** something, you speak very quietly, so that not many people can hear you.

  Didn't you see him ***murmur*** *something to his partner?*

- If you **mutter**, you speak very quietly, often because you are complaining about something.

  Don't just ***mutter*** *to yourself—speak up!*

- If you **point out** a fact or mistake, you speak to someone about it.

  I'd like to ***point out*** *that it was not my idea in the first place.*

- If you **prattle**, you talk a great deal about something unimportant.

  When I'm feeling nervous or shy, I tend to ***prattle***.

- If you **ramble**, you talk but do not make much sense because you keep going off the subject.

  At first, her story was interesting, but then she started to ***ramble*** *about people I've never met.*

- If you **remark** on something, you are making a comment about it.

  You were heard to ***remark*** *that you liked me.*

- If you **reply** to someone who has just spoken, you say something back to them.

  She thought about the question for a few moments, then began to ***reply***.

- If you **respond** to something that has been said, you react to it by saying something yourself.

  How can I ***respond*** *when I don't understand what you are saying?*

- If you **retort**, you reply angrily to someone. This is a formal word.

  If you accuse me, I can only ***retort*** *that the accident was your own fault.*

- If you **snap** at someone, you speak to them in a sharp, unfriendly way.

  I get upset when you ***snap*** *at me.*

- If you **snarl** something, you say it in a fierce, angry way.

  Don't ***snarl*** *like that, just calm down and tell me why you're so angry.*

- If you **state** something, you say it in a formal or definite way.

  Please ***state*** *your name and address.*

- If you **utter** sounds or words, you say them.

  He didn't ***utter*** *a word the whole evening.*

- If you **wheeze** something, you say it with a whistling sound, for example because you cannot get your breath.

  "I can't run any farther," he managed to ***wheeze***.

- If you **whisper**, you speak very quietly, using your breath rather than your throat.

  It's a secret, so I'll just ***whisper*** *it to you.*

S

scale
VERB
He tried to scale the fence, but it was too high.
▷ ascend, climb

scandal
NOUN
The scandal was reported in every newspaper for days.
▷ disgrace, shame, slander

scanty
ADJECTIVE
We have only a scanty supply of potatoes left.
▷ meager, sparse
ANTONYM abundant

scarce
ADJECTIVE
Wildflowers are becoming scarce in this region.
▷ rare, uncommon, unusual
ANTONYM common

scarcely

ADVERB

She had scarcely arrived when the class started.
▷ barely, hardly

scarcity

NOUN

There may be a scarcity of water this summer.
▷ insufficiency, lack, shortage

scare

VERB

The purpose of horror movies is to scare people.
▷ frighten, startle, terrify, unnerve

scary

ADJECTIVE

The owl's hoot sounded scary in the dark.
▷ alarming, chilling, eerie, frightening, terrifying, unnerving

scatter

VERB

Please scatter some birdseed out in the yard.
▷ spread, sprinkle

ANTONYM gather

scene

NOUN

1 *I've drawn a scene of fields in winter.*
▷ landscape, panorama, view

2 *Firefighters are at the scene of the accident.*
▷ location, place, site, spot

3 *He was not accustomed to the entertainment scene.*
▷ arena, business, environment, world

scenery

NOUN

We were awed by the scenery in the Northwest Territories.
▷ landscape, panorama, surroundings, view

scent

NOUN

The scent of cookies drew us into the kitchen.
▷ aroma, fragrance, perfume, smell

scheme

NOUN

The town council rejected the scheme.
▷ idea, plan, plot, project, proposal

scheming

ADJECTIVE

The scheming thieves planned to rob a bank.
▷ crafty, devious, sly

scoff at

VERB

Please do not scoff at my suggestion.
▷ belittle, mock, ridicule, scorn

scold

VERB

She did not scold me for spilling her coffee.
▷ chide, rebuke, reprimand

scoop

NOUN

Can you give me the scoop on the hockey scores?
▷ details, information

scope

NOUN

His scope of knowledge comes from reading a lot.
▷ breadth, extent, range

scorch

VERB

If the iron is too hot, it will scorch your shirt.
▷ burn, sear, singe

scorn

NOUN

The dishonest politician deserves public scorn.
▷ contempt, derision, disrespect, mockery

scornful

ADJECTIVE

The scornful audience booed and hissed.
▷ contemptuous, disdainful, sneering

scoundrel

NOUN

The con artist was a scoundrel.
▷ crook, rascal, rogue

scour

VERB

1 *Scour the sink after you wash the dishes.*
▷ clean, scrape, scrub

2 *I had to scour my locker for my missing journal.*
▷ comb, ransack, search

scowl

VERB

Why did you scowl at me like that?
▷ frown, glare, glower

scrap

NOUN

She begged for a scrap of information.
▷ bit, fragment, morsel, piece

VERB

They had to scrap their unsuccessful project.
▷ abandon, demolish, discard

ANTONYM preserve

scrape

VERB

Scrape the mud off your shoes.
▷ scour, scrub

NOUN

We are in a real scrape this time.
▷ fix, jam, predicament

S

scratch
NOUN
I fell and got a scratch on my knee.
▷ cut, graze, nick, scrape

scream
VERB
The fans began to scream when the music started.
▷ howl, screech, shout, shriek, squeal, yell

scrub
VERB
Scrub the chocolate off your face!
▷ clean, cleanse, scour, wash

scruffy
ADJECTIVE
We all looked scruffy after our camping trip.
▷ messy, shabby, sloppy, slovenly, unkempt
ANTONYM smart

scrutinize
VERB
Scrutinize the documents carefully.
▷ examine, inspect, study

scuffle
NOUN
He had a scuffle with another player.
▷ skirmish, tussle

scurry
VERB
We had to scurry around to collect the books.
▷ bustle, hurry, rush

seal
VERB
Seal the hole in the tent where the flies are getting in.
▷ close, plug, secure

search
VERB
Please search for the flashlight.
▷ hunt, look
NOUN
My search for a gift for my mom was successful.
▷ hunt, pursuit, quest

second-rate
ADJECTIVE
I ended up with a second-rate MP3 player.
▷ cheap, inferior

secret
ADJECTIVE
The desk has a secret drawer.
▷ concealed, confidential, hidden

section
NOUN
She liked the last section of the book the best.
▷ part, piece, portion, segment

secure
VERB
1 *He was able to secure four tickets to the play.*
▷ acquire, gain, obtain
2 *This glue will secure the handle to the cup.*
▷ attach, bind, fasten, fix, lock
ANTONYM release
ADJECTIVE
1 *They felt secure in the basement.*
▷ fortified, protected, safe, shielded
ANTONYM unsafe
2 *We were secure in the knowledge that we had done our best.*
▷ confident, protected, reassured, relaxed, safe

see
VERB
1 *What did you see through the window?*
▷ glimpse, notice, observe, perceive, spot
2 *I didn't see the point of the story.*
▷ appreciate, comprehend, follow, realize, understand
3 *Please see what your brother wants.*
▷ determine, discover

MAKE IT MORE FORMAL

see about find out about
see eye to eye agree
see red become very angry
see something through finish something
see to take care of

seek
VERB
1 *How do I learn the best way to seek information on the Internet?*
▷ hunt, look for, search for
2 *He says he will not seek re-election.*
▷ attempt, strive for, try for

seize
VERB
1 *The baby tried to seize the fork.*
▷ grab, grasp, snatch
2 *The town will seize the property for non-payment of taxes.*
▷ appropriate, confiscate, impound

select
VERB
Which book did you select?
▷ choose, decide on, pick
ADJECTIVE
We were represented by a select group of Canadian skiers.
▷ choice, first-class, first-rate, prime, special, superior

S

selfish

ADJECTIVE

The selfish children did not want to share the treat.
▷ greedy, inconsiderate, self-centred

send

VERB

Did you send the e-mail to the rest of the group?
▷ dispatch, forward, remit

MAKE IT MORE FORMAL

send in submit
send out emit

sensational

ADJECTIVE

We watched some sensational dancers on TV.
▷ exceptional, incredible, marvellous

sense

NOUN

1 *I had the sense that something was wrong.*
▷ feeling, impression, sensation
2 *Did she have enough sense to phone for help?*
▷ intelligence, judgment, wisdom

VERB

You always seem to sense when we have a problem.
▷ detect, feel, notice, realize, suspect

senseless

ADJECTIVE

I threw the senseless note into the garbage.
▷ foolish, meaningless, pointless, silly
ANTONYM wise

sensible

ADJECTIVE

A sensible idea is to save some of our money.
▷ down-to-earth, practical, prudent, rational, wise
ANTONYM foolish

sentimental

ADJECTIVE

I get sentimental when I hear that song.
▷ emotional, romantic

separate

ADJECTIVE

Keep your notes in a separate folder.
▷ distinct, unconnected

VERB

Separate the top and bottom forms.
▷ detach, disconnect, divide, part
ANTONYM connect

sequence

NOUN

Can you remember the sequence of events in the story?
▷ chain, series, string, succession

serene

ADJECTIVE

He looked so serene I didn't want to wake him.
▷ calm, peaceful, quiet, relaxed

series

NOUN

There was a series of thefts in the area.
▷ chain, sequence, string, succession

serious

ADJECTIVE

1 *The patient is in serious condition.*
▷ acute, critical, grave, severe
2 *Are you serious about hiking across Alberta?*
▷ genuine, honest, sincere

service

NOUN

My family went to the funeral service.
▷ ceremony, rite

set

NOUN

I have the whole set of 1987 baseball cards.
▷ batch, collection, group

VERB

1 *Just set your books on the table.*
▷ deposit, lay, place, position, rest
2 *Mom put the ice cream in the freezer to set.*
▷ harden, stiffen

ADJECTIVE

Do you have a set time for the meeting?
▷ firm, fixed, predetermined, scheduled

MAKE IT MORE FORMAL

all set ready to start
dead set against very determined not to do or allow
dead set on very determined to do or allow
set about begin
set aside reserve
set free release
set in your ways with stubbornly fixed habits
set loose free
set off explode
set up arrange
set upon attack

settle

VERB

The teacher helped us settle our argument.
▷ decide, resolve

several

ADJECTIVE

They donated several items to the sale.
▷ assorted, numerous, some, various

S

severe

ADJECTIVE

1 *He has a severe case of the flu.*

▷ acute, critical, grave, intense, serious

ANTONYM mild

2 *The severe look on her face made us nervous.*

▷ disapproving, grim, hard, harsh, stern, strict

severely

ADVERB

She has been severely ill all week.

▷ critically, dangerously, extremely, gravely

shabby

ADJECTIVE

I like my shabby jeans.

▷ dilapidated, ragged, scruffy, threadbare, worn

shady

ADJECTIVE

We were warned about those shady people.

▷ corrupt, crooked, suspicious

shake

VERB

1 *I began to shake with fear.*

▷ quiver, shiver, shudder, tremble

2 *Did the news shake you very much?*

▷ distress, disturb, rattle, shock, unnerve, upset

sham

ADJECTIVE

His sham grief did not fool us.

▷ artificial, counterfeit, fake, false, imitation, mock, phony

ANTONYM genuine

shame

NOUN

Her behaviour brought shame to the family.

▷ embarrassment, humiliation

VERB

This information will shame the people involved.

▷ disgrace, embarrass, humiliate

shameful

ADJECTIVE

Their shameful actions upset everyone.

▷ deplorable, disgraceful, scandalous

shameless

ADJECTIVE

What a shameless lie!

▷ barefaced, brazen, flagrant, unabashed

shape

NOUN

Please draw a triangular shape.

▷ figure, form, outline, structure

VERB

I tried to shape the clay into a horse.

▷ fashion, form, make, mould

share

VERB

Share the pizza with your friends.

▷ divide, split

NOUN

Give me a share of the grapes.

▷ part, portion, ration

sharp

ADJECTIVE

1 *Her sharp glance showed me that she wasn't fooled at all.*

▷ acute, alert, perceptive, shrewd

2 *He made a sharp turn into the plaza.*

▷ abrupt, marked, sudden

shatter

VERB

I saw the rock shatter the window.

▷ destroy, ruin, smash

sheer

ADJECTIVE

1 *The concert was sheer pleasure from start to finish.*

▷ absolute, complete, pure, total, unqualified, utter

2 *We looked up at the sheer face of the cliff.*

▷ perpendicular, steep, vertical

3 *She could see through the sheer fabric.*

▷ fine, lightweight, transparent

ANTONYM thick

shelter

NOUN

The stray cat found shelter in the barn.

▷ refuge, sanctuary

shield

VERB

Cover your face to shield it from the wind.

▷ guard, protect, safeguard, shelter

shifty

ADJECTIVE

He has shifty eyes.

▷ devious, dishonest, untrustworthy

shine

VERB

The lantern will shine through the darkness.

▷ beam, gleam, glow, radiate, shimmer, sparkle

shining

ADJECTIVE

A shining silver trophy sat on his desk.

▷ bright, brilliant, gleaming, luminous, radiant, sparkling

shirk

VERB

Do not shirk your duties.

▷ avoid, dodge, evade

S

shiver

VERB

The old house seemed to shiver in the wind.

▷ quiver, shake, shudder, tremble

shock

NOUN

The extent of the damage came as a shock.

▷ blow, fright, jolt, scare

VERB

1 *Did I shock you when I arrived early?*

▷ astonish, shake, stagger, stun

2 *That movie will shock many people.*

▷ appal, disgust, offend, outrage

shocking

ADJECTIVE

She made a shocking discovery.

▷ awful, frightful, horrible, terrible

shore

NOUN

I like to search for pretty stones along the shore.

▷ beach, lakeside, seashore, waterside

short

ADJECTIVE

1 *We got only a short peek at the celebrity.*

▷ brief, fleeting, momentary

ANTONYM long

2 *Keep your speech short, please.*

▷ brief, concise

3 See box at foot of this page.

shorten

VERB

I had to shorten my essay to fit on one page.

▷ abbreviate, condense, reduce

shout

NOUN

He heard the shout of the stranded kayakers.

▷ bellow, cry, roar, yell

VERB

Do not shout so loudly.

▷ bawl, bellow, call, cry, roar, yell

shove

VERB

Why did you shove me like that?

▷ elbow, jostle, push

show

VERB

Please show the class how you solved the problem.

▷ demonstrate to, instruct, teach

NOUN

The fall fair will have a motorcycle show.

▷ demonstration, display, exhibition, performance, presentation

MAKE IT MORE FORMAL

get the show on the road get started

run the show be in charge

show up appear

shower

VERB

Shower the roses with some water, please.

▷ spray, sprinkle

shred

NOUN

There is not a shred of truth in her statement.

▷ bit, fragment, particle, piece, scrap

S

REPLACE AN OVERUSED WORD: SHORT

Some adjectives used to describe a person who is **short** can be more hurtful or insulting than others.

- If you describe someone as **dumpy**, you mean they are short and fat. This is an uncomplimentary word.

  The store manager was a dumpy woman who always wore black.

- A person who is **little** is not large in physical size.

  He was too little to ride the roller coaster.

- If you describe a woman as **petite**, you are politely saying that she is short and not fat. This is a complimentary word.

  I am taller than my mom, who is petite.

- A **small** person is not large in physical size.

  The team captain was small, but he was an excellent skater.

- If you describe someone as **squat**, you mean that they are short and thick, usually in an unattractive way.

  The speaker was a squat man with a mean look on his face.

- A **tiny** person is extremely short.

  My older sister is tiny, graceful, and a great dancer.

shrewd

ADJECTIVE

His shrewd choice pleased everyone.

▷ astute, crafty, perceptive, sharp, smart

shriek

VERB

The children began to shriek with joy.

▷ hoot, scream, screech, squeal

shrill

ADJECTIVE

The shrill alarm woke everyone up.

▷ penetrating, piercing, screeching

shrink

VERB

Lack of rain is causing the pond to shrink.

▷ contract, diminish, dwindle, lessen

ANTONYM grow

shudder

VERB

I'm sure that you will shudder at the terrible sight.

▷ quake, shake, tremble

shun

VERB

It was unkind to shun the new student.

▷ avoid, ignore, snub, spurn

shut

VERB

I must shut the window before it rains.

▷ close, fasten, seal

ANTONYM open

shy

ADJECTIVE

She is shy with people she does not know well.

▷ bashful, modest, self-conscious, timid

ANTONYM bold

sick

ADJECTIVE

1 *The farmer worried about the sick cow.*

▷ ailing, diseased, ill, unwell, unhealthy

ANTONYM well

2 *The motion of the car made him sick.*

▷ ill, nauseous, queasy

sick of

ADJECTIVE

I am sick of that sitcom.

▷ bored with, fed up with, tired of, weary of

side

NOUN

Which side collected the most bottles?

▷ camp, faction, group, party, team

sight

NOUN

1 *She is fortunate to have good sight.*

▷ eyesight, vision

2 *The Olympic parade is an awesome sight.*

▷ display, scene, spectacle

VERB

We were able to sight the eclipse of the moon.

▷ observe, see, spot

sign

NOUN

1 *The company sign is above the door.*

▷ emblem, icon, logo, symbol

2 *The agent put the for-sale sign on the lawn.*

▷ board, notice, placard

3 *If you have any sign of a cold, do not visit the hospital.*

▷ clue, evidence, hint, indication, symptom, trace

signal

NOUN

The choir waited for the signal to begin.

▷ cue, gesture, sign

VERB

Did you signal him to stop speaking?

▷ gesture, motion

significant

ADJECTIVE

She shows significant improvement in reading.

▷ considerable, impressive, marked, notable, pronounced, striking

ANTONYM insignificant

silence

NOUN

I like the silence of the woods.

▷ hush, lull, peace, quiet, stillness

ANTONYM noise

silent

ADJECTIVE

He just looked at me, silent with surprise.

▷ speechless, wordless

silly

ADJECTIVE

Her silly song made everyone laugh.

▷ absurd, foolish, idiotic, inane, ridiculous, stupid

similar

ADJECTIVE

The jewels look similar, but one is fake.

▷ alike, comparable

ANTONYM different

simple

ADJECTIVE

I am sure there is a simple explanation.

▷ easy, straightforward, uncomplicated

ANTONYM complicated

S

simply

ADVERB

It is simply a matter of time before we win back the trophy.

▷ absolutely, just, merely, only, purely

since

CONJUNCTION

I will go, since you are busy.

▷ as, because, considering that

sincere

ADJECTIVE

He seemed sincere about his offer to help.

▷ genuine, wholehearted

ANTONYM insincere

single

ADJECTIVE

1 *A single bird perched on the feeder.*

▷ lone, sole, solitary

2 *I have two single uncles.*

▷ unattached, unmarried

singular

ADJECTIVE

She has a singular singing voice.

▷ exceptional, extraordinary, rare, remarkable, uncommon, unique, unusual

sinister

ADJECTIVE

The villain in the movie had a sinister manner.

▷ menacing, ominous, threatening

sink

VERB

In horror, I watched my cellphone sink into the water.

▷ descend, drop, fall, plunge

ANTONYM rise

site

NOUN

The site for the new pool has not been decided.

▷ location, place, scene, spot

situation

NOUN

The situation you have described is serious.

▷ circumstance, plight, scenario, state

size

NOUN

Please tell me the size of the room.

▷ dimensions, extent, proportions

skeptical

ADJECTIVE

I'm definitely skeptical about the free offer.

▷ cynical, doubtful, incredulous, unbelieving

sketch

VERB

We had to sketch apples in a bowl in art class.

▷ draw, illustrate, outline, picture, portray

skilful

ADJECTIVE

She is skilful at playing the flute.

▷ able, accomplished, adept, competent, expert, proficient, skilled

ANTONYM incompetent

skill

NOUN

His skill in football is due to constant practice.

▷ ability, competence, expertise, facility, knack, proficiency

skin

NOUN

1 *Remove the skin before you eat the fruit.*

▷ husk, peel, rind

2 *The pond had a green skin on its surface.*

▷ crust, film, scum

skinny

ADJECTIVE

See box at **thin**.

skip

VERB

Skip the first three paragraphs.

▷ disregard, miss, omit

skirmish

NOUN

A skirmish began between the two gangs.

▷ clash, fight, scrap

slack

ADJECTIVE

1 *The jacket looked slack on him.*

▷ baggy, limp, loose

ANTONYM tight

2 *She has become slack about doing her homework.*

▷ idle, lazy, sluggish

ANTONYM busy

slander

VERB

Politicians will sometimes slander their opponents.

▷ insult, libel, malign, smear

slant

NOUN

Put the board on a slant.

▷ angle, incline, slope

slap

VERB

Slap the mosquitoes away.

▷ hit, smack, strike

S

slash

VERB

A bear managed to slash open the tent and eat the food.

▷ cut, rip, slit

slaughter

VERB

They used to slaughter beavers for their fur.

▷ butcher, kill, massacre, murder, slay

slave

VERB

We had to slave for hours to build the fence.

▷ labour, toil, work

sleek

ADJECTIVE

Seals have a sleek look.

▷ glossy, polished, shiny, slick, smooth

sleep

VERB

I can't sleep during the day.

▷ doze, drowse, slumber, snooze

slender

ADJECTIVE

See box at **thin**.

slight

ADJECTIVE

There is a slight flaw in the material.

▷ insignificant, minor, negligible, small

ANTONYM large

slim

ADJECTIVE

See box at **thin**.

sling

VERB

Just sling your bag into the trunk.

▷ hurl, throw, toss

slip

VERB

1 *Slip quietly away and nobody will notice.*

▷ creep, sneak, steal

2 *The cars began to slip on the icy bridge.*

▷ skid, slide, slither

NOUN

You don't often make a slip like that.

▷ blunder, error, mistake, slip-up

MAKE IT MORE FORMAL

a slip of the tongue a remark made by mistake

give someone the slip evade someone

let slip tell without meaning to

slip one over on get the advantage of, especially by trickery

slip up make a mistake

slippery

ADJECTIVE

1 *The polished floor was slippery.*

▷ glassy, slick, smooth

2 *The slippery fox got into the henhouse.*

▷ cunning, sneaky, tricky

slit

VERB

Make a slit in the top crust of the pie.

▷ cut, gash

slope

NOUN

The slope of the ski hill is steep.

▷ angle, gradient, incline, slant

sloppy

ADJECTIVE

I can't hand in sloppy work.

▷ careless, messy, slipshod, slovenly, untidy

ANTONYM neat

slow

ADJECTIVE

It was slow of me not to understand your meaning.

▷ dense, dim, stupid

ANTONYM quick

sluggish

ADJECTIVE

The little creek is sluggish in the summer.

▷ sleepy, slow, slow-moving

ANTONYM fast

slumber

NOUN

The barking dog disturbed her slumber.

▷ doze, sleep, snooze

sly

ADJECTIVE

I avoid sly people.

▷ cunning, devious, scheming, sneaky, underhanded

smack

VERB

Try to smack the ball over the net.

▷ hit, slap, strike

small

ADJECTIVE

See box at top of next page.

smart

ADJECTIVE

1 *He always looks smart.*

▷ elegant, fashionable, stylish

ANTONYM scruffy

2 *She is smart, but she also studies hard.*

▷ bright, clever, intelligent

ANTONYM stupid

S

REPLACE AN OVERUSED WORD: SMALL

Depending on the sense of **small** that you mean, there are a number of adjectives that you can use to vary your writing and make it more interesting.

- **small things**

  Use the **little** plates for dessert.

  All cellphones are **miniature** nowadays.

  You need only a **minute** amount of this spice.

  She collects **tiny** wood carvings from Africa.

- **a small distance or area**

  We went for a **little** walk around the neighbourhood.

  The front yard is a **modest** size.

  You won't get the furniture through that **narrow** doorway.

  The mall is only a **short** distance from here.

- **small people** See box at **short**.

- **of small importance**

  My problems are **insignificant** compared to yours.

  She had a **minor** role in the play but she acted very well.

  We are wasting time on **petty** details.

  There is a **slight** difference between these two DVD players.

  Do not interrupt my work for such a **trifling** matter.

  You made one **trivial** error.

  I don't consider that the cost of the trip is an **unimportant** detail.

smash
VERB
Did you smash the mirror?
▷ break, demolish, destroy, shatter, wreck

smell
NOUN
The smell quickly filled the room.
▷ aroma, fragrance, odour, perfume, scent, stench, stink

smile
NOUN
Is that a smile on your face?
▷ beam, grin, smirk

smooth
ADJECTIVE
This fabric is smooth and silky.
▷ glassy, sleek, slick
ANTONYM rough

smother
VERB
He tried to smother his laughter.
▷ choke, stifle

smudge
NOUN
You have a smudge on the front of your T-shirt.
▷ mark, smear, spot, stain

smug
ADJECTIVE
He had a smug look on his face.
▷ complacent, conceited, self-satisfied

snag
NOUN
The snag is that I have other plans that day.
▷ catch, difficulty, disadvantage, drawback, problem

snap
VERB
I actually heard my ankle bone snap.
▷ break, crack, pop

snatch
VERB
The dog tried to snatch the cookie from my hand.
▷ grab, grasp, seize

sneak
VERB
I saw someone sneak around the back of the house.
▷ prowl, skulk, slink

sneaky
ADJECTIVE
She is sneaky and a gossip.
▷ crafty, deceitful, devious, dishonest, slippery, sly, untrustworthy

sneer at
VERB
He will often sneer at other people's ideas.
▷ jeer at, mock, ridicule, scoff at

snobbish
ADJECTIVE
That whole family is snobbish.
▷ condescending, haughty

S

snoop

VERB

A private detective is paid to snoop.

▷ eavesdrop, pry, spy

snooze

VERB

My old cat likes to snooze most of the day.

▷ doze, nap, sleep, slumber

snub

VERB

Did he snub you on purpose?

▷ insult, slight, spurn

snug

ADJECTIVE

We were snug in our sleeping bags.

▷ comfortable, cozy, sheltered, warm

so

ADVERB

We had some time, and so we went to the mall.

▷ accordingly, therefore, thus

soak

VERB

Soak the soil before you plant the seeds.

▷ drench, saturate, wet

sociable

ADJECTIVE

Our whole group is sociable.

▷ friendly, gregarious, outgoing

society

NOUN

1 *Canada is a multicultural society.*

▷ civilization, community

2 *Our society meets every Thursday afternoon.*

▷ association, club, group, organization, union

soft

ADJECTIVE

1 *We gave the baby a soft toy.*

▷ flexible, pliable, supple, yielding

ANTONYM hard

2 *They enjoyed the soft music in the restaurant.*

▷ gentle, low, mellow, muted, quiet, subdued

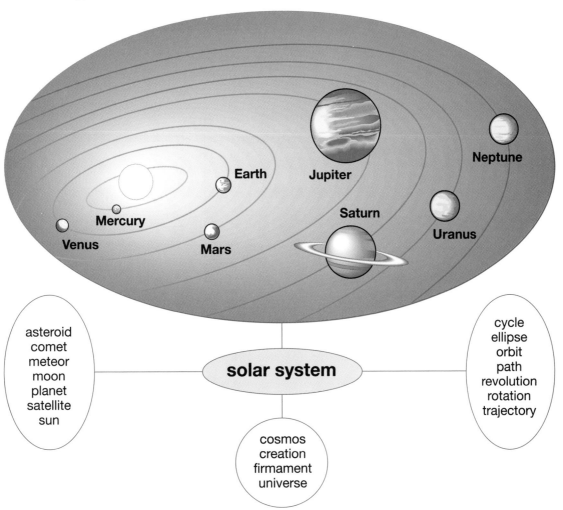

solar system

asteroid
comet
meteor
moon
planet
satellite
sun

cosmos
creation
firmament
universe

cycle
ellipse
orbit
path
revolution
rotation
trajectory

S

soften
VERB
*The wind will **soften** as the day goes on.*
▷ diminish, moderate, weaken

soil
NOUN
*Brush the **soil** off your boots.*
▷ clay, dirt, earth, ground

solar system
NOUN
See picture on previous page.

sole
ADJECTIVE
*She was the **sole** person to stay and help.*
▷ lone, one, only, single

solemn
ADJECTIVE
*It was a **solemn** moment for everyone.*
▷ grave, serious, sober

solid
ADJECTIVE
1 *The pond was frozen **solid**.*
▷ firm, hard, stiff
ANTONYM liquid
2 *This table is **solid** enough.*
▷ stable, steady, sturdy
ANTONYM shaky

solitary
ADJECTIVE
*I was the **solitary** witness to the crime.*
▷ lone, only, single, sole

solution
NOUN
*Do you have a **solution** to our problem?*
▷ answer, explanation

solve
VERB
*Can you **solve** the mysterious code?*
▷ crack, decipher, resolve, unravel

sombre
ADJECTIVE
*The day was **sombre**, but we hiked anyway.*
▷ dark, drab, dull, gloomy

some
ADJECTIVE
*I have **some** candies to share.*
▷ several, various

sometimes
ADVERB
Sometimes they travel by train.
▷ at times, now and then, occasionally, once in a while

song
NOUN
*I really like that **song**.*
▷ melody, number, tune

> ### MAKE IT MORE FORMAL
>
> **for a song** very cheaply
> **song and dance** long, pointless explanation

soon
ADVERB
*My sister will graduate from high school **soon**.*
▷ in the near future, presently, shortly
ANTONYM later

soothe
VERB
*The father tried to **soothe** the crying baby.*
▷ calm, comfort, pacify

sore
ADJECTIVE
1 *I can see you have a very **sore** thumb.*
▷ painful, raw, sensitive, tender
2 *She was really **sore** about losing the game.*
▷ annoyed, miffed, upset

sorrow
NOUN
*He expressed his **sorrow** in a poem.*
▷ grief, heartache, sadness, unhappiness, woe
ANTONYM joy

sorry
ADJECTIVE
1 *They were **sorry** about interrupting the party.*
▷ apologetic, regretful
2 *The whole school was **sorry** to hear about the tragedy.*
▷ distressed, grieved, sad
3 *A wet kitten is a **sorry** sight.*
▷ miserable, pathetic, pitiful, sad, wretched

sort
NOUN
*What **sort** of food do you like?*
▷ category, class, group, kind, style, type
VERB
Sort the votes by positives and negatives.
▷ arrange, categorize, classify, group

sound
NOUN
*There was a strange **sound** coming from the cellar.*
▷ din, hubbub, noise, racket
ANTONYM silence
ADJECTIVE
1 *The doctor told him his health was perfectly **sound**.*
▷ fine, fit, robust, well
2 *He came up with a **sound** plan.*
▷ firm, reliable, solid

S

sour

ADJECTIVE

1 *I like the sour taste of lemon.*
▷ acid, bitter, pungent, sharp, tart
ANTONYM sweet
2 *The milk is sour.*
▷ curdled, off, rancid
3 *Change that sour look on your face to a happy one.*
▷ disagreeable, peevish, sullen

source

NOUN

Her good report is the source of her happiness.
▷ cause, origin

souvenir

NOUN

We bought a souvenir of Vancouver in the gift shop.
▷ keepsake, memento, reminder, token

space

NOUN

1 *Our new apartment has enough space for my mom's office.*
▷ capacity, room
2 *There is a huge space between us for you to sit.*
▷ distance, gap

spacious

ADJECTIVE

Our school is enjoying its spacious new gym.
▷ extensive, huge, roomy

spare

ADJECTIVE

I've lost the spare key.
▷ extra, reserve, surplus
VERB
Can you spare a couple of dollars for the homeless?
▷ afford, give

sparkle

VERB

The full moon made the lake sparkle.
▷ gleam, glisten, glitter, shimmer, twinkle

sparse

ADJECTIVE

The population is sparse in the Northwest Territories.
▷ meagre, scanty, thin
ANTONYM dense

speak

VERB

See box at **say**.

special

ADJECTIVE

1 *Childhood was a special time in his life.*
▷ exceptional, important, significant
ANTONYM ordinary
2 *She gave a special gift to each guest.*
▷ distinctive, individual, particular

specific

ADJECTIVE

Are there any specific instructions for me?
▷ definite, precise, special

specimen

NOUN

Which tree has this leaf specimen come from?
▷ example, sample, type

speck

NOUN

You have a speck of dirt on your cheek.
▷ dot, particle, spot

spectacle

NOUN

They liked the spectacle of the Canada Day parade.
▷ display, scene, sight, wonder

spectacular

ADJECTIVE

He went to a spectacular concert last Friday.
▷ dramatic, fabulous, sensational, wonderful

spectator

NOUN

I was a spectator at the winning game.
▷ bystander, eyewitness, observer, onlooker, witness

speech

NOUN

Practise your speech in front of a mirror.
▷ address, lecture, talk

speed

NOUN

She worked with great speed to finish on time.
▷ haste, hurry, rapidity, swiftness, velocity
VERB
She likes to speed around on her scooter.
▷ race, rush, tear

speedy

ADJECTIVE

The speedy squirrel went from branch to branch.
▷ fast, quick, rapid, swift

spell

NOUN

We had a spell of hot weather in July.
▷ period, stretch, term, time

sphere

NOUN

A sphere is round.
▷ ball, globe, orb

spice

NOUN

I'm going to add a bit of spice.
▷ flavouring, seasoning, zest
See picture at **herb**.

S

spicy
ADJECTIVE
Some of those mixed nuts were spicy.
▷ hot, savoury, zesty

spill
VERB
Water began to spill over the top of the rain barrel.
▷ leak, overflow, pour

spin
VERB
We watched the skater spin until she was just a blur.
▷ pirouette, rotate, turn, whirl

spirit
NOUN
1 *The story is about a kind-hearted spirit.*
▷ apparition, ghost, phantom, spectre
2 *The team had lots of spirit, and were eager for a win.*
▷ energy, enthusiasm, fire, force, vigour, zest

spite
NOUN
She spilled paint on me out of spite.
▷ ill will, malice

spiteful
ADJECTIVE
He sent me a spiteful message.
▷ malevolent, malicious, nasty, snide, vindictive

splash
VERB
The baby likes to splash water around.
▷ shower, spatter, spray, sprinkle

splendid
ADJECTIVE
What a splendid idea!
▷ excellent, glorious, magnificent, wonderful

split
NOUN
1 *There is a split in my shoe.*
▷ crack, rip, tear
2 *The split between us happened two years ago.*
▷ breach, breakup, rift

spoil
VERB
1 *Pesticides can spoil the soil.*
▷ damage, harm, ruin, wreck
2 *They like to spoil their young cousins.*
▷ indulge, pamper

spoof
NOUN
Your spoof of the movie star was brilliant.
▷ parody, roast, satire, takeoff

spooky
ADJECTIVE
The campers told spooky stories in the darkness.
▷ eerie, frightening, ghostly, scary, supernatural, uncanny

spot
NOUN
There is still a spot on my shirt.
▷ blotch, mark, smudge, speck
VERB
Dad, did you spot that parking space?
▷ detect, observe

MAKE IT MORE FORMAL
hit the spot be exactly what is required
in a spot in a difficult situation
on the spot at the scene of an event

spray
VERB
The fountain will spray water into the pond.
▷ shower, splash, sprinkle, squirt

spread
VERB
1 *Spread the newspaper out on the floor.*
▷ unfold, unfurl, unroll
2 *He asked me to spread honey on his bread.*
▷ cover, slather, smear

sprightly
ADJECTIVE
She is sprightly and full of fun.
▷ active, lively, vivacious

spurn
VERB
If you spurn my help, I will not offer it again.
▷ refuse, reject, scorn

spurt
NOUN
A spurt of water came from the broken tap.
▷ gush, jet, stream

squabble
NOUN
Our squabble was foolish, and I apologize.
▷ argument, disagreement, dispute, quarrel, row, tiff

squad
NOUN
The football squad practises every day.
▷ band, group, team

squash
VERB
Please squash the boxes and tie them up.
▷ crush, flatten, mash

S

squeal

VERB

The fans began to squeal as soon as the singer appeared.
▷ squawk, squeak, yelp

squeeze

VERB

Can you squeeze another coat into the closet?
▷ cram, force, stuff

squirm

VERB

The students began to squirm in their seats.
▷ fidget, wriggle, writhe

stab

NOUN

Have another stab at spelling that word.
▷ attempt, try

stable

ADJECTIVE

Is the bench stable enough to stand on?
▷ firm, secure, solid, steady

stack

VERB

Stack the CDs on the bottom shelf.
▷ heap, load, pile

stage

NOUN

At this stage, we add the eggs and sugar.
▷ phase, point, step

VERB

They wanted to stage a protest outside the school.
▷ arrange, organize

stagger

VERB

1 *He began to stagger and finally fell down.*
▷ lurch, reel, totter
2 *This news will stagger you!*
▷ amaze, shock, surprise

stain

NOUN

There's an ink stain on my textbook.
▷ blot, mark, spot

VERB

He always manages to stain his clothes.
▷ dirty, mark, soil

stale

ADJECTIVE

Put out the stale bread for the birds.
▷ dry, old
ANTONYM fresh

stalk

VERB

The detective made plans to stalk the suspect.
▷ follow, hunt, tail, track

stamina

NOUN

You will have more stamina if you exercise.
▷ endurance, energy, strength

stand

VERB

How can you stand his rudeness?
▷ abide, bear, endure, tolerate

MAKE IT MORE FORMAL

stand by wait
stand for put up with
stand up for defend
stand up to defy

standard

NOUN

We must develop a better standard for recycling plastics.
▷ criterion, guideline, requirement

ADJECTIVE

The store has a standard rule for exchanges and refunds.
▷ customary, normal, regular, routine

star

NOUN

The star was gracious about giving autographs.
▷ celebrity, idol, personality

stare

VERB

It is bad manners to stare at someone.
▷ gape, gaze, peer

stark

ADJECTIVE

With no carpet or drapes, the room looked stark.
▷ bare, bleak, plain, severe

start

VERB

1 *When did the program start?*
▷ begin, commence
ANTONYM finish
2 *Start your silent reading now, please.*
▷ begin, commence, proceed with
ANTONYM stop
3 *They should start an investigation right away.*
▷ begin, establish, initiate, launch, open
ANTONYM close

NOUN

I was against the idea from the start.
▷ beginning, opening, outset
ANTONYM finish

startle

VERB

Sorry, I didn't mean to startle you.
▷ alarm, frighten, scare

S

state

NOUN
Citizens of a state must obey its laws.
▷ country, land, nation

VERB
The witness was asked to state his name.
▷ declare, specify

stationary

ADJECTIVE
The subway train remained stationary for over an hour.
▷ motionless, still

stationery

NOUN
See picture below.

status

NOUN
The last game improved the baseball team's status in the league.
▷ position, rank, standing

staunch

ADJECTIVE
He is a staunch friend.
▷ faithful, firm, steadfast, trusty

stay

VERB
Can you stay a little longer?
▷ linger, loiter, remain, wait

steady

ADJECTIVE
1 *The drummer kept a steady beat.*
▷ even, regular, uninterrupted
2 *The bridge over the river seemed steady.*
▷ firm, secure, stable

steal

VERB
1 *I know you tried to steal my project idea.*
▷ appropriate, pilfer, swipe, take
2 *I saw someone steal across the yard.*
▷ creep, slink, sneak, tiptoe

stealthy

ADJECTIVE

*Her **stealthy** movements made me suspicious.*
▷ furtive, sly, sneaky
ANTONYM open

steep

ADJECTIVE

*There is a fence at the edge of the **steep** cliff.*
▷ sheer, vertical
ANTONYM gradual

steer

VERB

*I tried to **steer** them to a better place to eat.*
▷ direct, guide, manoeuvre

step

NOUN

*You missed a **step** in the science experiment.*
▷ phase, stage

stern

ADJECTIVE

*All the people in the old photograph look **stern**.*
▷ grim, harsh, serious, severe, strict

stick

NOUN

*Hand me that **stick**, please.*
▷ bat, cane, pole, rod

VERB

1 *Stick the candles into the birthday cake.*
▷ insert, jab, poke, push, shove, thrust
2 *Stick a label on this package, please.*
▷ adhere, attach, glue, paste

MAKE IT MORE FORMAL

stick around wait nearby
stick in your throat be hard for you to accept
stick it out put up with unpleasant
  circumstances
stick it to someone treat someone harshly
stick out bulge
stick up for someone support someone

sticky

ADJECTIVE

*The paint on the floor was still **sticky**.*
▷ gluey, gummy, tacky

stiff

ADJECTIVE

1 *We need stiff paper to build our model.*
▷ firm, rigid
ANTONYM limp
2 *His conversation is a bit stiff.*
▷ formal, stilted
ANTONYM relaxed

3 *She did not deserve such a stiff punishment.*
▷ hard, severe
ANTONYM lenient

still

ADJECTIVE

*We enjoyed the **still** summer evening.*
▷ calm, peaceful, tranquil

ADVERB

*Keep **still** while I remove that splinter.*
▷ motionless, stationary

stink

NOUN

*There was a **stink** coming from under the house.*
▷ reek, smell, stench

stock

NOUN

*Where is your emergency **stock** of food?*
▷ reserve, stockpile, store, supply

stocky

ADJECTIVE

*That **stocky** teen over there is a terrific hockey player.*
▷ chunky, sturdy, thickset

stop

VERB

1 *Will he ever stop complaining?*
▷ cease, desist, discontinue, halt, quit
ANTONYM start
2 *The lesson will stop at 4 p.m.*
▷ conclude, end, finish
ANTONYM begin
3 *Do you know a way to stop the hiccups?*
▷ block, check, prevent

store

NOUN

*The pirates' **store** of gold was buried on the island.*
▷ cache, hoard, reserve, stock, stockpile, supply

VERB

*She will **store** our belongings until we return.*
▷ keep, save

storm

VERB

*The soldiers were told to **storm** the fort.*
▷ assault, attack, charge

NOUN

*The **storm** lasted four days.*
▷ blizzard, gale, hailstorm, hurricane, rainstorm, snowstorm, thunderstorm

story

NOUN

*I enjoyed every **story** in the book.*
▷ anecdote, fable, legend, tale, yarn

S

straightforward

ADJECTIVE

1 *The directions were straightforward.*
▷ basic, easy, routine, simple, uncomplicated
ANTONYM complicated

2 *Give us a straightforward answer.*
▷ candid, direct, frank, honest, open, plain

strain

NOUN

The strain of waiting made him bite his nails.
▷ anxiety, pressure, stress, tension

VERB

Do not strain yourself.
▷ overwork, tax

strange

ADJECTIVE

1 *Some of our customs must seem strange to you.*
▷ abnormal, bizarre, curious, extraordinary, odd, peculiar, unusual

2 *I like to try strange foods.*
▷ exotic, foreign, unfamiliar

streak

NOUN

He painted a streak of red on his skateboard.
▷ band, line, strip

strength

NOUN

1 *Gorillas have immense strength.*
▷ might, muscle

2 *She has great strength of will.*
▷ force, intensity, power
ANTONYM weakness

strengthen

VERB

Which walls did they have to strengthen?
▷ bolster, brace, fortify, reinforce, support
ANTONYM weaken

stress

NOUN

The stress of losing her job made her ill.
▷ anxiety, pressure, strain, tension, worry

VERB

Please stress the importance of healthy eating.
▷ accentuate, emphasize, highlight, underline

stretch

VERB

I would like to stretch the camping trip to two weeks.
▷ extend, lengthen
ANTONYM shorten

strict

ADJECTIVE

My piano teacher is strict, and doesn't let me fool around.
▷ firm, stern

strike

VERB

Strike the ball with the bat.
▷ hit, smack, whack

striking

ADJECTIVE

He bears a striking resemblance to his brother.
▷ eye-catching, noticeable, remarkable

stripe

NOUN

Paint a stripe on the model airplane.
▷ band, bar, line

strive

VERB

We always strive to do our best.
▷ attempt, seek, try

stroke

VERB

The baby likes to stroke his toy bear.
▷ caress, pat, rub

stroll

NOUN

She went for a stroll through the park.
▷ ramble, saunter, walk

strong

ADJECTIVE
See box at top of next page.

struggle

VERB

I had to struggle to get the cat into the carrier.
▷ strain, strive, toil, work

NOUN

The struggle between the debating teams was entertaining.
▷ battle, conflict, contest

stubborn

ADJECTIVE

The stubborn child refused to go to bed.
▷ dogged, obstinate, persistent

stuck-up

ADJECTIVE

Are all actors stuck-up?
▷ arrogant, conceited, haughty, proud, snobbish

study

VERB

1 *Did you study the history of Canada yet?*
▷ learn, read up on

2 *Study the map before you go.*
▷ contemplate, examine, pore over

S

REPLACE AN OVERUSED WORD: STRONG

Strong is an overused adjective. Depending on what you are referring to, there are many substitutes that you can use in its place to add variety and interest to your writing.

- **strong muscles**

  He exercises daily to maintain his **athletic** build.

  The top gymnast was a tall and **muscular** girl.

  Swimmers have **powerful** shoulders.

  We're both **well-built**, but my brother is taller than me.

- **strong in health**

  She is **blooming** with health.

  The coach won't let me play until I'm completely **fit** again.

  He isn't very **robust**, and often has a cold.

  Make sure you are in **sound** condition before going on the canoe trip.

- **strong in confidence and courage**

  Be **brave** and face your fears.

  Terry Fox made a **courageous** attempt to run across Canada.

  The early settlers must have been a **feisty** lot.

  You have to be **tough** to survive in the bush.

- **able to withstand rough treatment**

  These jeans are made of **durable** cotton denim.

  I need a pair of **hard-wearing** boots.

  She bought a **heavy-duty** hockey bag.

  Dad and I built a **sturdy** fence around the yard.

- **strong feelings**

  At the first performance of the musical, the lead player had an **acute** feeling of stage fright.

  We are all **ardent** hockey fans.

  The two of them formed a **deep** friendship.

  My sister has an **intense** dislike of snakes.

- **a strong argument**

  You had better provide some **convincing** reasons.

  He gave an **effective** reply to the charges against him.

  Your **persuasive** argument has made me change my mind.

  She presented a **sound** case against eating fast food.

- **a strong smell**

  The café was filled with the **intense** aroma of coffee.

  The perfume that you are wearing is **overpowering**.

  There's a **powerful** smell of smoke coming from the barbecue.

  The dog came inside, and we immediately became aware of the **pungent** scent of skunk.

- **a strong flavour**

  Vindaloo is a **hot** curry.

  The **overpowering** taste of garlic spoilt the salad.

  I liked the **sharp** tang of lemon in the pie.

  Spicy foods make me sweat.

- **a strong colour**

  I never wear **bold** colours.

  The team jackets are **bright** green.

  The cloudless sky was a **brilliant** blue.

  In some countries, firetrucks are painted a **glaring** yellow.

stuff

NOUN

*He put his **stuff** in the hall.*

▷ belongings, equipment, gear

VERB

***Stuff** all the paper in the recycling box.*

▷ cram, force, jam, push, ram, shove, squeeze, thrust

stuffy

ADJECTIVE

*It is **stuffy** in here, so please open the window.*

▷ close, muggy, stifling

ANTONYM airy

stump

VERB

*He claims that no puzzle can **stump** him.*

▷ baffle, mystify, perplex

stun

VERB

*The improvement in our team will **stun** you.*

▷ amaze, shock, surprise

stupid

ADJECTIVE

*Almost everyone does **stupid** things sometimes.*

▷ foolish, idiotic, silly, unwise

ANTONYM smart

S

sturdy

ADJECTIVE

The table is sturdy and will not collapse.

▷ durable, solid, strong, substantial, well-built

ANTONYM fragile

style

NOUN

1 *He has an unusual style of keyboarding.*

▷ manner, method, technique, way

2 *She dresses with style.*

▷ elegance, flair, taste

subdue

VERB

The knight swore to subdue the dragon.

▷ crush, defeat, overcome, overpower, vanquish

subject

NOUN

The subject under discussion is water pollution.

▷ issue, matter, point, question, theme, topic

substitute

VERB

I want to substitute some of the ingredients in the recipe.

▷ swap, switch

ADJECTIVE

The substitute pitcher ran onto the field.

▷ alternative, replacement

succeed

VERB

He worked hard to succeed in life.

▷ flourish, prosper, thrive, triumph

success

NOUN

Her success came after years of study.

▷ prosperity, triumph, victory

ANTONYM failure

successful

ADJECTIVE

The successful business began in a small garage.

▷ flourishing, prosperous, thriving

sudden

ADJECTIVE

The sudden noise woke the baby.

▷ abrupt, unexpected

ANTONYM gradual

suffer

VERB

We had to suffer the discomfort of freezing rain.

▷ bear, endure, experience, undergo

sufficient

ADJECTIVE

Do you have sufficient money to buy your lunch?

▷ adequate, ample, enough

ANTONYM insufficient

suggest

VERB

I suggest that you drive to Brandon on the Trans-Canada Highway.

▷ advise, propose, recommend

suggestion

NOUN

The whole class agreed with his suggestion.

▷ plan, proposal, recommendation

suit

VERB

Does my idea for our project suit you?

▷ please, satisfy

suitable

ADJECTIVE

Can you think of a suitable gift for him?

▷ acceptable, appropriate, satisfactory

sulky

ADJECTIVE

I am tired of her sulky behaviour.

▷ glum, huffy, moody, sullen

sullen

ADJECTIVE

He gets sullen when he cannot have his own way.

▷ grumpy, moody, sulky

summary

NOUN

Please give us a summary of the story.

▷ outline, rundown

summit

NOUN

She climbed to the summit of the mountain.

▷ height, peak, pinnacle, top

sumptuous

ADJECTIVE

The actor arrived wearing a sumptuous cape.

▷ costly, magnificent, rich, splendid

sunny

ADJECTIVE

They had a sunny day for their picnic.

▷ bright, clear, cloudless, fine

superb

ADJECTIVE

I have a superb part in the school play.

▷ excellent, magnificent, marvellous, outstanding, splendid, wonderful

S

superfluous

ADJECTIVE

I think you have packed a lot of superfluous clothing for a weekend trip.
▷ excess, surplus
ANTONYM essential

superior to

ADJECTIVE

1 *His language skills are superior to mine.*
▷ better than, greater than, higher than
ANTONYM inferior
2 *It is rude to behave in such a superior way.*
▷ condescending, disdainful, haughty, patronizing, snobbish

supervise

VERB

Who will supervise the group?
▷ direct, manage, oversee, run

supple

ADJECTIVE

Acrobats must be supple.
▷ flexible, pliable

supplies

NOUN

They got their supplies from the camping store.
▷ provisions, rations, stores

supply

VERB

We can supply you with some extra food.
▷ equip, furnish, provide
NOUN

Our supply of wood is behind the shed.
▷ cache, reserve, stock, stockpile, store

support

VERB

1 *A celebrity has agreed to support that charity.*
▷ back, champion, promote
ANTONYM oppose
2 *I will continue to support him in his new project.*
▷ encourage, help
3 *We need to support the wobbly fence.*
▷ bolster, brace, reinforce

supporter

NOUN

I am a supporter of the local soccer team.
▷ fan, follower

suppose

VERB

I suppose this is very important to you.
▷ assume, believe, expect, guess, imagine, presume, reckon, think

suppress

VERB

1 *The police arrived to suppress the riot.*
▷ crush, quash, quell
2 *We had to suppress our laughter during the speech.*
▷ conceal, restrain, stifle

supreme

ADJECTIVE

Whoever wins this game becomes the supreme champion.
▷ chief, foremost, greatest, highest, leading, principal, top, ultimate

sure

ADJECTIVE

1 *She was sure that she had the correct answer.*
▷ certain, convinced, positive, satisfied
2 *Cold weather is a sure sign that winter is near.*
▷ definite, dependable, foolproof, infallible, reliable, trustworthy

---

MAKE IT MORE FORMAL

for sure without doubt
sure enough definitely

---

surly

ADJECTIVE

Your surly behaviour is annoying.
▷ bad-tempered, cross, sullen

surpass

VERB

I am trying to surpass my previous best score.
▷ beat, exceed, pass, top

surplus

ADJECTIVE

Return any surplus paper to the shelf.
▷ excess, spare

surprise

NOUN

1 *The team's loss was a surprise.*
▷ jolt, revelation, shock
2 *We laughed at the surprise on their faces.*
▷ amazement, astonishment, incredulity, wonder
VERB

I wanted to surprise you by arriving early.
▷ amaze, astonish, astound, stagger, stun

surrender

VERB

The wounded soldiers were ordered to surrender to the enemy.
▷ submit, yield

S

surround

VERB

Surround the tree with flowers.

▷ encircle, enclose, encompass, envelop

survey

NOUN

The class did a survey on least favourite foods.

▷ analysis, overview, study

suspect

VERB

1 *I suspect the bus will be late.*

▷ believe, feel, guess, think

2 *I suspect everything she says.*

▷ distrust, doubt, mistrust

suspend

VERB

They had to suspend the game due to rain.

▷ cease, delay, postpone

suspicious

ADJECTIVE

1 *She has a suspicious mind.*

▷ distrustful, doubtful, skeptical, wary

2 *A suspicious character cannot be trusted.*

▷ shady, shifty

Greek alphabet

α β γ δ ε ζ
η θ ι κ λ μ
ν ξ ο π ρ σ
τ υ φ χ ψ ω

Latin alphabet

A B C D E F G H I J K L M
N O P Q R S T U V W X Y Z

Ancient Egyptian hieroglyphs

Chinese ideogram

好 朋

badge emblem logo

symbol

speech
alphabet
hieroglyph
ideogram
rune

number
figure
numeral
sign

S

swamp

NOUN

Many animals and birds live in the swamp.
▷ bog, marsh, morass, muskeg, quagmire, wetland

swap

VERB

I like to swap hockey cards with my friend.
▷ barter, exchange, switch, trade

sway

VERB

You cannot sway me, since I am determined to go.
▷ affect, influence, persuade

sweet

ADJECTIVE

1 *That juice drink has a very sweet taste.*
▷ sugary, syrupy
ANTONYM sour

2 *Lilacs have a sweet smell.*
▷ aromatic, fragrant, perfumed

3 *Her voice is low and sweet.*
▷ mellow, melodious
ANTONYM harsh

4 *The child has a sweet personality.*
▷ adorable, lovable
ANTONYM unpleasant

swell

VERB

The bump on my head began to swell.
▷ bulge, enlarge, expand, inflate

swerve

VERB

The bicyclist had to swerve around the puddle.
▷ turn, veer

swift

ADJECTIVE

His swift action saved the child.
▷ fast, prompt, quick, rapid, speedy
ANTONYM slow

swindle

VERB

She is too smart to allow someone to swindle her.
▷ cheat, con, rob

NOUN

It was a clever swindle, but they got caught.
▷ fraud, racket, scam

switch

VERB

My friend and I want to switch seats.
▷ change, exchange, swap

symbol

NOUN

See picture on previous page.

sympathetic

ADJECTIVE

He was sympathetic when I told him my problem.
▷ compassionate, kind, thoughtful, understanding
ANTONYM hostile

synopsis

NOUN

We had to give a synopsis of the speech.
▷ outline, summary

system

NOUN

I have a good system for studying.
▷ arrangement, method, procedure, technique

S

T t

tackle
VERB
1 *Did he tackle the quarterback?*
▷ attack, block, intercept
2 *I will tackle my homework after supper.*
▷ attempt, begin

tacky
ADJECTIVE
They wore tacky clothes to the costume party.
▷ flashy, gaudy, tasteless

tact
NOUN
Thank you for your tact in the situation.
▷ delicacy, diplomacy, discretion, judgment, sensitivity

tactful
ADJECTIVE
She was tactful and did not embarrass us.
▷ diplomatic, discreet, sensitive
ANTONYM tactless

tactic
NOUN
Your tactic was successful.
▷ approach, method, strategy

tactless
ADJECTIVE
I am sorry I was so tactless.
▷ blunt, inconsiderate, insensitive
ANTONYM tactful

tag
NOUN
The clerk put a "reduced" tag on the coat.
▷ label, sticker, ticket

taint
VERB
Pesticides taint lakes and rivers.
▷ contaminate, pollute, spoil
ANTONYM purify

take
VERB
1 *I'll take this end of the rope.*
▷ grab, grasp, seize
2 *Can you take the garbage out?*
▷ carry, transport
3 *Take me home, please.*
▷ escort, guide, lead
4 *Which one would you take?*
▷ choose, pick, select

take care of
VERB
1 *I have to take care of my little sister this evening.*
▷ mind, tend, watch
ANTONYM neglect
2 *He will take care of all the details.*
▷ handle, manage, see to

take in
VERB
I could not take in what the speaker said.
▷ absorb, assimilate, comprehend, digest, grasp, understand

take (someone) in
VERB
Did she really take you in with that lie?
▷ con, deceive, fool, mislead, trick

MAKE IT MORE FORMAL

on the take accepting bribes
take aback surprise
take advantage of impose on
take after resemble
take away subtract
take down write
take five take a break
take for mistake
take into account consider
take it or leave it accept or reject something without changing it
take it out of tire out
take lying down accept something undesirable without a protest
take off remove; depart
take on assume
take out get rid of
take over possess
take over from replace
take part participate
take place happen

tale
NOUN
He always has some tale to make us laugh.
▷ account, anecdote, story

talent
NOUN
She has quite a talent for drawing.
▷ flair, gift, skill

talk

VERB

See box at **say**.

NOUN

1 *My friend and I had a talk at recess.*
▷ chat, conversation, discussion
2 *The speaker gave a talk on healthy living.*
▷ address, lecture, speech

> ### MAKE IT MORE FORMAL
>
> **look who's talking** the person criticizing is equally guilty
> **now you're talking** now you're saying what I want to hear
> **talk about** discuss
> **talk back** answer disrespectfully
> **talk big** boast
> **talk down** speak in a condescending way
> **talk into** persuade
> **talk over** discuss
> **you should talk** you are guilty of the thing you are criticizing

talkative

ADJECTIVE

He is talkative, but not boring.
▷ chatty, communicative

tall

ADJECTIVE

There are tall mountains in the eastern region of Nunavut.
▷ high, lofty, soaring, towering

tame

ADJECTIVE

1 *The injured bird became quite tame.*
▷ domesticated, housebroken
ANTONYM wild
2 *The merry-go-round is too tame for me.*
▷ bland, dull, safe

VERB

I do not believe you can tame that raccoon.
▷ domesticate, train

tamper

VERB

Did anyone tamper with the DVD remote?
▷ fiddle, interfere, meddle

tangle

NOUN

The wind blew her long hair into a tangle.
▷ jumble, knot

VERB

Do not tangle the fishing line.
▷ snarl, twist

tap

VERB

Tap on the door lightly.
▷ drum, pat, rap

NOUN

1 *The tap needs to be fixed.*
▷ faucet, nozzle, spout, valve
2 *We heard a tap on the window.*
▷ knock, rap

target

NOUN

The food drive has a target of one item from each student.
▷ aim, goal, objective

tart

ADJECTIVE

The lemonade was tart.
▷ bitter, sharp, sour
ANTONYM sweet

NOUN

May I have another piece of tart?
▷ pastry, pie

task

NOUN

Each member of the group has a task.
▷ assignment, duty, job

taste

VERB

Taste this yogurt and see if you like it.
▷ try, sample

NOUN

1 *I'll have just a taste of your ice cream.*
▷ bite, mouthful
2 *Do you like the taste of grapefruit?*
▷ flavour, tang
3 *My brother and I have a taste for hiking.*
▷ fondness, liking

tasteful

ADJECTIVE

She chose a tasteful outfit for the presentation.
▷ elegant, refined, stylish

tasteless

ADJECTIVE

1 *I added some pepper to the tasteless soup.*
▷ bland, flat, weak
ANTONYM tasty
2 *Some people think lawn ornaments are tasteless.*
▷ flashy, garish, gaudy, tacky
ANTONYM tasteful

tasty

ADJECTIVE

Lunch was really tasty.
▷ appetizing, delicious, flavourful

T

taunt
VERB
Do not taunt your brother.
▷ mock, ridicule, tease

taut
ADJECTIVE
The muscles in your neck are taut.
▷ rigid, tense, tight

tax
NOUN
Is there any tax on shoes?
▷ duty, levy, tariff
VERB
Carrying a heavy backpack will tax your strength.
▷ drain, exhaust, sap

teach
VERB
She will teach younger children after school.
▷ coach, instruct, train, tutor

teacher
NOUN
My teacher helped me after class.
▷ coach, educator, instructor, professor, tutor

team
NOUN
She's part of a team of acrobats.
▷ gang, group, squad, troupe

team up
VERB
We should team up to get the job done.
▷ collaborate, join forces, unite, work together

tear
NOUN
My bicycle tire has a tear in it.
▷ rip, slash, split
VERB
1 *How did you tear your pants?*
▷ rip, slash, split
2 *He had to tear to the library before it closed.*
▷ dart, dash, fly, race

tearful
ADJECTIVE
The tearful child wanted her mother.
▷ crying, sobbing, weepy

tease
VERB
My uncle likes to tease me about my short hair.
▷ kid, needle, taunt

technique
NOUN
I have my own technique for studying.
▷ method, system, procedure

tedious
ADJECTIVE
The movie was tedious and too long.
▷ boring, monotonous, uninteresting
ANTONYM interesting

tell
VERB
1 *Please tell me when you are ready.*
▷ advise, inform, notify
2 *Will you tell him to be on time, please?*
▷ ask, order
3 *He could tell that the child was unhappy.*
▷ deduce, discern, see
4 *You can tell your story now.*
▷ narrate, recount, relate, report

MAKE IT MORE FORMAL

tell a lie lie
tell apart distinguish
tell it like it is tell the plain truth
tell me about it I have experienced exactly what you mean
tell off scold
tell on inform on
tell the difference distinguish
tell time know what time it is by looking at a clock
you're telling me I agree completely

temper
NOUN
I did not let my temper show.
▷ anger, annoyance, displeasure, rage

tempo
NOUN
The tempo of that song is too slow!
▷ beat, pace, rhythm

tempt
VERB
Can I tempt you into having another piece of cake?
▷ entice, lure, persuade

tend
VERB
1 *Our family members tend to be tall.*
▷ be apt, be inclined, be liable
2 *She will tend her flowers all summer.*
▷ care for, cultivate, look after
ANTONYM neglect

tender
ADJECTIVE
1 *She gave the sleeping child a tender glance.*
▷ affectionate, caring, gentle, loving
2 *My heel is tender from too much running.*
▷ inflamed, painful, sensitive, sore

T

tense

ADJECTIVE

1 *She was tense waiting for the election results.*
▷ anxious, edgy, nervous
ANTONYM calm

2 *The tense silence made everyone nervous.*
▷ nerve-racking, stressful

3 *His face was tense with excitement.*
▷ rigid, strained, taut, tight
ANTONYM relaxed

tension

NOUN

The tension showed in her voice.
▷ strain, stress, worry

term

NOUN

1 *Her term in office was three years.*
▷ duration, period, stretch, time

2 *The formal term for "stamp collector" is "philatelist."*
▷ name, word

terrain

NOUN

The terrain is rocky.
▷ earth, ground, land, landscape

terrible

ADJECTIVE

The car accident was a terrible sight.
▷ appalling, awful, dreadful, horrendous, horrible

terrific

ADJECTIVE

We had a terrific trip to Cypress Hills in Saskatchewan.
▷ remarkable, tremendous, wonderful
ANTONYM dreadful

terrify

VERB

Horror movies are meant to terrify the audience.
▷ frighten, petrify, scare
ANTONYM calm

terror

NOUN

He had never felt such terror before.
▷ fear, fright, horror

terrorize

VERB

The tiger continued to terrorize the village.
▷ frighten, scare, terrify

test

VERB

We are going to test tap water in class today.
▷ analyze, assess, evaluate, examine

NOUN

Is there a test next week?
▷ assessment, exam, quiz

texture

NOUN

I like the texture of velvet.
▷ consistency, feel

thankful for

ADJECTIVE

He was thankful for their help.
▷ appreciative of, grateful for
ANTONYM ungrateful

thanks

NOUN

I sent her a note of thanks for the gift.
▷ appreciation, gratitude

thaw

VERB

Keep ice cream in the freezer or it will thaw.
▷ defrost, melt, soften
ANTONYM freeze

theme

NOUN

What is the main theme of the story?
▷ message, subject, topic

theory

NOUN

The scientist must test her theory.
▷ concept, hypothesis, idea

therefore

ADVERB

They lost the game and are therefore out of the playoffs.
▷ as a result, consequently, for that reason, hence, thus

thick

ADJECTIVE

1 *There is a thick white line painted down the middle of the road.*
▷ broad, fat, wide
ANTONYM thin

2 *Thick liquids are difficult to pour.*
▷ concentrated, condensed, syrupy
ANTONYM runny

3 *The forest is thick with evergreen trees.*
▷ dense, lush, luxuriant
ANTONYM sparse

thicken

VERB

The pudding will thicken as it cools.
▷ congeal, set, solidify
ANTONYM thin

thief

NOUN

The thief stole a woman's purse.
▷ burglar, crook, pickpocket, robber

T

thin

ADJECTIVE

See box at foot of this page.

thing

NOUN

Pliers are just the thing to pull the nail from the wood.
▷ article, device, gadget, item, object

MAKE IT MORE FORMAL

know a thing or two be experienced
make a (big) thing (out) of give too much importance to
make a good thing of profit from

things

NOUN

Get your things ready for the hike.
▷ belongings, effects, gear, possessions, stuff

think

VERB

I think I will be ready to leave in an hour.
▷ believe, consider, feel, reckon

think about

VERB

Dad said he would think about my request.
▷ consider, contemplate, ponder

thirsty

ADJECTIVE

We were all thirsty after the run.
▷ dry, parched

thorough

ADJECTIVE

They made a thorough search for the lost watch.
▷ detailed, exhaustive, painstaking

though

CONJUNCTION

I will go to the game, though I will be late.
▷ although, but

thought

NOUN

Give the question some thought before answering.
▷ consideration, deliberation, reflection

REPLACE AN OVERUSED WORD: THIN

When describing someone who is **thin**, some adjectives are complimentary, some are neutral, and others are definitely uncomplimentary.

- If you describe someone as **bony**, you mean that he or she has very little flesh.

  He is pale and bony after being ill for such a long time.

- A person or animal that is **emaciated** is very thin and weak from illness or lack of food.

  The TV program showed footage of emaciated lions trying to survive during the dry season.

- If you say someone is **lanky**, you mean that he or she is tall and thin and moves rather awkwardly.

  The chubby little girl grew to be a lanky teenager.

- If you describe someone as **lean**, you mean that he or she is thin, but looks strong and healthy.

  Like many runners, she was lean and muscular.

- A **light** person does not weigh very much.

  The ballerina was fairly tall, but very light.

- If you say a person is **scrawny**, you mean that he or she looks unattractively thin.

  He eats enormous meals, but still looks like a scrawny child.

- A **skinny** person is extremely thin, in a way that you find unattractive. This is an informal word.

  Do you have to be skinny to be a supermodel?

- A **slender** person is thin and graceful.

  One after the other, four slender dancers drifted across the stage.

- A **slight** person has a fairly thin and delicate-looking body.

  I have a slight figure, but I am stronger than I look.

- A **slim** person has a thin and well-shaped body.

  My sister is quite slim, and I tease her by calling her "Skinny."

- Someone who has a **spare** figure is tall and not at all fat. This is a formal word.

  We smiled to see my uncle, who has a spare figure, fold himself into the back seat of the car.

- If someone is **underweight**, he or she is too thin and therefore not healthy.

  Some designers are refusing to use models who are underweight.

T

thoughts
NOUN
May we hear your thoughts on the topic?
▷ ideas, opinion, views

thoughtful
ADJECTIVE
1 *She closed her eyes and looked thoughtful.*
▷ contemplative, pensive, reflective
2 *The thoughtful girl mowed her neighbour's lawn.*
▷ attentive, considerate, kind
ANTONYM thoughtless

thoughtless
ADJECTIVE
She is thoughtless and often hurts my feelings.
▷ inconsiderate, insensitive, tactless
ANTONYM thoughtful

threat
NOUN
There is a threat of a hurricane.
▷ danger, hazard, risk

threaten
VERB
1 *I am not afraid, so do not bother to threaten me.*
▷ bully, intimidate, pressure
2 *Arguing will threaten the success of our project.*
▷ endanger, jeopardize, put at risk

threatening
ADJECTIVE
The sky was full of dark, threatening clouds.
▷ foreboding, menacing, ominous, sinister

thrifty
ADJECTIVE
I know how to be thrifty and save money.
▷ careful, economical, frugal
ANTONYM wasteful

thrill
VERB
It will thrill us to see our friends again.
▷ delight, excite, overjoy

thrilling
ADJECTIVE
We loved the thrilling rides at the fair.
▷ exciting, exhilarating, gripping

thrive
VERB
The kitten should thrive now that it has good food.
▷ flourish, grow, prosper

throb
VERB
My heart began to throb with excitement.
▷ beat, pound

throng
NOUN
We pushed our way through the throng.
▷ crowd, horde, mass, mob

throw
VERB
He can throw the football a long way.
▷ cast, fling, hurl, pitch, toss

MAKE IT MORE FORMAL
throw about scatter
throw away discard
throw cold water on discourage
throw in add as a bonus
throw off produce something in a casual way
throw out discard
throw together make hurriedly
throw up vomit
throw yourself into do enthusiastically

thud
NOUN
The books fell off the shelf with a thud.
▷ bang, bump, clunk, thump

thug
NOUN
A thug thinks it is funny to scare people.
▷ bully, delinquent, hoodlum, hooligan

thus
ADVERB
I received some money and thus was able to buy the DVD.
▷ consequently, so, therefore

ticket
NOUN
Did you get a ticket to go backstage?
▷ coupon, pass, voucher

tidy
ADJECTIVE
His room is always tidy.
▷ neat, orderly, uncluttered, well-kept
VERB
Tidy your locker before you leave school.
▷ arrange, neaten, organize, straighten

tie
VERB
Tie your shoelaces tightly.
▷ bind, fasten, knot, secure
NOUN
1 *If the game ends in a tie, there will be a rematch.*
▷ dead heat, deadlock, draw, stalemate
2 *I have a close tie with one of my cousins.*
▷ bond, connection, relationship

tight
ADJECTIVE
1 *Six people in that car is a tight fit.*
▷ cramped, snug
ANTONYM loose
2 *Make sure the knot is tight.*
▷ firm, secure
3 *Massage can help if your muscles are tight.*
▷ rigid, taut, tense
ANTONYM slack

tilt
VERB
The axle broke and the wagon began to tilt.
▷ incline, lean, slant, tip
NOUN
The house on the hill is built on a tilt.
▷ angle, gradient, incline, slant, slope

time
NOUN
1 *There was a time when he did not like school.*
▷ period, spell, stretch, term
2 *I wish I lived at the time of dinosaurs.*
▷ age, epoch, era, period
VERB
Time your visit so that you get here before dark.
▷ schedule, set

timetable
NOUN
The teacher handed out a timetable.
▷ agenda, program, schedule

timid
ADJECTIVE
The timid child hid her face.
▷ bashful, coy, nervous, shy
ANTONYM bold

tinge
NOUN
I like water with a tinge of lemon juice.
▷ bit, drop, hint, touch, trace

tint
NOUN
I like the light yellow tint.
▷ colour, hue, shade, tone
VERB
Are you sure you want to tint your hair?
▷ colour, dye

tiny
ADJECTIVE
A tiny insect crawled onto my hand.
▷ diminutive, microscopic, minute
ANTONYM huge

tip
NOUN
1 *You can see only the tip of an iceberg.*
▷ peak, point, top
2 *I know a tip on how to remove the stain.*
▷ hint, pointer, suggestion
VERB
The building is starting to tip because the foundation is weak.
▷ incline, lean, slant, tilt

tire
VERB
The long hike will tire us.
▷ drain, exhaust, weaken

tired
ADJECTIVE
They were tired and went to bed early.
▷ drained, exhausted, fatigued, weary

tiresome
ADJECTIVE
His long story became tiresome.
▷ boring, dull, tedious

title
NOUN
Does this chapter have a title?
▷ heading, name

toast
VERB
1 *Please stand to toast the bride and groom.*
▷ hail, honour, salute
2 *She plans to toast her snack in the oven.*
▷ bake, brown

toddler
NOUN
The toddler played with the teddy bear.
▷ child, kid, youngster

together
ADVERB
The members of the team worked well together.
▷ collectively, jointly
ANTONYM alone

toil
VERB
He had to toil for long hours to earn a living.
▷ labour, slog, work

token
NOUN
1 *Take this key chain as a token of your visit.*
▷ keepsake, memento, souvenir
2 *Use this token to get into the show.*
▷ coupon, ticket, voucher

T

tolerable

ADJECTIVE

1 *The speech was tolerable because it was short.*
▷ bearable, endurable

ANTONYM unbearable

2 *We felt the extra charge was tolerable.*
▷ acceptable, reasonable

tolerant

ADJECTIVE

My parents are tolerant and easy to talk to.
▷ broad-minded, open-minded, understanding

ANTONYM narrow-minded

tolerate

VERB

Do not tolerate rude behaviour.
▷ accept, permit, put up with

toll

NOUN

They had to pay a toll to use the new highway.
▷ charge, duty, fee, levy

tomb

NOUN

The ancient tomb held gold and jewels.
▷ grave, mausoleum, sepulchre, vault

too

ADVERB

1 *That sweater is too big for me.*
▷ extremely, overly, ridiculously, unduly

2 *I'm hungry, and thirsty too.*
▷ also, as well, besides

tone

NOUN

1 *His singing voice has a good tone.*
▷ note, pitch, sound, timbre

2 *Do you like that tone of blue?*
▷ colour, hue, shade

tool

NOUN

I used the wrong tool and broke the pipe.
▷ implement, instrument

top

NOUN

1 *Wait for me at the top of the hill.*
▷ apex, crest, peak, summit

ANTONYM bottom

2 *I cannot get the top off the jar.*
▷ cap, cover, lid

ADJECTIVE

She is the top scorer in the league.
▷ head, highest, leading

VERB

1 *I am trying to top my previous high-jump record.*
▷ exceed, go beyond, surpass

2 *No one can top that excuse for being late.*
▷ beat, better, improve on, outdo, surpass

MAKE IT MORE FORMAL

from top to bottom completely
off the top of your head without preparation
over the top to an exaggerated degree
top up add to

topic

NOUN

Has the group chosen a topic to research?
▷ question, subject

topple

VERB

The tower of toy blocks began to topple over.
▷ collapse, fall, tumble

torment

VERB

They began to torment the caged monkey.
▷ annoy, bully, persecute, provoke, tease

torrent

NOUN

The stream became a torrent of rushing water.
▷ burst, cascade, flood

torture

NOUN

The torture of my broken leg was unbearable.
▷ agony, anguish, pain

toss

VERB

We used to toss coins into the fountain.
▷ cast, fling, hurl, pitch

tot

NOUN

He put the tot into the car seat.
▷ child, infant, kid

total

NOUN

The total was more than she expected.
▷ amount, sum

VERB

Please total how much I owe you.
▷ add up, calculate

ADJECTIVE

The school play was a total success.
▷ absolute, complete, outright, utter

totally

ADVERB

I am totally against that idea.
▷ completely, entirely, utterly

ANTONYM partially

T

touch

VERB

1 *Touch both surfaces and describe them in your notebooks.*
▷ feel, finger, handle

2 *The branches were close enough to touch the bedroom window.*
▷ brush, contact, graze, meet

3 *Did the sad part of the movie touch you?*
▷ affect, move, stir

NOUN

The soup needs a touch more salt.
▷ hint, shade, trace

MAKE IT MORE FORMAL

touch down land
touch on mention

---

touching

ADJECTIVE

He gave a touching farewell speech.
▷ affecting, moving, poignant

touchy

ADJECTIVE

She is touchy, so do not upset her.
▷ easily offended, moody, quick-tempered, sensitive

tough

ADJECTIVE

1 *Our school has a tough wrestling team.*
▷ hardy, robust, rugged, strong

2 *My jacket is made from a tough fabric.*
▷ durable, resilient, solid, sturdy
ANTONYM fragile

3 *Climbing the rope was tough.*
▷ arduous, difficult
ANTONYM easy

tour

NOUN

We want to go on a tour to Fort Simpson.
▷ excursion, journey, trip, voyage

tournament

NOUN

Did you play in the tennis tournament?
▷ competition, contest, match

tow

VERB

We need a hitch to tow the trailer.
▷ drag, haul, lug, pull

toy

NOUN

The child asked for a new toy.
▷ game, plaything
See picture on next page.

trace

VERB

He tried to trace his lost relatives.
▷ locate, track down

NOUN

1 *There was no trace of the missing money.*
▷ evidence, record, sign

2 *She did not have a trace of sympathy for me.*
▷ dash, drop, tinge

track

NOUN

They walked along the track in single file.
▷ path, road, trail

VERB

The hunters will track their prey through the woods.
▷ follow, pursue, stalk

MAKE IT MORE FORMAL

track down locate
track record reputation

---

trade

NOUN

1 *The company does trade with other countries.*
▷ business, commerce

2 *He is learning the trade of computer programmer.*
▷ business, livelihood, occupation, profession

VERB

Will you trade your baseball for my skipping rope?
▷ barter, exchange, swap

trader

NOUN

The trader buys and sells used CDs.
▷ dealer, merchant

tradition

NOUN

What is your favourite Canada Day tradition?
▷ custom, practice, ritual

traditional

ADJECTIVE

Describe a traditional activity in your family.
▷ customary, established

tragedy

NOUN

The earthquake was a terrible tragedy.
▷ calamity, catastrophe, disaster

tragic

ADJECTIVE

Carelessness was the cause of the tragic accident.
▷ disastrous, distressing, heartbreaking

trail

NOUN

Be careful of poison ivy along the trail.
▷ path, road, route, track

T

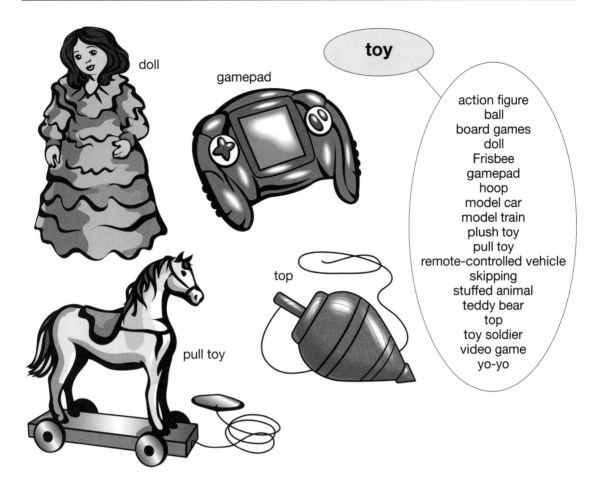

doll

gamepad

toy

action figure
ball
board games
doll
Frisbee
gamepad
hoop
model car
model train
plush toy
pull toy
remote-controlled vehicle
skipping
stuffed animal
teddy bear
top
toy soldier
video game
yo-yo

top

pull toy

train
VERB
She is going to train Olympic athletes.
▷ coach, guide, instruct, teach

trait
NOUN
Which human trait is the most important?
▷ attribute, characteristic, quality

tranquil
ADJECTIVE
I would like to have a tranquil holiday.
▷ calm, peaceful, quiet

transfer
VERB
Transfer to the bus behind this one.
▷ move, pass, switch

transform
VERB
The actor used makeup to transform himself into a vampire.
▷ alter, change

transmit
VERB
During the war, the armed forces used to transmit messages in code.
▷ broadcast, communicate, send

transparent
ADJECTIVE
The moon shone clearly through the transparent curtains.
▷ clear, see-through, sheer

transport
VERB
The moving truck will transport our furniture.
▷ carry, convey, haul, ship

trap
NOUN
I set a trap for whoever was stealing my lunch.
▷ net, snare
VERB
1 *We tried to trap the mouse.*
▷ capture, corner, snare
2 *Can you trap them into admitting the theft?*
▷ dupe, lure, trick

T

trash

NOUN

Our club offered to pick up the trash in the park.

▷ garbage, refuse, waste

travel

VERB

Can we travel by car to Inuvik?

▷ journey, voyage

See picture on next page.

treacherous

ADJECTIVE

1 *A treacherous friend is worse than an enemy.*

▷ disloyal, unfaithful, untrustworthy

ANTONYM loyal

2 *Those roads are treacherous in winter.*

▷ dangerous, hazardous, perilous

treasure

NOUN

The pirates buried their treasure on a small island.

▷ fortune, riches, wealth

VERB

I treasure the time I spend reading.

▷ cherish, prize, value

treat

VERB

1 *Treat other people the way you would like to be treated.*

▷ act toward, behave toward, deal with

2 *Did the doctor treat you when you were ill?*

▷ care for, medicate

treaty

NOUN

The treaty was signed by both countries.

▷ accord, agreement, pact

trek

NOUN

It's a long trek to other end of the island.

▷ hike, journey, walk

tremble

VERB

I began to tremble with excitement.

▷ quake, shake, shiver

tremendous

ADJECTIVE

She has a tremendous interest in music.

▷ enormous, immense, wonderful

trend

NOUN

1 *We refused to follow the silly trend.*

▷ craze, fad, fashion

2 *There is a trend toward more recycling.*

▷ direction, movement, tendency

trendy

ADJECTIVE

Black is the trendy colour every year.

▷ fashionable, latest, stylish

trial

NOUN

His illness has been a trial for him.

▷ hardship, ordeal

trick

NOUN

That trick was cruel, not funny or clever.

▷ hoax, joke, prank

VERB

Someone tried to trick her into giving her credit-card number.

▷ con, deceive, dupe, fool

trickle

NOUN

Only a trickle of water came out of the tap.

▷ dribble, drip, drop

tricky

ADJECTIVE

The directions for building the model airplane were tricky.

▷ complex, complicated, difficult

ANTONYM simple

trim

VERB

My neighbour likes to trim his shrubs into spheres.

▷ clip, crop, prune, shear

ADJECTIVE

They live in a trim little cottage.

▷ neat, orderly, tidy

ANTONYM scruffy

trip

NOUN

Our trip to the country had to be postponed.

▷ excursion, journey, outing, voyage

VERB

Move the box or someone will trip over it.

▷ fall, stumble, tumble

triumph

NOUN

His triumph gave us a chance to cheer him.

▷ achievement, success, victory

ANTONYM failure

trivial

ADJECTIVE

The council wasted time on trivial matters.

▷ insignificant, minor, petty, unimportant

ANTONYM important

troop

NOUN

Our entire troop went on a camping trip.

▷ band, group, squad, team

T

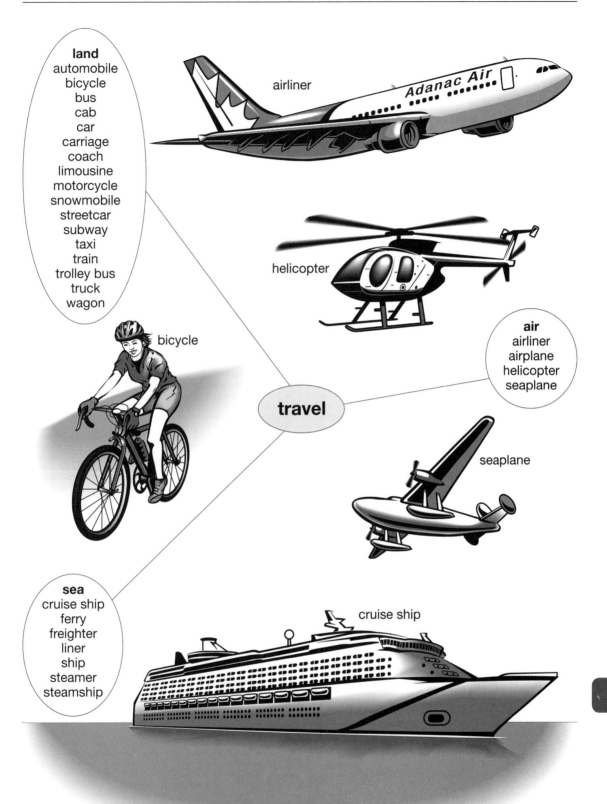

land
automobile
bicycle
bus
cab
car
carriage
coach
limousine
motorcycle
snowmobile
streetcar
subway
taxi
train
trolley bus
truck
wagon

airliner

helicopter

air
airliner
airplane
helicopter
seaplane

bicycle

travel

seaplane

sea
cruise ship
ferry
freighter
liner
ship
steamer
steamship

cruise ship

trophy
NOUN
I received a trophy for my science project.
▷ award, cup, plaque, prize, title

trouble
NOUN
The trouble was that I could not stop laughing.
▷ difficulty, dilemma, problem
VERB
1 *Do not trouble him right now.*
▷ bother, concern, disturb, worry
2 *May I trouble you for the time?*
▷ bother, disturb, impose upon, inconvenience

true
ADJECTIVE
1 *The witness gave a true account of the accident.*
▷ accurate, correct, factual
ANTONYM inaccurate
2 *You are a true pal.*
▷ faithful, genuine, loyal, real

trunk
NOUN
1 *She found some family pictures in the old trunk.*
▷ box, case, chest
2 *His trunk is covered with a rash.*
▷ body, torso

trust
VERB
Can I trust you to deliver the message?
▷ count on, depend on, have confidence in, have faith in, rely upon
NOUN
I know you have trust in her.
▷ confidence, faith

trustworthy
ADJECTIVE
Trustworthy employees have keys to the store.
▷ dependable, honest, reliable
ANTONYM unreliable

truth
NOUN
How much truth is in that statement?
▷ accuracy, fact

truthful
ADJECTIVE
Be truthful and tell us what happened.
▷ candid, frank, honest, open, straight

try
VERB
1 *I will try to get to your house by five o'clock.*
▷ attempt, endeavour, strive
2 *I am going to try a new recipe for chili.*
▷ test, try out

NOUN
Let me have a try at solving the puzzle.
▷ attempt, crack, shot

MAKE IT MORE FORMAL
try out test
try your hand at attempt

tube
NOUN
I can feel warm air coming out of this tube.
▷ duct, hose, pipe, spout

tuck
VERB
Tuck some tissues in your pocket.
▷ insert, place, stick, stuff

tug
VERB
They tried to tug the box from under the bed.
▷ jerk, pull, wrench, yank

tumble
VERB
He tripped and started to tumble down the stairs.
▷ fall, plunge, topple

tune
NOUN
I know the tune but not the words.
▷ melody, song

tunnel
NOUN
They found a tunnel between the rocks.
▷ channel, passageway
VERB
Moles will tunnel under the grass for grubs.
▷ burrow, dig, excavate

turn
VERB
1 *The children watched the pinwheel turn.*
▷ rotate, spin, twirl, twist
2 *When will the caterpillar turn into a butterfly?*
▷ change, convert, transform
NOUN
Finally, it was my turn to ask a question.
▷ chance, opportunity

MAKE IT MORE FORMAL
turn back return
turn down decline
turn red blush
turn under fold
turn up appear

T

tutor

NOUN
He is a good math tutor.
▷ instructor, teacher

VERB
Is it difficult to tutor more than one student?
▷ educate, instruct, teach

twinge

NOUN
He got a twinge in his injured leg.
▷ ache, cramp, pang, spasm

twinkle

VERB
I saw the lights twinkle in the distance.
▷ flash, gleam, glitter, sparkle

twirl

VERB
1 *Twirl the string around your fingers.*
▷ coil, curl, wind
2 *The ballet dancer started to twirl on one foot.*
▷ pirouette, revolve, rotate, spin

twist

VERB
1 *Twist the rope around that thick branch.*
▷ bend, curl, wind
2 *High heat will twist plastic.*
▷ distort, mangle, warp
3 *How did you twist your ankle?*
▷ sprain, wrench

NOUN
Could you follow every twist in the plot?
▷ change, development, turn

twitch

VERB
She was nervous and began to twitch.
▷ fidget, jerk, shudder, tremble

type

NOUN
What type of music do you like?
▷ form, kind, style, variety

typical

ADJECTIVE
There's no such thing as a typical teen.
▷ average, characteristic, normal, representative, standard

T

U u

ugly
ADJECTIVE
The garbage in the park was an ugly sight.
▷ hideous, unattractive, unsightly
ANTONYM beautiful

ultimate
ADJECTIVE
What was his ultimate choice of dessert?
▷ eventual, final, last

umpire
NOUN
The umpire stopped the argument.
▷ arbiter, mediator, referee

unacceptable
ADJECTIVE
Your behaviour is unacceptable.
▷ improper, unsatisfactory, unsuitable

unaccustomed to
ADJECTIVE
He is unaccustomed to speaking in public.
▷ unacquainted with, unfamiliar with

unaffected
ADJECTIVE
She behaves in a very unaffected way.
▷ genuine, natural, sincere
ANTONYM insincere

unafraid
ADJECTIVE
He was unafraid and got the cat out of the tree.
▷ bold, brave, courageous, intrepid

unappreciative of
ADJECTIVE
She seemed unappreciative of our help.
▷ ungrateful for, unthankful for
ANTONYM grateful

unashamed
ADJECTIVE
He bragged about his win in an unashamed way.
▷ brazen, conceited, immodest, shameless

unassuming
ADJECTIVE
The speaker had an unassuming manner.
▷ humble, modest, reserved
ANTONYM arrogant

unattractive
ADJECTIVE
The vegetables looked dry and unattractive.
▷ ugly, unappealing, unsightly

unavoidable
ADJECTIVE
The crash seemed unavoidable.
▷ certain, inescapable, inevitable

unaware of
ADJECTIVE
She was unaware of the danger she was in.
▷ ignorant of, oblivious to, uninformed about

unbearable
ADJECTIVE
The constant noise became unbearable.
▷ impossible, intolerable, unendurable
ANTONYM tolerable

unbelievable
ADJECTIVE
1 *It was unbelievable how quickly they did the job.*
▷ astonishing, incredible, stupendous
2 *The news story about aliens from outer space is unbelievable.*
▷ implausible, improbable, inconceivable, preposterous

uncanny
ADJECTIVE
He has an uncanny talent for predicting the weather.
▷ eerie, mysterious

uncertain
ADJECTIVE
I'm uncertain about switching to another school.
▷ doubtful, hesitant, tentative
ANTONYM sure

unclean
ADJECTIVE
The flood victims had to drink unclean water.
▷ contaminated, dirty, impure, polluted, tainted
ANTONYM pure

unclothed
ADJECTIVE
The baby was unclothed except for a diaper.
▷ bare, naked, nude, uncovered, undressed

uncomfortable
ADJECTIVE
1 *My new shoes were uncomfortable at first.*
▷ cramped, ill-fitting, painful
2 *He was uncomfortable talking about his problem.*
▷ awkward, ill at ease, self-conscious, uneasy

uncommon
ADJECTIVE
A rainbow is an uncommon sight.
▷ extraordinary, infrequent, rare, unusual

U

uncomplicated

ADJECTIVE

The plot of the story was uncomplicated.

▷ basic, simple, straightforward

unconditional

ADJECTIVE

They give unconditional love to their children.

▷ absolute, total, unrestricted

unconscious of

ADJECTIVE

She seemed unconscious of her bleeding knee.

▷ oblivious to, unaware of

ANTONYM aware

unconventional

ADJECTIVE

She likes to wear unconventional outfits.

▷ eccentric, strange, unorthodox, unusual

uncoordinated

ADJECTIVE

I have always been uncoordinated.

▷ awkward, clumsy, ungainly

uncover

VERB

Reporters work hard to uncover scandal and wrongdoing.

▷ expose, reveal

under

PREPOSITION

I picked up the spoon that was under the table.

▷ below, beneath, underneath

ANTONYM above

MAKE IT MORE FORMAL

under par unwell

under the weather sick

undergo

VERB

She had to undergo another operation.

▷ endure, experience

underground

ADJECTIVE

The underground organization was a network of secret paths and hiding places.

▷ clandestine, hidden, secret

underhand

ADJECTIVE

Lying is an underhand way to blame others.

▷ deceitful, devious, sly, sneaky

underline

VERB

The teacher planned to underline the importance of studying.

▷ emphasize, highlight, stress, underscore

underneath

PREPOSITION

Place the chair underneath the window.

▷ below, beneath, under

ANTONYM above

understand

VERB

1 *Did you understand the meaning of the story?*

▷ comprehend, follow, get, grasp, see

2 *I understand classes will begin tomorrow.*

▷ believe, gather, hear

understanding

ADJECTIVE

I have a very understanding teacher.

▷ compassionate, considerate, supportive, sympathetic

undertaking

NOUN

Organizing the school picnic was a huge undertaking.

▷ job, operation, project, task

undesirable

ADJECTIVE

The practical joke had an undesirable result.

▷ unfavourable, unwanted, unwelcome

undivided

ADJECTIVE

We gave the speaker our undivided attention.

▷ complete, entire, exclusive, total, whole

undo

VERB

She cannot undo the knot in her shoelace.

▷ loosen, open, unfasten, untie

ANTONYM fasten

undressed

ADJECTIVE

The children got undressed and put pyjamas on.

▷ bare, naked, nude, unclothed

unearth

VERB

Did you unearth anything interesting from the basement?

▷ discover, find, reveal, uncover

uneasy

ADJECTIVE

He was uneasy about leaving his bicycle outside.

▷ anxious, nervous, uncomfortable, worried

ANTONYM comfortable

U

unemployed

ADJECTIVE

The company closed and now my mom is unemployed.

▷ idle, jobless, laid off

uneven

ADJECTIVE

1 *The top of the stone wall is uneven.*

▷ bumpy, irregular, jagged, rough

ANTONYM smooth

2 *The tennis player's game was uneven.*

▷ inconsistent, irregular, variable

unexpected

ADJECTIVE

There was an unexpected thunderstorm.

▷ abrupt, sudden, unforeseen

unfair

ADJECTIVE

A rule is unfair if it treats people unequally.

▷ unjust, unreasonable, wrong

unfamiliar

ADJECTIVE

Look up unfamiliar words in the dictionary.

▷ new, novel, strange, unknown

unfasten

VERB

Did you unfasten the gate?

▷ open, release, undo, unhook, unlatch

unfinished

ADJECTIVE

My unfinished project got a poor mark.

▷ incomplete, rough

ANTONYM complete

unfit

ADJECTIVE

Violent movies are unfit for young children.

▷ inappropriate, unsuitable

unfold

VERB

How did the story unfold?

▷ develop, expand, progress

unforeseen

ADJECTIVE

The game has been cancelled due to unforeseen circumstances.

▷ unanticipated, unexpected

unforgettable

ADJECTIVE

We had an unforgettable drive along the Caribou Trail in Newfoundland.

▷ cherished, memorable, treasured

unfriendly

ADJECTIVE

Our neighbour was unfriendly at first.

▷ aloof, cold, disagreeable, distant, unkind, unsociable

unhappiness

NOUN

Her unhappiness showed in her face.

▷ grief, misery, sadness, sorrow

unhappy

See box at foot of this page.

unhealthy

ADJECTIVE

1 *Cigarette smoke is unhealthy for everyone.*

▷ damaging, harmful, noxious, unsanitary, unwholesome

2 *The unhealthy child missed a lot of school.*

▷ ailing, ill, sick, unwell

unhurried

ADJECTIVE

He has an unhurried way of walking.

▷ casual, leisurely, slow

REPLACE AN OVERUSED WORD: UNHAPPY

Depending on the sense of **unhappy** that you mean, there are a number of other adjectives that you can use instead.

- **not happy**

  *My best friend has gone away on vacation, and I'm feeling **depressed**.*

  *He seemed a little **down** when I spoke to him this morning.*

  *I think the cry of a loon is a **melancholy** sound.*

  *For many people, Remembrance Day is a **sad** occasion.*

- **not satisfactory or not fortunate**

  *His brightly coloured outfit was an **inappropriate** choice for a formal dance.*

  *By an **unfortunate** coincidence, we both reached for the last cookie at the same time.*

  *In the **unlucky** chance that the fire alarm rings, all doors will automatically unlock.*

  *Don't you think a goat is an **unsuitable** pet for someone who lives in a city?*

uniform
ADJECTIVE
Cut all the ribbons into a uniform length.
▷ consistent, identical, regular, unvarying

unimportant
ADJECTIVE
The details are unimportant.
▷ insignificant, irrelevant, minor, slight, trivial

uninhabited
ADJECTIVE
The uninhabited house burned down.
▷ abandoned, deserted, empty, unoccupied, vacant

uninterested
ADJECTIVE
Are you uninterested or just sleepy?
▷ bored, indifferent, nonchalant, unresponsive

uninteresting
ADJECTIVE
This story is uninteresting.
▷ boring, dull, monotonous, unexciting

uninterrupted
ADJECTIVE
We had an uninterrupted conversation.
▷ constant, continuous, endless, nonstop

union
NOUN
The union helped the miners improve their working conditions.
▷ association, coalition, confederation, federation, league

unique
ADJECTIVE
Each snowflake is unique.
▷ distinctive, original, special
ANTONYM common

unite
VERB
Let us all unite to fight hunger.
▷ collaborate, join together, pull together, work together
ANTONYM divide

universal
ADJECTIVE
Poverty is a universal problem.
▷ common, general, widespread, worldwide

unjust
ADJECTIVE
The reporter wrote an unjust article.
▷ biased, prejudiced, unfair

unkind
ADJECTIVE
That was an unkind comment to make.
▷ cruel, mean, nasty, spiteful, thoughtless

unknown
ADJECTIVE
She realizes that the future is unknown.
▷ hidden, mysterious, unfamiliar, unidentified

unlikely
ADJECTIVE
That's a very unlikely excuse.
▷ doubtful, implausible, unbelievable, unconvincing

unlucky
ADJECTIVE
The unlucky boy broke his leg again.
▷ doomed, hapless, luckless, unfortunate

unnatural
ADJECTIVE
We saw unnatural flashes of colour in the sky.
▷ abnormal, mysterious, strange, unusual

unnecessary
ADJECTIVE
These warnings are unnecessary.
▷ excessive, needless, pointless

unoccupied
ADJECTIVE
The apartment was unoccupied for a month.
▷ deserted, empty, uninhabited, vacant

unpaid
ADJECTIVE
You have an unpaid library fine.
▷ due, outstanding, overdue, owing

unpleasant
ADJECTIVE
1 *Too much salt in food is unpleasant.*
▷ disagreeable, distasteful, nasty, repulsive
2 *She was quite unpleasant to me this morning.*
▷ nasty, obnoxious, rude, unfriendly

unpopular
ADJECTIVE
These rules are unpopular.
▷ detested, disliked, shunned

unpredictable
ADJECTIVE
Her moods are unpredictable.
▷ changeable, erratic, irregular

unprotected
ADJECTIVE
The soldiers left the village unprotected.
▷ defenceless, exposed, unguarded, vulnerable

U

unqualified

ADJECTIVE

The boy is unqualified for that job.

▷ untrained, unskilled

unreasonable

ADJECTIVE

1 *She received an unreasonable punishment.*

▷ excessive, extreme, unfair

2 *Please do not be unreasonable.*

▷ difficult, irrational

unreliable

ADJECTIVE

An unreliable helper will not be much help!

▷ irresponsible, untrustworthy

ANTONYM dependable

unruly

ADJECTIVE

The bus driver reported the unruly children.

▷ disobedient, disorderly, rowdy, unmanageable

ANTONYM well-behaved

unsafe

ADJECTIVE

The unsafe playground slide was repaired.

▷ dangerous, hazardous, perilous, risky

ANTONYM secure

unsatisfactory

ADJECTIVE

Your computer skills are unsatisfactory.

▷ disappointing, inadequate, mediocre, poor, unacceptable

unseen

ADJECTIVE

An unseen actor spoke from behind the curtain.

▷ hidden, invisible

unselfish

ADJECTIVE

He is always helpful and unselfish.

▷ charitable, considerate, generous, selfless

unsightly

ADJECTIVE

Clean up that unsightly mess!

▷ hideous, ugly, unattractive

unsound

ADJECTIVE

The scientist's theory was proved to be unsound.

▷ faulty, flawed, illogical

unstable

ADJECTIVE

I don't want the desk if it's unstable.

▷ rickety, unsafe, unsound, unsteady

unsteady

ADJECTIVE

The baby took a few unsteady steps.

▷ shaky, tottering, wobbly

unsuitable

ADJECTIVE

Casual clothing is unsuitable for the occasion.

▷ improper, inappropriate, unacceptable

unsuspecting

ADJECTIVE

Crooks cheated the unsuspecting girl.

▷ innocent, naive

ANTONYM wary

unthinkable

ADJECTIVE

It was unthinkable that we might lose the game.

▷ impossible, unbelievable, unimaginable

untidy

ADJECTIVE

Our untidy hall closet is an embarrassment.

▷ cluttered, disorderly, jumbled, messy, unkempt

untie

VERB

Please untie the dog's leash.

▷ disentangle, undo, unfasten, unknot

until

PREPOSITION

Wait until noon before you leave.

▷ till, up to

untimely

ADJECTIVE

They were not pleased at our untimely arrival.

▷ early, premature

untrue

ADJECTIVE

The information was untrue.

▷ false, fictitious, incorrect

untrustworthy

ADJECTIVE

He has a reputation for being untrustworthy.

▷ undependable, unreliable

ANTONYM dependable

unusual

ADJECTIVE

I have an unusual Canadian stamp.

▷ curious, extraordinary, rare, uncommon

ANTONYM common

unwell

ADJECTIVE

I have been unwell with a fever.

▷ ailing, ill, queasy, sick

U

unwilling

ADJECTIVE
He was unwilling to have his picture taken.
▷ averse, loath, reluctant

unwise

ADJECTIVE
She made an unwise decision.
▷ foolish, irresponsible, rash, reckless

upbeat

ADJECTIVE
I like upbeat music.
▷ bubbly, cheerful, happy, positive

upcoming

ADJECTIVE
Our upcoming trip to Manitoba will include a visit to the Sunflower Festival.
▷ approaching, forthcoming, future, imminent, impending

upheaval

NOUN
We could see some kind of upheaval on the other side of the arena.
▷ commotion, disruption, disturbance, turmoil

uphold

VERB
Judges must uphold the law.
▷ maintain, support, sustain

upright

ADJECTIVE
1 *I set the lamp upright, but it fell over again.*
▷ erect, standing, vertical
2 *He did the upright thing and confessed.*
▷ decent, honest, honourable, moral, respectable

uproar

NOUN
There was complete uproar when the referee awarded a penalty.
▷ chaos, pandemonium, turmoil, upheaval

upset

ADJECTIVE
They were clearly upset by the bad news.
▷ agitated, distraught, distressed, troubled
VERB
1 *Do not upset everyone with your complaints.*
▷ agitate, bother, displease, distress, disturb
2 *Did you upset the glass of milk?*
▷ capsize, knock over, overturn, spill

urge

NOUN
I have an urge to see that movie again.
▷ compulsion, desire, impulse, longing, yearning
VERB
Urge your parents to come to the meeting.
▷ beg, beseech, plead, press

urgent

ADJECTIVE
There is an urgent need for food donations.
▷ critical, immediate, pressing, vital

use

VERB
How do you use this gadget?
▷ employ, operate, utilize
NOUN
1 *Was the use of force necessary?*
▷ application, employment
2 *What is the use of taking extra shoes?*
▷ benefit, object, point, purpose

MAKE IT MORE FORMAL

have no use for not need or want; dislike
make use of use for a purpose
used to accustomed to; formerly did
use up consume entirely; tire out

---

useful

ADJECTIVE
A thesaurus is a useful book.
▷ beneficial, helpful, practical, valuable, worthwhile
ANTONYM useless

useless

ADJECTIVE
1 *A flashlight is useless without a battery.*
▷ ineffective, ineffectual, worthless
ANTONYM useful
2 *That person was useless in the emergency.*
▷ hopeless, inept, pathetic

usual

ADJECTIVE
His usual breakfast is fruit and cereal.
▷ customary, normal, regular, standard

utilize

VERB
She will utilize her cooking skills at camp.
▷ employ, use

utter

ADJECTIVE
That movie was an utter waste of time.
▷ absolute, complete, outright, sheer, total

U

V v

vacant
ADJECTIVE
Is the apartment vacant?
▷ empty, uninhabited, unoccupied
ANTONYM occupied

vacation
NOUN
I'm looking forward to my next vacation.
▷ break, holiday

vague
ADJECTIVE
The instructions were vague and not helpful.
▷ hazy, indefinite, uncertain, unclear
ANTONYM clear

vain
ADJECTIVE
1 *He's a show-off, and vain about his looks.*
▷ conceited, egotistical, proud
ANTONYM modest
2 *She made a vain attempt to catch the ball.*
▷ fruitless, futile, unsuccessful, useless
ANTONYM successful

valiant
ADJECTIVE
Be valiant, and defend yourself.
▷ brave, courageous, fearless, heroic
ANTONYM cowardly

valid
ADJECTIVE
Make sure your password is valid.
▷ genuine, legal, official, proper
ANTONYM invalid

valley
NOUN
The river runs through a valley between the two hills.
▷ canyon, chasm, coulee, depression, gorge, gulch, gully, ravine

valour
NOUN
In the Middle Ages, knights fought to prove their valour.
▷ bravery, courage, fortitude, heroism
ANTONYM cowardice

valuable
ADJECTIVE
1 *Learning how to find information on the Internet is a valuable lesson.*
▷ beneficial, helpful, useful, worthwhile
ANTONYM useless
2 *My collection of baseball cards may be valuable.*
▷ costly, expensive, precious, priceless
ANTONYM worthless

value
NOUN
1 *We all know the value of regular exercise.*
▷ advantage, benefit, importance, merit, worth
2 *Computers drop in value every year.*
▷ cost, price
VERB
I value your friendship.
▷ appreciate, cherish, prize, respect, treasure

vanish
VERB
The moon is about to vanish behind a cloud.
▷ disappear, fade
ANTONYM appear

vanity
NOUN
Vanity seems to be everywhere in the movie business.
▷ conceit, ego, egotism, pride
ANTONYM modesty

vanquish
VERB
The hero must vanquish all the villains in the last scene.
▷ beat, conquer, crush, defeat, overcome

vapour
NOUN
The vapour over the lake was gone by noon.
▷ fog, mist, steam

variable
ADJECTIVE
Lately, my moods have been variable.
▷ changeable, erratic, fickle, unpredictable
ANTONYM constant

variety
NOUN
1 *She put a variety of cookies on the plate.*
▷ array, assortment, collection, medley, mixture, range
2 *Is this a new variety of apple?*
▷ category, class, kind, sort, strain, type

various
ADJECTIVE
I have a little box where I keep various personal items.
▷ assorted, different, diverse, miscellaneous

vary
VERB
1 *The number of classes I go to does not vary from day to day.*
▷ alter, change, differ, fluctuate
2 *Don't forget to vary the length of your sentences.*
▷ alter, alternate, change
ANTONYM preserve

vast

ADJECTIVE

There are vast stretches of farmland on the Prairies.
▷ colossal, enormous, extensive, gigantic, great, huge, immense
ANTONYM tiny

vault

NOUN

The underground vault was damp and dark.
▷ cellar, crypt, dungeon, tomb

VERB

The fence looked too high to vault over.
▷ bound, hurdle, jump, leap, spring

veer

VERB

A witness saw the car veer off the road.
▷ swerve, swing, turn

vehement

ADJECTIVE

My brothers were having a vehement argument.
▷ forceful, heated, intense, passionate, violent

vehicle

NOUN

In the movie, the villain stole a vehicle and escaped.
▷ ambulance, automobile, bicycle, bus, cab, car, carriage, cart, chariot, coach, fire engine, jeep, limousine, motorcycle, sled, snowmobile, stagecoach, streetcar, subway train, taxi, toboggan, tractor, train, trap, travois, tricycle, trolley bus, truck, wagon

vengeance

NOUN

The accused threatened the witness with vengeance.
▷ reprisal, retaliation, revenge

vent

NOUN

Warm air comes from that vent in the wall.
▷ opening, outlet

venture

NOUN

The venture was poorly planned, and is sure to fail.
▷ endeavour, enterprise, project, undertaking

verbal

ADJECTIVE

He insisted that a verbal promise was not a real promise.
▷ oral, spoken, unwritten
ANTONYM written

verdict

NOUN

The judges' verdict is final.
▷ conclusion, decision, finding, judgment, opinion

verify

VERB

Please key in your password again to verify that it is correct.
▷ confirm, prove
ANTONYM contradict

vertical

ADJECTIVE

The vertical cliff was too dangerous to climb.
▷ perpendicular, sheer, steep, upright
ANTONYM horizontal

very

ADVERB

See box at foot of this page.

vessel

NOUN

1 *The large ocean-going vessel is carrying oil.*
▷ boat, craft, ship
2 *Choose a vessel big enough to hold all the water.*
▷ basin, bowl, canister, container, jar, pot

vestige

NOUN

These ruins are only a vestige of a huge city.
▷ remainder, remnant, trace

REPLACE AN OVERUSED WORD: VERY

The adverb **very** is greatly overused. Make your language more interesting and use one of the following instead.

- **to a great degree**
  I am deeply grateful for your help.
  We are exceedingly pleased to be invited.
  Your non-stop chatter is extremely annoying.
  She was greatly upset at being ignored.
  It is highly likely that the concert will be cancelled.

  She was intensely interested in what I had to say.
  He's been really ill all week.
  Your writing is remarkably good.
  I'm terribly sorry that I kept you waiting.
  The weather is unusually warm today.
  The team played wonderfully well all season.

V

veteran
NOUN
*If you want to learn, you could ask a **veteran**.*
▷ expert, professional
ANTONYM novice

veto
VERB
*It takes only one person to **veto** this proposal.*
▷ ban, disallow, forbid, overturn, prohibit, reject, stop

vibrate
VERB
*The washing machine will **vibrate** on the spin cycle.*
▷ quiver, shake, shudder, tremble

vice
NOUN
*Greed and **vice** are associated with gangsters.*
▷ corruption, evil, immorality, wickedness
ANTONYM virtue

vicious
ADJECTIVE
*Children should be kept away from **vicious** dogs.*
▷ savage, violent
ANTONYM gentle

victory
NOUN
*That was the team's first **victory** this season.*
▷ success, triumph, win
ANTONYM defeat

view
NOUN
1 *In my **view**, the protesters went too far.*
▷ attitude, belief, feeling, opinion, viewpoint
2 *This is a **view** of Baffin Island.*
▷ panorama, scene
VERB
*We **view** all of you as our friends.*
▷ consider, regard

viewpoint
NOUN
*Try to look at things from my **viewpoint**.*
▷ point of view, position, standpoint

vigilant
ADJECTIVE
*Be **vigilant** in guarding against computer viruses.*
▷ alert, attentive, careful, observant, wary, watchful
ANTONYM careless

vigorous
ADJECTIVE
*He does twenty minutes of **vigorous** exercise every day.*
▷ active, energetic, enthusiastic, forceful, lively, strenuous
ANTONYM weak

vigour
NOUN
*The younger team members played with great **vigour**.*
▷ energy, power, strength

vile
ADJECTIVE
*The smell from the blocked drain was **vile**.*
▷ disgusting, filthy, foul, nasty, offensive

villain
NOUN
*In the story, she tricks the **villain** and escapes.*
▷ criminal, crook, outlaw, rogue, scoundrel
ANTONYM hero

vindictive
ADJECTIVE
*The **vindictive** student told lies about her classmate.*
▷ cruel, malicious, spiteful

violence
NOUN
1 *We are against the use of **violence**.*
▷ bloodshed, brutality, force, savagery, terrorism
2 *He shook his fist with **violence**.*
▷ fervour, force, harshness, severity

violent
ADJECTIVE
1 ***Violent** crime horrifies all of us.*
▷ brutal, cruel, savage, vicious
2 *The **violent** winter storm destroyed many trees.*
▷ intense, powerful, severe, wild

VIP
NOUN
*We were told there was a **VIP** on the plane.*
▷ celebrity, dignitary, personage, star

virtue
NOUN
*The old king's life had been full of generosity and **virtue**.*
▷ decency, goodness, honesty, morality
ANTONYM vice

virtuous
ADJECTIVE
*Keeping a promise is a **virtuous** thing to do.*
▷ decent, good, honest, honourable, moral

visible
ADJECTIVE
*She became angry, but there was no **visible** change in her expression.*
▷ apparent, clear, evident, noticeable, observable, obvious

vision
NOUN
*Your **vision** of the future is different from mine.*
▷ dream, fantasy, ideal, image

V

vital

ADJECTIVE
1 *The snowstorm has cut off* vital *food supplies to the village.*
▷ critical, crucial, essential, indispensable, necessary
ANTONYM unimportant
2 *Our dog is fifteen years old, but is still* vital*.*
▷ active, energetic, lively, spirited

vitality

NOUN
He's always busy, and seems to have lots of vitality*.*
▷ drive, energy, life, spirit, strength, vigour

vivacious

ADJECTIVE
The audience appreciated hearing such a vivacious *speaker.*
▷ active, alive, animated, lively, vital
ANTONYM monotonous

vivid

ADJECTIVE
I like to wear vivid *clothing on a rainy day.*
▷ bold, bright, brilliant, colourful
ANTONYM dull

vogue

NOUN
Black seems to be always in vogue*.*
▷ fashion, style

voice

VERB
I must voice *my disapproval of your behaviour.*
▷ express, speak, utter
See picture below.

void

ADJECTIVE
The guarantee will be void *if the seal is broken.*
▷ cancelled, invalid, useless
NOUN
The snow bridge had collapsed, leaving a dark void*.*
▷ abyss, chasm, emptiness, hole

volatile

ADJECTIVE
Living with a volatile *younger brother is not always fun.*
▷ changeable, moody, unpredictable
ANTONYM steady

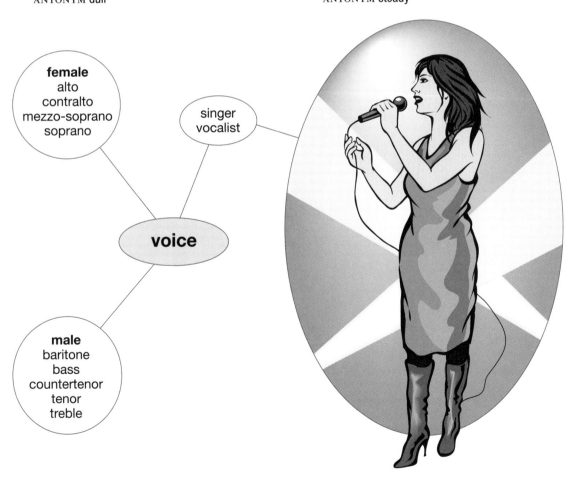

female
alto
contralto
mezzo-soprano
soprano

singer
vocalist

voice

male
baritone
bass
countertenor
tenor
treble

V

volume

NOUN

I have a huge volume of paper to be recycled.
▷ amount, bulk, mass, quantity

vote

VERB

I vote that we go to the mall.
▷ propose, recommend, suggest

NOUN

What was the result of the vote?
▷ ballot, referendum

vow

VERB

Will you vow that you will always be my friend?
▷ guarantee, pledge, promise

NOUN

If you make a vow, you should keep it.
▷ assurance, pledge, promise

vulgar

ADJECTIVE

Vulgar language is not acceptable in school.
▷ coarse, crude, rude, tasteless, uncouth

ANTONYM polite

vulnerable

ADJECTIVE

We must protect all vulnerable parts of our environment.
▷ defenceless, exposed, unprotected, weak

ANTONYM protected

V

W w

waft
VERB

*Shut the door so the smell doesn't **waft** into the next room.*
▷ drift, float

wage
NOUN

*She earns a decent **wage**.*
▷ income, salary

wail
VERB

*The baby began to **wail**.*
▷ cry, howl, sob, weep

wait
VERB

*I will **wait** in the library.*
▷ remain, stay

NOUN

*Will there be a long **wait** for the bus?*
▷ delay, holdup

wake
VERB

*The baby will **wake** if you make too much noise.*
▷ awaken, stir

walk
VERB

See box at foot of this page and top of next page.

wall
NOUN

*They built a **wall** around their yard.*
▷ barrier, divider, fence, partition

wander
VERB

*I like to **wander** along the beach.*
▷ meander, ramble, roam, stroll

wane
VERB

*Interest in hockey tends to **wane** in the spring.*
▷ diminish, subside, weaken

wangle
VERB

*Try to **wangle** things so that we can both go to the party.*
▷ arrange, contrive, manipulate

want
VERB

1 *I **want** a new MP3 player.*
▷ crave, desire, fancy
2 *My essay will **want** proofreading.*
▷ need, require

NOUN

*The explorers were weak from **want** of food and water.*
▷ absence, lack, shortage
ANTONYM abundance

REPLACE AN OVERUSED WORD: WALK

There are a number of more interesting or creative words that you can use in place of the basic verb **walk**, if you want to say something about the way in which a person walks.

- If you **hike**, you walk some distance in the countryside for pleasure.
  *We plan to **hike** in Yukon's Tombstone Park next summer.*

- If you **march**, you walk quickly and in a determined way, perhaps because you are angry.
  *You should **march** right back to the store and get your money back.*

- If you **pace**, you walk up and down a small area, usually because you are anxious or impatient.
  *He was very upset, and kept getting up to **pace** up and down the hallway.*

- If you **plod**, you walk slowly, with heavy steps, often because you are tired.
  *Toward the end of the day we were very tired, but we managed to **plod** home before it got dark.*

- If you **reel**, you walk about in an unsteady way as if you are going to fall.
  *The smell from the skunk made us **reel** backwards.*

- If you **saunter**, you walk in a slow, casual way.
  *The others were eager to get to school, so I couldn't **saunter** along as I usually do.*

- If you **stagger**, you walk very unsteadily, often because you are ill.
  *The patient said that he went to the washroom, but felt so dizzy that he could only **stagger** back to bed.*

- If you **stamp**, you put your feet down very hard when you walk, usually because you are angry.
  *"I'm not staying here!" he shouted, and began to **stamp** out of the room.*

W

Here are some more words you can use in place of the basic verb **walk**,
if you want to say something about the way in which a person walks.

- If you **stalk**, you walk in a stiff, proud, or angry way.

  *She turned and tried to **stalk** away, but we persuaded her to stay.*

- If you **step** in a particular direction, you move your foot in that direction.

  ***Step** over here, please, and help me move this desk.*

- If you **stride**, you walk with quick, long steps.

  *He is happiest when he can **stride** along by himself.*

- If you **stroll**, you walk in a slow, relaxed way.

  *We have lots of time, so we plan to **stroll** through the mall before going home.*

- If you **stumble**, you trip while you are walking and almost fall.

  *Don't leave your boots in the doorway for everyone to **stumble** over.*

- If you **tiptoe**, you walk very quietly without putting your heels on the ground, so as not to be heard.

  *You won't wake him if you just **tiptoe** in and out.*

- If you **tread** in a particular way, you walk in that way. This is rather a formal word.

  ***Tread** carefully here—there is ice beneath the snow.*

- If you **trudge**, you walk slowly, with heavy steps, often because you are tired.

  *We missed the last bus, and had to **trudge** all the way home.*

- If you **wander**, you walk around in a casual way, often without intending to go anywhere in particular.

  *The sun was shining, so I was happy to **wander** around in the park.*

war
NOUN
The war lasted for five years.
▷ battle, conflict, fighting, hostilities
ANTONYM peace

wardrobe
NOUN
My winter wardrobe is warm and practical.
▷ apparel, attire, clothing

warm
ADJECTIVE
1 *The warm spring day lifted our spirits.*
▷ balmy, mild, pleasant, temperate
ANTONYM cold
2 *He has a warm personality.*
▷ affectionate, amiable, friendly, genial
ANTONYM unfriendly

warmth
NOUN
She shows great warmth toward all animals.
▷ affection, kindness, tenderness

warn
VERB
Will you warn us if there is a problem?
▷ advise, alert, inform, notify

warning
NOUN
We had no warning before the tornado struck.
▷ alert, notice, notification, word

warp
VERB
Direct heat will warp a CD.
▷ bend, deform, distort, twist
ANTONYM straighten

wary
ADJECTIVE
The dog is wary of strangers.
▷ cautious, distrustful, suspicious

wash
VERB
1 *Wash the stain before it sets.*
▷ launder, rinse, scrub, sponge
2 *You will need to wash after playing in the mud.*
▷ bathe, shower

come out in the wash be resolved over time
That won't wash. That won't be acceptable.
wash away erode
wash out fade

waste

VERB

Do not waste your money on junk food.

▷ fritter away, squander, throw away

ANTONYM save

ADJECTIVE

All waste material will be recycled.

▷ excess, remaining, surplus, unused, unwanted

NOUN

Put your waste in the appropriate container.

▷ garbage, litter, trash

watch

VERB

1 *We like to watch the orangutans at the zoo.*

▷ observe, study, view

2 *Watch my bike while I go into the store.*

▷ guard, mind, protect

MAKE IT MORE FORMAL

watch out be alert

watch over guard

watchful

ADJECTIVE

He is a very watchful babysitter.

▷ attentive, vigilant

water

VERB

He will water the garden and I will mow the lawn.

▷ hose, irrigate, spray, sprinkle

NOUN

There are many species of fish in the water.

▷ lake, ocean, pond, river, sea, stream

waterway

NOUN

See picture at foot of this page.

wave

NOUN

1 *He was overcome by a wave of emotion.*

▷ flood, surge

2 *The wave knocked the surfer off his board.*

▷ breaker, swell

VERB

You should not wave sharp objects in the air.

▷ brandish, flourish

brook
canal
channel
creek
estuary
river
rivulet
stream
tributary
watercourse
waterfall

waterway

waterfall

W

way

NOUN

1 *Our teacher showed a way to solve the problem.*
▷ manner, means, method, procedure, technique

2 *The way is rocky, so be careful!*
▷ lane, path, road, route

MAKE IT MORE FORMAL

go out of your way make a special effort
no way absolutely not
under way in progress
way in entrance

weak

ADJECTIVE

1 *The operation left him weak and tired.*
▷ feeble, frail, infirm, sickly
ANTONYM strong

2 *I feel weak after running the marathon.*
▷ drained, exhausted, tired

3 *He was too weak to stand up for himself.*
▷ cowardly, powerless, spineless
ANTONYM resolute

4 *The apple juice was so weak, I actually thought it was water.*
▷ diluted, thin
ANTONYM strong

5 *A weak light shone through the curtain of her bedroom window.*
▷ dim, faint, low, soft

weaken

VERB

1 *Any strong wind will weaken the rickety dock.*
▷ damage, destabilize
ANTONYM strengthen

2 *Did his health continue to weaken?*
▷ decline, deteriorate, flag
ANTONYM strengthen

weakness

NOUN

1 *Your compassion for others is a strength, not a weakness.*
▷ fault, flaw, imperfection
ANTONYM strength

2 *We both have a weakness for chocolate.*
▷ fondness, liking, taste
ANTONYM dislike

wealth

NOUN

1 *She inherited her wealth from her grandmother.*
▷ assets, fortune, money, riches

2 *This book has a wealth of information on mammals.*
▷ abundance, bounty, variety
ANTONYM shortage

wealthy

ADJECTIVE

My wealthy uncle paid for my riding lessons.
▷ affluent, prosperous, rich
ANTONYM poor

wear

VERB

We will wear pirate costumes in the play.
▷ be clothed in, be dressed in, don, sport

NOUN

My skateboard wheels are showing signs of wear.
▷ abrasion, friction

weary

ADJECTIVE

We were too weary to walk another step.
▷ drained, exhausted, fatigued, tired, worn out

weather

NOUN

See picture on next page.

weave

VERB

Let's weave our way through the crowd.
▷ twist, wind, zigzag

wedge

VERB

She tried to wedge the books into her backpack.
▷ cram, force, pack, squeeze, stuff

NOUN

I would like a small wedge of cake.
▷ chunk, piece, section, slice

weep

VERB

I always weep at sad movies.
▷ bawl, blubber, cry, snivel, sob, wail

weigh

VERB

Weigh the pros and cons before making a decision.
▷ assess, consider, evaluate, ponder

weight

NOUN

1 *The weight on the scale must not exceed 100 kilograms.*
▷ burden, load, mass

2 *Her opinion has weight in our group.*
▷ importance, influence, power

weird

ADJECTIVE

I had a weird dream last night.
▷ bizarre, eerie, odd, peculiar, strange

W

welcome

VERB

It was my job to welcome the guests.

▷ greet, meet, receive

ADJECTIVE

The warm weather is a welcome change.

▷ delightful, pleasant, pleasing, refreshing

NOUN

His welcome was warm and sincere.

▷ greeting, reception

well

ADVERB

1 *The project is going well.*

▷ satisfactorily, smoothly, splendidly, successfully

ANTONYM badly

2 *He dances very well.*

▷ admirably, expertly, skilfully

ANTONYM badly

3 *Wash your hands well after taking out the garbage.*

▷ completely, fully, properly, thoroughly

4 *She always treats her pets well.*

▷ compassionately, humanely, kindly

ADJECTIVE

He feels well when he exercises regularly.

▷ fit, healthy, robust, sound, strong

ANTONYM sick

MAKE IT MORE FORMAL

well-behaved polite
well-being health
well-built sturdy
well-known prominent
well-liked popular
well-mannered polite
well off rich
well-to-do wealthy
well-versed experienced

fair weather
balmy
clear
dry
fine
hot
humid
mild
muggy
sunny
warm

cold weather
cold
icy
freezing
snowy

wet weather
damp
drizzly
misty
rainy
showery

weather

windy weather
blustery
breezy
stormy
thundery

cloudy weather
cloudy
dull
foggy
overcast

W

wet

ADJECTIVE
1 *My bathing suit is still wet.*
▷ damp, drenched, moist, soaked, sodden, waterlogged
ANTONYM dry
2 *It was a cool, wet day.*
▷ misty, rainy, showery
ANTONYM dry
VERB
Wet the cloth and wipe the table down.
▷ dampen, moisten, soak
ANTONYM dry

whim

NOUN
I felt a sudden whim to audition for the play.
▷ desire, fancy, impulse, notion, urge

whine

VERB
You whine too much.
▷ complain, gripe, grumble, moan

whip

VERB
Whip the eggs before adding the flour.
▷ beat, mix, stir, whisk

white

ADJECTIVE
He wore a white shirt with a black tie.
▷ cream, ivory, off-white, pearl, snow-white

whole

ADJECTIVE
I spent the whole day reading a book.
▷ complete, entire, total

wholesome

ADJECTIVE
Bread is a wholesome food.
▷ beneficial, healthy, nutritious

wide

ADJECTIVE
See box at foot of this page.

wild

ADJECTIVE
1 *The bush is full of wild berries.*
▷ natural, uncultivated, undomesticated
ANTONYM cultivated
2 *The wild weather kept us inside for the day.*
▷ blustery, rough, stormy, violent
ANTONYM calm
3 *We were wild on the last day of school.*
▷ boisterous, rowdy, uncontrolled, unruly
ANTONYM orderly

will

NOUN
He does not have the will to give up chocolate.
▷ determination, motivation, purpose, resolve, willpower

willing

ADJECTIVE
My little brother is a very willing helper.
▷ eager, enthusiastic, keen
ANTONYM reluctant

wilt

VERB
Flowers wilt if you forget to water them.
▷ droop, sag, shrivel, wither

REPLACE AN OVERUSED WORD: WIDE

There are a number of ways in which the adjective **wide** can be used, depending on what you are referring to. Make your language more interesting by using one of the following instead.

- **wide in area**

  *Are **baggy** pants in fashion this year?*

  *The path is **broad** enough for four people to walk side by side.*

  *The new sports complex stretches over an **extensive** area.*

  *I like shirts with very **full** sleeves.*

  *The Pacific Ocean is an **immense** body of water.*

  *This jacket is so **roomy** that I can wear two sweaters under it.*

  *The house is small, but the garden is **spacious**.*

  *The wheat fields in Saskatchewan cover **vast** stretches of land.*

- **wide in scope**

  *There is **ample** opportunity for you to take up any sport that you like.*

  *She has a **broad** range of interests.*

  *I'm looking for a website that gives a **comprehensive** list of books on global warming.*

  *He has an **encyclopedic** knowledge of sports and games.*

  *The art gallery has an **extensive** collection of Canadian paintings.*

  *Climate change has **far-ranging** consequences for all of us.*

  *The bakery offers a **large** variety of cakes.*

W

win

VERB

1 *All of the players hope to win.*
▷ be victorious, succeed, triumph
ANTONYM **lose**

2 *She is trying to win the trust of the stray cat.*
▷ achieve, attain, earn, gain, secure

NOUN

A win in the next match will put us into the finals.
▷ triumph, victory
ANTONYM **defeat**

wind

NOUN

The wind blew some shingles off the roof.
▷ Alberta clipper, breeze, chinook, cyclone, gale, gust, hurricane, tornado, typhoon, whirlwind

VERB

Wind the rope around the fence post.
▷ coil, twine, twist, weave

MAKE IT MORE FORMAL

put the wind up someone alarm someone
wind down relax
wind up conclude

winner

NOUN

The winner will receive a trophy.
▷ champion, title holder, victor
ANTONYM **loser**

wipe

VERB

1 *Wipe the table before you set it.*
▷ clean, wash

2 *Please do not wipe that dirt on your pants.*
▷ rub, smear, spread

wisdom

NOUN

I admire her wisdom.
▷ insight, judgment, knowledge

wise

ADJECTIVE

He is a very wise individual.
▷ astute, clever, informed, intelligent, shrewd
ANTONYM **foolish**

wish

NOUN

What is your greatest wish?
▷ desire, hope, longing, yearning

withdrawn

ADJECTIVE

He tends to be shy and withdrawn.
▷ antisocial, distant, reserved, solitary
ANTONYM **outgoing**

wither

VERB

Those flowers will wither in the hot sun.
▷ droop, fade, shrivel, wilt

without

PREPOSITION

She is completely without fear.
▷ devoid of, lacking

MAKE IT MORE FORMAL

without charge free
without delay now

witness

NOUN

I was a witness and saw the whole accident.
▷ bystander, observer, onlooker, spectator

woman

NOUN

That woman is my doctor.
▷ female, lady

wonder

NOUN

Finding the cure was a wonder of modern science.
▷ marvel, miracle, phenomenon

wonderful

ADJECTIVE

We had a wonderful time at the park.
▷ excellent, fabulous, marvellous, superb

wood

NOUN

Add the wood to that pile.
▷ board, log, plank

word

NOUN

1 *My teacher asked to have a word with me.*
▷ chat, conversation, discussion, talk

2 *We have had no word from them since they left.*
▷ communication, information, news

3 *I gave my word that I would attend his recital.*
▷ assurance, pledge, promise

MAKE IT MORE FORMAL

eat your words take back what you have said
have the last word make the final statement in an argument
take the words out of my mouth say what I was about to say
word for word in the exact words

W

work

VERB

1 *We work at my aunt's farm on weekends.*
▷ labour, toil
ANTONYM laze

2 *Do you know how to work that machine?*
▷ control, drive, operate, run

NOUN

Her work is in the technology sector.
▷ employment, job, livelihood, occupation, profession

world

NOUN

She completed a solo voyage around the world.
▷ globe, planet

worn

ADJECTIVE

My running shoes are old and worn.
▷ damaged, shabby, tattered

worn out

ADJECTIVE

I was worn out after gym class.
▷ exhausted, fatigued, tired

worried

ADJECTIVE

His dog had run away, and he was worried about it.
▷ anxious, concerned, uneasy
ANTONYM unconcerned

worry

VERB

1 *Try not to worry; the storm will pass.*
▷ be anxious, feel uneasy, fret

2 *I do not want to worry them with my problems.*
▷ bother, pester, trouble

NOUN

For some, health is a major source of worry.
▷ anxiety, apprehension, concern, unease

worsen

VERB

Your grades will worsen unless you study.
▷ decline, deteriorate
ANTONYM improve

worship

VERB

Some people worship actors and musicians.
▷ adore, idolize, revere
ANTONYM despise

worth

NOUN

Those toys no longer have any worth to my brother.
▷ importance, significance, value

worthless

ADJECTIVE

Anything in that pile is worthless and can be thrown away.
▷ meaningless, useless, valueless
ANTONYM valuable

worthwhile

ADJECTIVE

That is a very worthwhile cause.
▷ beneficial, meaningful, valuable

wound

VERB

The knight managed to wound the dragon.
▷ hurt, injure, maim

NOUN

The wound has not healed properly.
▷ abrasion, gash, injury

wreck

VERB

They plan to wreck that abandoned building.
▷ demolish, destroy, ruin, shatter, smash

wrinkle

VERB

Try not to wrinkle the piece of paper.
▷ crease, crinkle, crumple
ANTONYM smooth

write

VERB

1 *They will write the soldiers' names on the monument.*
▷ inscribe, record

2 *You should write a thank-you note.*
▷ compose, draft

MAKE IT MORE FORMAL

write down record
write off dismiss someone or something as insignificant

writhe

VERB

I always writhe in discomfort at the sight of blood.
▷ squirm, wriggle

wrong

ADJECTIVE

1 *I had only one wrong answer on the quiz.*
▷ false, incorrect
ANTONYM correct

2 *It is wrong to steal.*
▷ criminal, evil, immoral, wicked

XYZ xyz

yank
VERB
*It was rude to **yank** the letter out of my hand.*
▷ pull, snatch, tug

yap
VERB
*The small dog began to **yap** loudly.*
▷ bark, yelp

yard
NOUN
*A skunk dug up our **yard** last night.*
▷ garden, lawn

yarn
NOUN
1 *He told us a **yarn** about dragons.*
▷ fable, legend, story, tale
2 *Wind the **yarn** into a ball.*
▷ thread, twine, wool

yearn for
VERB
*I **yearn for** the sound of the ocean.*
▷ crave, desire, hunger for, long for, pine for

yearning
NOUN
*She had a **yearning** for strawberry ice cream.*
▷ craving, desire, hunger, longing

yell
VERB
*The speaker had to **yell** because the crowd was so noisy.*
▷ bellow, scream, screech, shout, shriek
ANTONYM whisper

yield
VERB
1 *Do not **yield** to unreasonable demands.*
▷ give in, submit, surrender
2 *Our garden will **yield** lots of tomatoes this year.*
▷ produce, provide, supply

yielding
ADJECTIVE
*The clay was **yielding** and easy to work with.*
▷ flexible, soft, unresisting

young
ADJECTIVE
*The **young** students did not behave very well on the bus.*
▷ adolescent, immature, junior, juvenile, little, youthful
ANTONYM old

youngster
NOUN
*Why is the **youngster** crying?*
▷ boy, child, girl
ANTONYM adult

youth
NOUN
*The **youth** asked for permission to see the movie.*
▷ adolescent, juvenile, minor, teenager
ANTONYM adult

zany
ADJECTIVE
*It is sometimes fun to behave in a **zany** way.*
▷ comical, eccentric, foolish, wild
ANTONYM serious

zeal
NOUN
*Their **zeal** for recycling is admirable.*
▷ devotion, eagerness, enthusiasm, passion
ANTONYM indifference

zealous
ADJECTIVE
*She is **zealous** about practising the guitar every day.*
▷ devoted, enthusiastic, fervent, passionate
ANTONYM indifferent

zenith
NOUN
*His athletic skill was at its **zenith** in the last game.*
▷ apex, peak, pinnacle, summit, top
ANTONYM nadir

zero
NOUN
*They ate all the cookies and left **zero** for everyone else.*
▷ nil, none, nothing, nought

zest
NOUN
*Her **zest** for winter activities sets a good example for the rest of us.*
▷ appetite, enthusiasm, gusto, relish, vigour

zone
NOUN
*My cellphone will not work in your **zone**.*
▷ area, district, region, territory

zoom
VERB
*It was thrilling to watch the motorcycles **zoom** around the track.*
▷ flash, fly, rush, streak

XYZ

ANSWERS TO ACTIVITIES

Activity 1: Vivid Verbs

1. announce (loud, calm)
   babble (medium loud, excited)
   gasp (soft, excited)
   groan (medium soft, calm)
   retort (medium loud, medium excited)

2. Answers will vary. Here are some possible answers:
   bolt (fast, medium jerky)
   crawl (slow, a little jerky)
   creep (slow, smooth)

Activity 2: More Vivid Verbs

1. Answers will vary. Here are some possible answers:
   snigger
   announce
   hike
   dashed
   whacked, raced

2. Answers will vary.

Activity 3: Specific Nouns

1. Answers will vary. Here are some possible answers:
   boat—canoe
   hate—despise
   lake—pond
   mark—smudge
   picture—painting
   pain—ache

2. Answers will vary.

Activity 4: Adjectives—Size, Appearance

1. Answers will vary. Here are some possible answers:
   wide—broad, full, roomy
   old—ancient, aging, elderly
   short—little, petite, small
   orange—apricot, peach, tangerine

2. Answers will vary.

Activity 5: Adjectives—Smell, Taste, Sound, Feel

Answers will vary. Here are some possible answers:

1. hard

2. fragrant

3. soft

4. noisy

5. sweet

6. loud

7. aromatic

8. delicious

Activity 6: Antonyms

Answers will vary.